Latino Muslims:
Our Journeys to Islam

Edited by Juan Galvan

Cover Photo: Silvia Cosimini
Cover Art: Al Haqq Media
Back Cover: Debora McNichol
LatinoMuslims.net

Copyright © 2017 Juan Galvan
All rights reserved.

San Antonio, TX

ISBN 978-1530007349 (Paperback Edition)
ISBN 978-1538062715 (Hardcover Edition)

In Remembrance of
Khadijah Rivera,
Ibrahim Gonzalez,
Benjamin Perez.

Table of Contents

Dedication

Dear Allah (Glorious and Exalted Is He):

This book is dedicated to you. Thank you for everyone who has put his or her trust in this book. Thank you for everyone you have brought into my life. Thank you for everyone who has made this book possible.

Thank you for my beautiful wife, Haneme Idrizi, for her love and support. Thank you for my wonderful children - Juan, Adam, and Daniel. Thank you for my parents, Roberto and Yolanda Galvan, for their unconditional love. Thank you for my seven siblings, including my deceased sister Elizabeth.

Thank you for Benjamin Perez and Khadijah Rivera, who taught me that the value of generosity extends the test of time. Thank you for Ibrahim Gonzalez who encouraged me to value the individuality of every Muslim.

Thank you for all the dedicated Latino Muslims in the United States including Samantha Sanchez, Juan Alvarado, Isa Contreras, Aaron Siebert-Llera, Rocio Martinez-Mendoza, Marta Galedary, Wilfredo Ruiz, Yusef Maisonet, Nylka Vargas, Michael Ramos-Lynch, Mujahid Fletcher, Isa Parada, Hazel Gomez, Walter Gomez, Justin Benavidez, Reymundo Nur, Cesar Dominguez, Abdul Khabeer Muhammad, Yahya Figueroa, Rahim Ocasio, Jorge Fabel Pabon, Shareefa Carrion, Rafael Narbaez, Michelle Raza, Rebecca Abuqaoud, Ricardo Pena, Yahya Lopez, Edmund Arroyo, Alma Campos, Diana Cruz, RuthAldape Saleh, Shinoa Matos, Joaquin Jule, Maria Rodriguez, Alex Robayo, Hamza Perez, Abu Sumayyah Lebron, Jalil Navarro, Nahela Morales, Wendy Diaz, Hernan Guadalupe, Mikhael Nicasio, Khalil Salgado, Daniel Hernandez, Daniel Montenegro, Yusuf Rios, Zane Alsareinye, Gabriel Martinez, and Jehan Sanchez. My list of admired Latino Muslims gets longer every year, and I apologize for anyone I have inadvertently not included.

Thank you for everyone associated with the North Hudson Islamic Educational Center (NHIEC), particularly Mariam Abbassi. Thank you for all the Austin Muslims who brought me closer to Islam. Thank you for Golam who taught me how to perform my daily prayers, Jahanara who encouraged me to go to a mosque, and to her cousin Mamun for becoming a friend. And, for Abdul Razzaque who was there when I needed help the most. Thank you for my friends at ISNA, ICNA, MAS, CAIR, WhyIslam, LADO, ALMA, IslamInSpanish, HablamosIslam, PIEDAD, and LALMA, Alianza Islamica, the Bism Rabbik Foundation, Latino Muslims of the Bay Area, Latino Muslims of Arizona, and the Latino Muslims of Chicago. Indeed, thank you for all the Islamic institutions that work regularly with Latino Muslims.

I must also say thank you for the growing Muslim community of Latin America: Juan Suquillo, Omar Weston, Muhammad Ruiz, Isa Garcia, Anas Amer Quevedo, Isa Rojas, and the late Dawud Herrera. And, I thank you for the late Malcolm X, W.D. Muhammad, and T.B. Irving. Thank you for anyone who has ever contributed to the ever-growing body of information about Latino Muslims. Thank you for Aminah McCloud, Debora McNichol, Camilla Stein, Clay Chip Smith, Gaston Espinoza, Harold Morales, Patrick Bowen, Ken Chitwood, Hjamil Martinez-Vazquez, and the late Linda Delgado.

Allah, thank you for giving me the courage to complete this book. Please forgive me if I have offended anyone. Everything that I do is solely for you. Thank you for your guidance.

Juan Jose Galvan

Sr. Khadijah – The People's Sister

Nylka Vargas

We all have specific gifts, characteristics, and traits we imprint on this planet and its inhabitants that remain etched-long after our passing. Blessed are some with an abundance of this innate, natural ability. Such is the case for Sister Khadijah.

Khadijah was born in Puerto Rico as Vita Milagros Rivera on August 14, 1950, into a Catholic, Ecuadorean-Puerto Rican family. Everyone whose life she touched, including her children and close friends, describes her as compassionate, fierce and determined to serve others.

I first met Khadijah in 2009, at the Seventh Annual Latino Muslim Day in New Jersey. She was a guest speaker and I felt honored to meet her. She was such an accomplished woman, radiating light and love. I recall complimenting her on her unwavering commitment to service; however, she immediately rebuked me and explained how only through Allah is anything possible. I admired how she embodied a selfless ability to serve and lead by example. She was forever committed to the objective, both in triumph and in failure. She always refused any claim to leadership or self-praise. I learned through Khadijah how not to fear challenges and how to keep persevering despite the demands of maintaining a non-profit.

I knew Khadijah best through her work in *dawah*, or "call to Islam". Her dawah manifested in many ways: Women's Dawah, Latino Dawah, and leadership training. Khadijah brought knowledge of Islam to countless individuals. The organization she co-founded in 1988 in New York City, PIEDAD, is her legacy. Piedad, or *Taqwa*, means piety or God-fearing. Its acronym stands for Propagación Islámica para la Educación de Devoción a Aláh el Divino. PIEDAD began as outreach directed towards overlooked Latinas in NYC, but the founders of PIEDAD were not all Spanish speaking. Members have always been encouraged to speak freely and Khadijah urged members to have a lifelong thirst for knowledge.

Under her leadership, PIEDAD organized Islamic speaking conferences at Colombia University, Masjid At-Taqwa in Brooklyn in addition to the Islamic Circle of North America (ICNA) and Islamic Society of North America (ISNA) conferences. She also organized, through PIEDAD, Chicago's first Latino Muslim conference with prominent guest speakers such as Jamal Badawi, Imam Siraj Wahhaj,

Mohammed Nasim, Dr. Thomas Irving, Dr. Omar Kasule, and others. Khadijah represented PIEDAD at the Second Annual Latino Islamic Congress in Spain.

Following the tragic events of 9-11, Khadijah made herself available to the media. She appeared on "Telemundo" and the "Christina Show" to demystify Islam for the Latinos of Miami. In 2007, Khadijah was one of several sisters of PIEDAD interviewed to be a part of a 3-part series entitled, "Muslims in America". She spoke candidly about why she helped found the organization and the challenges Muslim face with the rise of Islamophobia.

The most significant impact Khadijah had was with one-on-one dawah. This personalization of the deen (religion) was the most powerful. She was practical in how she handled the reality of the dawah and acknowledged the difficulties one may face after embracing Islam, laying out sister-friendly plans. She always ensured there was something for us to be active and contribute to the betterment of the world. Through it all, Khadijah was a great source of hope. Khadijah told all her sisters in faith to be proud and empowered, without sacrificing their Muslim identity. The message resonated with me deeply.

In addition to her work with PIEDAD, Khadijah served as a community activist with faith-based organizations. She fought for civil rights, justice, and was involved in causes that help fight hunger and the exploitation of farm workers. At least once a month, Khadijah was volunteering with organizations feeding the hungry or collecting donations to buy needy kids new bicycles. She served as a second mother to many students in the socio-disadvantaged Tampa Bay area school where she worked. She offered genuine advice and guidance when it was needed the most. Those she mentored will never forget her counsel.

Khadijah was a Latina Muslim pioneer. She, along with other Latina leaders, helped pave the way for the rest of us. They were courageous enough to try to make a difference with limited resources. They had the foresight and ingenuity to connect with a global audience before the age of social media. It is up to us to honor their lifetime of achievements and continue down their path.

Our Ummah lost a humanitarian and activist with the death of Khadijah, and her shoes have not been filled since.

Khadijah Rivera
August 14, 1950 - November 22, 2009

Remembering Ibrahim Gonzalez

Rahim Ocasio

Latino Muslims are relative newcomers to the American Islamic landscape, and their history is for the most part unknown. I would like to speak of one who made a difference in the portrayal of Latino Muslims, empowering them in ways that are not fully appreciated today.

I met Ibrahim Gonzalez when he was twelve years old. He was deeply thoughtful and sensitive; those qualities led him to a lifelong habit of looking beyond convention and to a penchant for artistic expression. He developed a love for music and became a gifted guitarist, pianist, and percussionist. His sensitivity, however, also made him acutely aware of the oppressive nature of life in El Barrio. With a stubborn, unyielding sense of justice, he made it his life's mission to stand up and fight injustice at every turn.

As a very young teenager, he was organizing high schoolers as part of the Third World Students League, a mass organization of the Young Lords Party. He would also arrange security for campus takeovers, always willing to take the first watch and to put himself on the front line. He remained until the day he breathed his last breath, committed to the struggle for better conditions for all oppressed people.

Ibrahim became a Muslim in 1973. Like other Latino Muslims from El Barrio who came from an environment steeped in militancy and resistance, he looked to continue the struggle from an Islamic perspective. Alas Ibrahim was to experience frustration upon frustration. Latino Muslims were few in number, and were dismissed by the older established Muslim groups as insignificant.

This manifested during Ibrahim's employment at Islamic Society of North America (ISNA) headquarters in Indiana. Noticing the absence of Spanish Islamic material, he took it upon himself to put together a translation of a famous Islamic brochure, even preparing the printing plates. ISNA brass, however, turned him down and showed absolutely no interest in Latinos or Latino *dawah*. Ibrahim was deeply hurt and troubled with the little regard his fellow Muslims held for Latinos. Before his conversion, he was a tireless worker for the rights of Latinos. Now, his Muslim brothers made it abundantly clear that regarding his people, they could not care less.

Ibrahim was undeterred. With the same tenacity he displayed as a teenager, he masterminded a Latino Muslim event at El Museo del

Barrio in 1985 that was so impactful, Latino Muslims were courted to participate in conferences and *dawah* programs by the same established organizations that had rebuffed and ignored them previously. Prior to Ibrahim's historic "coup", there existed a feeling in some circles that Latinos should just disappear, subsuming themselves into existing immigrant or African-American groups. After the event at El Museo del Barrio, it was understood that Latino Muslims could no longer be discounted.

Ibrahim continued to be a key figure in the growth of the Latino Muslim community. He co-founded Alianza Islamica, the first Islamic organization to ever serve the needs of a Latino community. In fact, Ibrahim represented Alianza Islamica at a convention sponsored by the same ISNA that had repeatedly ignored him. He went on to become a noted radio personality, hosting two programs, and was a presence on a local cable channel in the Bronx.

He never lost his love of music, going on to become a composer and producer. He also loved to perform onstage, often traveling the country with his quintet. Ibrahim had a profound spiritual dimension and remained to the end a faithful adherent to the Naqshbandi Sufi order.

Ibrahim Gonzalez was indeed one of the most critical and influential Latino Muslims in our short history and a true pioneer. He changed the way Latino Muslims are perceived today, opening the gates toward dignity and respect - something I believe is taken for granted by the current generation. His loss was immense, but his legacy lives on. May Allah have mercy on him and admit him into His Paradise. Ameen.

Ibrahim Gonzalez
January 26, 1956 - June 4, 2013

A Tribute to Benjamin Perez

Juan Galvan

Benjamin Perez was born on June 7, 1933, in Carlsbad, New Mexico. He was of Mexican-American and Native American (Seminole and Yaqui) descent and the second eldest of eight children. His family remained in New Mexico until their move to Dinuba, California, when Benjamin was 9 years old. He moved to Oakland shortly after where he married Cecilia Perez in 1955. Together, they had a long, fruitful marriage of 54 years with four children and nine grandchildren. After a long battle with cancer, he died peacefully in his home on December 8, 2009, surrounded by his family.

After an honorable discharge from the Air Force in order to care for his aging parents, Benjamin took a job at Calo Pet Foods, a cannery for dog and cat food in Oakland. While employed at the cannery, he met a co-worker who invited him to a Nation of Islam (NOI) meeting. In a 2002 interview with Deborah Kong of the Associated Press, Benjamin described his first foray into Islam, "I saw there was a lot of knowledge in their teachings to black people. Their food was delicious. They were friendly. I liked it there and I stayed." He joined the NOI in 1957 and became known as Benjamin X.

After some initial rejection, Benjamin was permitted to join the Fruit of Islam (FOI), a male-only subgroup within NOI. He began attending classes that included topics like public relations, which as per NOI leader Elijah Muhammad, would allow Benjamin to reach more Latinos. He ultimately becomes the chaplain of Indian and Latin American Outreach at Muhammad's Temple of Islam. Among acquaintances within the NOI, Benjamin considered Malcolm X to be a respected and beloved friend. They initially met when Malcolm X came to Oakland and expressed an interest in learning Spanish. During this period, Benjamin introduced the NOI teachings to his friend Cesar Chavez, the farmworker activist. Cesar Chavez would later give an in-depth interview in a 1972 issue of *Muhammad Speaks*.

Benjamin eventually left the NOI after questioning some of its teachings and converted to mainstream Sunni Islam. He became a chaplain of the World Community of Al-Islam in the West under the leadership of Imam W.D. Muhammad, the son of Elijah Muhammad, who after his father's death would bring the NOI closer to Sunni Islam.

In 1978, he became a member of the California Muslim Chaplain Council.

Benjamin was very active in the California prison system since 1963. He has lectured in eleven major California prisons and received seven awards. Some prisons he has worked at include San Quentin State Prison, Folsom State Prison, Solano State Prison, and Chino Correctional Institution. Benjamin traveled to all the significant Native American reservations in California, including Hoopa Valley Tribe, Round Valley Indian Tribes, and Checkerboard Reservation. He has served as the chairman of the Intertribal Friendship House in Oakland.

Benjamin became one of the first Latino Muslims from the United States to perform the Muslim pilgrimage to Mecca (Hajj) in 1977. He would return in 1997 and visit Jerusalem on his way home. Upon returning from Hajj, he lengthen his name to Hajji Ibrahim Benjamin Perez Mahomah. However, he was widely known as simply Imam Benjamin.

Much of Benjamin's life was dedicated to connecting Latino and Native Americans to Islam. He traveled the country, lecturing to English and Spanish-speaking audiences, and focused much of his energy on interfaith dialogue. He had an innate talent to move with ease within a variety of multi-cultural, multi-lingual, and multi-denominational settings. He was the founder of Spanish Speaking and Native American Islamic Outreach in Oakland, and was the first president of the California Latino Muslim Association (CALMA). Benjamin has spoken at various national Islamic conventions and has written several articles published in prominent Islamic journals.

Benjamin was a great Muslim pioneer who over the course of several decades touched the lives of countless people. Throughout this country, he is recognized for his exceptional contributions on behalf of Islam and Latinos. Brother Benjamin, you have paved the way for many and will always be remembered.

Introduction

Juan Galvan

The *shahadah* is the first of Islam's five pillars. It is the testimony in the belief of a single God and Muhammad being the Messenger of God; what makes someone a Muslim. By taking *shahadah*, new Muslims pledge to live by the precepts of Islam. Although the destination for those who recite the *Shahadah* is the same, each person's distinctive life experiences influence the unique path they take towards Islam. No group embodies this reality better than the diverse, dynamic, and ever-growing Latino Muslim population.

When learning of the increasing number of Latinos embracing Islam, many Muslims and non-Muslims react with surprise. Some hold the belief that being Latino and Muslim are incompatible. One can only imagine a similar response from the non-Muslims of the Arab Peninsula when witnessing the rapid spread of Islam during the lifetime of the Prophet Muhammad. Why would a people dominated by pagan practices reject all of their deities and accept the belief in a single God?

The earliest converts to Islam, the *Sahaba*, were loyal companions of the Prophet who came to Islam in different ways. Some staunchly fought Islam until their conversion, such as Omar. Some came to Islam early and freely, such as Abu Bakr. The *Sahaba* sacrificed much of their old lives and had to accustom themselves to a new, altered identity. In many ways, the stories of Latino Muslim converts are very similar. Although certainly not at the level of practice of the *Sahaba*, many Latinos who choose to follow Islam face the same struggles assimilating into a new reality. The story of the *Sahaba* is a fundamental way of understanding the idea behind this endeavor.

This book is about struggles. A struggle to accept Islam as a new faith and new way of life. A struggle to be patient and deal with the response of family and friends to their conversion. Some stories are positive and uplifting, with full acceptance by those in their lives. Others start with angst and conflict, but ultimately end with complete acceptance. For some new Muslims, issues remain unresolved to this day. Each story is as unique as its author. You will find stories by young and old, rich and poor, male and female, and many more.

Many find the very idea that I would compile, edit, and introduce a book about Latino Muslims surprising considering my background. As a third generation Mexican-American who grew up in the Texas

Panhandle, I do not fulfill the stereotypes that exist about Muslims. I still recall the first time someone asked why I embraced Islam. I was taken aback by the question and surprised by my inability to readily provide an answer. This question led to a great deal of self-reflection and in a way, this work became my personal search for answers.

My search of self-discovery led me to reach out and inquire why others converted. I have posed this question to hundreds of Latino Muslims. Their responses provided a colleague, Samantha Sanchez, and myself with the idea for this book in 2001. Being young and inexperienced, we did not foresee the complexities of such a vast undertaking. Among the most considerable difficulties, was deciding on the scope and title of the book. The title evolved to include the word "journey" to emphasize the process that Latino Muslims have taken on their way toward Islam. Despite Samantha being unable to further contribute to the creation of this book due to familial obligations, she insisted I push forward to complete the project without her. These stories were an inspiration to me and kept me returning to this book. Despite the scope of this project and its challenges, such as legal requirements for releases and the misplacement of contact information over time, I never wavered because of how much was at stake.

When I first converted, I was distressed and discouraged by the lack of information available about Latino Muslims. I remember taking great comfort in reading conversion stories of others. Keeping my experiences in mind, I understood the importance of gathering and centralizing these stories into written form. Latino Muslims want their stories told and shared with friends and family. This book allows us to preserve our individual history and to share a part of ourselves that is not well known and poorly understood. Books about Latinos and Muslims in the United States have until recently been devoid of information about Latino Muslims. I hope that other Latino Muslims will take comfort in learning about the similar struggles experienced by other Latino Muslims.

My hope is this book will educate about Latinos, Muslims, and Islam. Despite Latinos being the most rapid growing and largest minority group in the United States and Islam being the fastest growing religion in our nation, so much misinformation exists about both groups. In these divisive times, some Americans view Latinos and Muslims with a similar level of mistrust and contempt. This book may make people uncomfortable because it will challenge misconceptions. Contributors had the courage to open up and share their stories with everyone. I did my best to stay true to their original meanings and intentions. I avoided editing content, even statements some may find controversial, because everyone has a right to tell their story.

The table of contents will assist readers with familiarizing themselves to the scope of this book. This book follows a simple format, beginning with a few previously published articles of interest to Latino Muslims followed by conversion stories, and ends with a list of Islamic phrases and a bibliography.

This labor of love is for each Latino who decided to take a leap of faith. Each individual is part of the foundation of our great Latino Muslim community. I want to thank you, the reader, for your interest. By the time you complete this book, God willing, you will understand why Latinos are becoming Muslim. My hope is this book will become a part of your journey - whoever and wherever you may be. I present to you: *Latino Muslims: Our Journeys to Islam.*

Islam is for everyone. Islam es para todos.

The Rise Of Latino Muslims

Juan Galvan

In the Quran, Allah (SWT) says: "And We did not send any messenger but with the language of his people, so that he might explain to them clearly. Then Allah leaves astray whom He wills, and guides whom He wills. He is the Mighty, the Wise." (14:4). In the verse, language doesn't only mean language in its verbal form. Prophets addressed the concerns, values, beliefs, and needs of the people to whom they were sent. The Prophet Muhammad (PBUH) was born in Arabia and naturally spoke the language of his people. He knew his people and their customs, and was familiar with their way of thinking.

The Prophet would send companions to invite tribes and kings to Islam. By conveying the message in a manner which non-Muslims understood, his companions were able to clarify the message of Islam. This is why we educate other Latinos about the important role of the Virgin Mary and Jesus (PBUH) in Islam. This is also why all Muslims must seek to make the message of Islam accessible to non-Muslims in their own language. We are Latinos and Muslims, and as Latino Muslims want to call others to the beautiful religion of Islam.

We are Latinos. Latinos are generally identified by their descent. Latinos come from many countries. Although a majority are from Spanish-speaking countries, some Latinos from South and Central American speak English or Portuguese. Although Latinos do not always share the same culture, Latinos are generally known for their love of family. Some Latinos are recent immigrants to the United States, while others come from families who have been here for generations. Recent immigrants may have less command of the English language, whereas those Latinos who have lived here for generations may know little or no Spanish.

We are Muslims. As Muslims, we bear witness that there is no one and nothing worthy of worship except Allah, and we bear witness that Muhammad is His last Prophet and Messenger. We believe in the oneness and uniqueness of Allah, the sole Creator and Sustainer of the universe. We believe that Prophet Muhammad is the best example for humanity. We agree that salvation is gained, with the grace of Allah, through the five daily prayers, fasting the month of Ramadan, giving zakat, and making the pilgrimage to Mecca, if one is capable of doing so. We believe that Allah created the angels and sent honorable Messengers with Divine Books to guide humanity and warn of the Day of Judgment. We believe in Divine Decree, which is the knowledge and consequence of Allah over His creation. We seek perfection in worship, such that we worship Allah as if we see Him, and although we cannot see Him, we undoubtedly believe that He is continually watching over us.

We are Latino Muslims. The 2017 report based on the Latino Muslim Survey estimated the number of Latino Muslims between 50,000 to 70,000. Religious conversion is generally a personal choice. People, places, and events are all significant factors that affect a Latino's decision to embrace Islam. Most Latino Muslims embraced Islam because they believe the religion is true. Many Latinos believe that leaving Catholicism equates rejecting their identity. However, defining culture by faith is not very practical. Our ancestors were Christian, Muslim, Jewish, or pagan. One can argue that if most American Latinos are Muslim 100 years from now, the typical Latino would consider Islam to be inseparable from Latino culture. The Latino culture of today could become the Latino Muslim culture of tomorrow.

By calling non-Muslims to Islam, we are inviting them to join a universal brotherhood and sisterhood in Islam. We thank all Muslims who assist the growing Latino Muslim community. Any accomplishments are a success for all Muslims because we Muslims are one ummah. The most significant thing that Latino Muslims offer is not literature, events, or speakers, but instead hope, patience, and truth. We do this by our invitation to peace through submission to our Creator. Knowing that we have given the smallest deed for the sake of Allah (SWT) is most rewarding.

This piece is based on the editorial initially published in The Message International, November-December 2004, p. 7.

Thoughts Among Latino Muslims

Juan Galvan

While performing research for articles last year, I sent out ten questions to ten American Latino Muslims. Upon reviewing the answers I received, I realized that many Muslims could benefit from this valuable information. Consequently, I decided to write an article composed of the responses. Latino Muslims may relate to the responses. For sake of privacy, I either used first names or Muslim names of the respondents. I hope you may benefit from the following answers.

1. Why do Latinos convert to Islam in America?

Getsa: People convert to Islam for the same reasons others convert to other religions. People convert to Islam because they have a belief that Islam is the best and true religion.

Daniel: It's the same reasons why people convert to Islam anywhere else. They develop a love for Islam.

Teqwa: I think it's mostly about disillusionment with the Catholic Church. Many Catholics don't understand Christian concepts just like Baptists, Methodist, etc. Simplicity and unity are lacking in the Christian Church.

Farheed: I think maybe you are better off by asking the question: "Why do Latinos revert to Islam?" In my opinion, this question gets down to the crux of the issue, because you address all Latinos rather than analyzing a particular location.

Omar: Because converts had the opportunity to speak with Muslims, they opened their hearts to the message of Islam.

Aisha: I don't think it is a question of America. The question is more about a more precise definition of God and about how to worship, about personal experiences, education, and similarities in family values.

Yolanda: Disappointment in Christianity.

Gilberto: I don't know about others. I'm an Afro-Cuban raised in America, so in my case, I went through the route of reading about Malcolm X and the Nation of Islam, etc. along with more "religious" concerns about things like the Trinity, incarnation, and others. I am not sure what trajectory other Latinos take. Reasons for conversion are different for everyone.

Ricardo: People have their unique situation in terms of what they've been exposed to all their lives. Because Islam is all-encompassing, it typically addresses the average person's concerns. Concerning Latinos, those who convert will usually have traveled the road of knowledge. It is through knowledge of both their current religion in comparison with the knowledge of what Islam is all about that enlightens them and then inspires them to embrace Islam. Most Latinos are Catholic, and there is much negativity experienced by Latinos towards the Catholic religion. Those negative concerns are addressed in Islam, and the whole thing begins to make sense. Once their rationale makes sense of it, their hearts follow suit bringing a person to embrace Islam with their minds as well as their hearts. That's peace.

2. Why aren't there more Latino Muslims? For example, what have been your observations?

Daniel: The community is not well established yet. More dawah needs to be done towards the huge Latino population. My observation is that there has been no emphasis on dawah towards Latinos.

Getsa: I think that there are more Latino Muslims, but where are they hidden? Latinos in states like Texas have been Roman Catholic for a while now as has been Mexico. I think that has something to do with it as well.

Teqwa: Most non-Muslim Latinos that I have been in contact with think that being a Muslim is a race, not a religion. It's a lack of information. The Telemundo novela about Muslims, "El Clon," yes I know it's a novela, has had a positive effect. More Latinos are watching it, and between the drama, an uncle gives information about Islam in a very positive light. I wish they had it in English as well.

Aziz: The most important reason why there are not many Latino Muslims is that there is not much Spanish dawah. Dawah in Spanish is very important. This is because religion mixed with the Spanish language is a part of their culture. Dawah must address these issues.

Farheed: A possible answer to the question could be that Latinos are just unaware that there is such a thing as a Latino Muslim. In my opinion, it just boils down to education and knowing that they exist.

Omar: Because many people are Hispanic and not all of them speak English. They find it difficult to learn another language. But they must to get a better job and to learn about Islam. People have many responsibilities with work and family. Learning about Islam requires some commitment.

Yolanda: There aren't more Latino Muslims because of the lack of dawah work and proper cultural approach by those of us who are Muslims. There are not many of us. We are still growing, and the other Muslim communities have not done enough to train us new Muslims, so most of us are struggling on our own.

Gilberto: I really don't know. Perhaps some Latinos groups, such as NY Puerto Ricans, can identify with African-Americans more than others and find Islam that way.

Ricardo: From my observations, there are three main reasons. First and foremost, there aren't many people delivering the message to the Latino community, and many who do may not be very effective in doing so. Second, once there is someone who gives the message there is a barrier that must be overcome. If the person is a devout Catholic, many times their emotions make it difficult to cope with the message delivered. It causes a sort of "crushing" of their faith; hence, they become somewhat heart-broken and try to stay away from Islam. The third reason I believe has to do with those Latinos who don't think about religion much, to begin with, much less a religion that they feel is cult-like, "promotes terrorism," seemingly oppresses women, and that is very strict. Those who tend to listen have somewhat of a balance between being a rational person and a compassionate person.

Aisha: I think there are more Latino Muslims than we believe there are. They just do not always come to the mosque. I thought I knew all the Latina Muslims in the community - that was about four, but recently I held a get-together of Latina Muslims in our area alone and found that there were 10 to 15 that are known by one lady in the community. Imagine those who we don't know about. I just found out of another one just yesterday from the Dominican Republic who was not on the list of women I called to the gathering. I was astounded and pleased.

3. What are the main joys and difficulties of being a Latino Muslim?

Daniel: The joys include following the path of the Last Prophet of Allah and going back to our roots. Difficulties involve dealing with stereotypes.

Teqwa: Joys include spending time with my friends, and there is an automatic sense of unity. Difficulties? I think all Latinos, regardless of skin color, should feel welcome by the general Latino community.

Getsa: One joy is that since there are so many Muslims now, I can't really feel out of place. One difficulty is that as a woman, I have less contact with people.

Aziz: The main joy of being a Muslim is the peace of knowing that I'm on the Truth. This feeling is peaceful to the soul and the body. However, with all these great emotions, one cannot escape the reality of the state of the Ummah and the Muslims. One of the biggest trials is being patient with Muslims from Muslim countries who maintain a racist attitude toward other Muslims, especially towards converts. This type of Jahiliyyah still helps the enemies of Allah (SWT) to keep the Muslims disunited. Because of something so simple and easy to fall into, the Muslims hate each other and cannot even come together to make Allah's religion superior over all others.

Farheed: A joy I get from being a Latino Muslim is that I get to meet other Latino Muslims. I have the opportunity to link with Latino Muslims on two different levels. One, as Latinos, we have that instant connection through culture and language. Second, the initial relationship becomes stronger once the Islamic link is apparent. The only difficulty I encounter is when family members are partaking in a Catholic ceremony, and I choose not to be a part of it. In this type of situation, one feels awkward.

Yolanda: Islam gives me peace of mind. It brings me closer to my creator and gives me a purpose in life. It has brought me a clear and definite path to follow with other brothers and sisters. One difficulty concerns the issue of communities dividing by culture. For example, I am part of an Indo-Pakistani community. As a Musulmana, I've had to learn what is cultural and what Islam is. This is something that I'm open to since I work for a cultural institution, but what about those brothers and sisters that are converting? Where are they going? How do they feel when they become part of a mosque that is Arab? African American? Indo-Pakistani? Do they feel welcomed? If they don't learn about the culture, are they left out? If people leave Islam because communities make them feel "left out," who is responsible? This is a reality, and I am wondering how many communities choose cultural over religious. Is our goal as Latino Muslims to form our own mosques and separate ourselves culturally too?

Aisha: There are more joys, when one makes the decision to become a Muslim, regardless of where you are from - especially in a broader and more spiritual sense. The clarity of the Quran and the constant reminders for us to learn more and to use our powers of intelligence, observation, and reason when dealing with all matters including faith, is simply refreshing and enlightening. The most prominent negative for me as a Latino Muslim is merely the barriers one feels with family. At the outset, they were astounded by my decision to change my faith. As time progresses, they have learned to accept it, but it is never quite a full acceptance. I have to admit that I made things more difficult in the process by being very strict on myself and not allowing the adjustment to take time - mainly when I was around my family. Actions speak louder than words and although the path is steep, the benefits and results are always sweeter when one struggles.

Omar: We don't have the same chance to get involved with other Muslims because they have different customs than ours. They grew up in other places overseas, and in many ways, we do not and cannot think like them. I'm referring to people like Arabs and Pakistanis.

Gilberto: I'm not sure about joys specific to being a Latino Muslim. One difficulty is that since there are a small number of us, there is a certain degree of aloneness compared to other communities that are more represented.

Ricardo: The main joy of being a Latino Muslim has more to do with being a Muslim than about being Latino. There's fulfillment in Islam that has nothing to do with being Latino. The main difficulty with being a Latino Muslim is letting go of things that were part of your Latino background that is un-Islamic.

4. What needs to be done to call more Latinos to Islam?

Aisha: We need to have more knowledgeable Latino Muslims, for one. Second, they need to speak and write the Spanish language fluently. Personally, I think there is more need to merely educate Latinos about Islam, the beliefs, and practices, than to "call" them to the faith. The outcome of education would be of greater benefit towards building communities that tolerate and respect each other. If they knew about the similar values we share in our faiths, we could join hands to work together on many issues we have in common. The preaching mentality meets with much resistance. If we have a conversion mentality or demeanor, we will not get far. And let's face it; it is Allah who makes Muslims, not us. I cannot stress enough that the character of a person speaks louder than merely what we say.

Getsa: We need more publications and more open, publicized events. I don't know how you would become Muslim unless you have contact with other Muslims. I only came in contact with Islam by association through my husband. I don't know if Muslims venture out to other groups for the purpose of calling others to Islam.

Teqwa: More interaction. I spend a good deal of time in the Latino community as a bilingual/ESL teacher. I have parents who ask many questions, which is a good thing. I think that if more was put out there in Spanish, it would be much better. Just being around…allowing people to see you is critical.

Daniel: Organize.

Yolanda: We, Latinos, need to empower ourselves. We need to approach mosques and other local organizations to assist us in dawah work in our own communities.

Omar: We need more dawah at the mosque but in Spanish. Dawah at mosques is better for new Muslims. For non-Muslims, maybe, somewhere other than the mosque would bring bigger crowds.

Ricardo: I believe that there must be individuals who will deliver the message to Latino Muslims. These individuals must possess certain qualities. They must be very knowledgeable in at least the basics of Islam and the everyday practices. They must be articulate, and they must have a certain degree of eloquence. Some people deliver the message stronger than others do. However, the point is that there is no better way to get someone to subscribe to a belief than by giving the message by word-of-mouth.

Gilberto: Something that occurred to me a long time ago is that Latinos as a people have connections to Islam from three different directions. Spain was once a Muslim country, and Islam has made its imprint on Latino culture and language. The obvious is the African component. Some researchers say that Muslims arrived in the Pre-Columbian Americas and also left marks in the language and culture such as in names such as Tallahassee, Florida. Anyway, after the fall of Andalusia to Christians, Spanish culture has a tendency to define itself in opposition to "esos Moros" over there. More work has to be done to make Islam seem less foreign. A Chicano friend, who was considering Islam, partly because he was dating a Muslim woman, is drawn to the social justice element of Islam. Perhaps if Muslims stressed this aspect more, we would find more support in the Latino community. The mix of conservative "family values" and a radically progressive view of social justice would (insha'Allah) be appealing to many Americans who are generally not receptive to dawah.

5. What are ways to help Latinos abandon their misconceptions about Islam?

Ricardo: We accomplish this through educating them and by example. Muslims must first become less isolated from their non-Muslim neighbors. Increased positive interaction will create increased awareness.

Awareness brought about through positive interaction can overcome popular negative misconceptions. All Muslims must do this, not just Latino Muslims.

Aziz: One of the best ways to help Latinos get around the misconceptions is educating them about Islam and about Spanish history. By doing so, they can see for themselves how Islam relates to them.

Getsa: We should define the common misconceptions for one. Many Latinos think women have to be completely covered and are also afraid of how women are treated by Muslim men. This needs to be removed from people's minds by talking about positive role models. There is a lack of positive Muslim role models in our society. I can think of three instances that play in my mind when it comes to negative role models, though: 1. Ali - the movie. Muhammad Ali converts and cheats on his wife. 2. The harsh treatment of women in Afghanistan. 3. OZ - an HBO series. The Muslims in that prison kill. I know that two out of the three are fictitious but all three play on people's minds just as the real thing does.

Daniel: We could begin by organizing media outlets for spreading Islam.

Farheed: A right approach is to tell Latino brothers and sisters that many Spanish words are similar to Arabic words. In addition, you could say to them that Islam had an enormous influence on the Spanish daily life and culture for hundreds of years.

Omar: We should speak with people who are interested in Islam. I mean Latinos watch the media, and media says wrong things or lies. Many Latinos are interested in Islam but no one is telling them what it really is.

Aisha: I think the first step is to not marginalize ourselves when we become Muslim. There are many ways we can work with the Latino community to help the injustices and social problems occurring in the Latino community and that means we have to volunteer in human rights organizations, immigrant organizations, domestic violence organizations, and so on. We must be active in both the Latino community and the Muslim community. After all, we have more similarities than differences when it comes to hardships we face here in the west as minorities. Once a person becomes active without a conversion agenda, both Latinos and Muslims will start to build bridges of respect and tolerance. Education, involvement, and activity are essential.

Gilberto: I don't know of a fast way. In terms of my mom, it has mainly taken slow, patient explanations about various things.

6. Do you know any statistics about the number of Muslims in a particular state? Is there a way to get these figures?

Ricardo: I'd have to do research. The US Census is the first place I would look to get these figures. After that, I would think involving mosques in data gathering efforts would be the best way to get the information. The question of whether it is worth doing or even if it matters must be addressed first.

Gilberto: I have no idea about finding the numbers other than by calling all the mosques to ask what percentage of mosque attendees are Latino. You could also call Latinos around the country to ask about their religious affiliation. You could also poll Latino organizations to ask what percentage of members is Muslim. There are problems with whatever method you choose though.

Aisha: There really is not a system to attain demographic information about our community - unless you become a member of a mosque. Even then, they don't keep records about your background or nationality. This is sad but true. This kind of "census" work is essential for our communities, locally and nationally, but mosques have not taken on the task. Organizations, such as CAIR and AMC, have conducted some studies.

7. There seems to be a positive correlation between mosque size and rate of conversion. Why?

Teqwa: At larger mosques, there are more activities at all hours.

Yolanda: Larger mosques are more diverse and open.

Getsa: At larger mosques, there will be more positive role models. If more Muslims are in the community, more Muslims will be practicing

Islam so there's higher quality in the overall community. More people are available to speak about Islam so more conversion. It's like with everything. The more resumes you send out, the more chances you'll be called for an interview.

Ricardo: I can only speculate as to why this correlation exists. Maybe it is the fact that there are more Muslims living closer to larger mosques, thereby, creating a higher concentration of Muslims that in turn interacts with non-Muslims. Again, I believe that more interaction of Muslims with non-Muslims will increase awareness, which will increase the number of people who convert.

Omar: I disagree. Although there isn't a mosque in Monterrey, Mexico, many people are interested in Islam there. I'm originally from Mexico.

Farheed: I would like to know more about how the information was collected to come up with the correlation.

8. Most Latinos who leave Catholicism choose the Pentecostal religions. Why? What can Muslims learn from this?

Daniel: Perhaps, they are tired of the same liturgy in the Catholic Church. They are looking to be active in their faith. Muslims can learn a lot from this. We need to be as effective as the Evangelicals or Pentecostals.

Yolanda: Protestant religions have always been more consistent and adamant about providing free social services and information about their religion. For example, Jehovah's Witnesses have seen a dramatic increase in the last ten years because they are organized, focused, and persistent.

Farheed: I have no knowledge of the Pentecostal religions and cannot form an objective opinion.

Omar: I was Pentecostal, and I knew about Islam. I think people prefer to convert to Christianity because there are Hispanic churches where they can learn about Christianity in their own language. In general, it's easier to find a church than a mosque in America. More people would convert if there were more mosques.

Teqwa: They probably leave the Catholic Church for lack of support. Alhamdulillah, I have been Muslim for a long time. If I were a new Muslim and didn't have friends who could be a sounding board, I might have dropped out.

Aisha: I am curious to know why myself, but I can tell you that the trend I have seen is that they tend to leave Catholicism because of the idol worship, the pressures of the "high" social classes, and general hierarchy existing within the churches. They tend to go to other Christian denominations because they firmly believe in the divinity of Jesus (PBUH). In addition, I think that it also appeals to them that in different sects they read the Bible more than in Catholicism.

Gilberto: (getting on soapbox). I think Latino, African-American, and European-American Muslims need to realize the extent to which they can be themselves and still be Muslim. While riding my bike around campus, I found these people playing congas outside on one Sunday afternoon a few years ago. I stopped to listen for a while. Eventually, one Latino starts speaking in Spanish. I listen to what he's saying, and it's some generally positive stuff about God. And, then I hear a little longer, and I realize that they are Muslim. Subhanallah! We need to first learn the difference between being Muslim and being Arab, Indo/Pak, Malay, African-American, etc. Arabs, Indo/Paks, and other groups have developed their own ways of being Muslim. This is something that needs to happen among Americans as well. By doing so, we can confidently and naturally find means to be a Muslim and a Latino. To get back to your original question, the idea of "Pentecostal Muslims" is apparently really messed up. In general, I would say that mosques don't really run the gamut of what would be a permissible preaching style. And if there are styles that for some reason are more appealing to specific groups, mosques ought to be encouraged to include them along with others.

9. What kinds of Dawah activities would you suggest? What works and what doesn't work?

Teqwa: We have to be accessible to the public and not be afraid to talk. Hispanic women love to talk so get some sisters out there and make sure they know what they are going to say and aren't scared to say it in a nice way. Another thing is to draw parallels. I make sure that I use things that are common in the Hispanic community to explain Islamic beliefs.

Remember that you are dealing with people who have an allegiance to the Church and have a special place in their heart for Mary and traditions. You have to make sure that you are still positive about their beliefs and show them how Islam is different but also has many of the same thoughts. If not, forget it. They will shut down completely. Please don't forget those who are Cuban, Dominican, Venezuelan or Puerto Rican. Just because someone doesn't look mestizo doesn't mean they should be overlooked.

Omar: There should be regular meetings at mosques or wherever for non-Muslims and/or for new Muslims. Dawah is more successful if it frequent, not only once a year. You have to be available. Non-Muslims have to be able to come to you when they are ready. We also should not expect or wait for them to come to us. Latinos need to know we are Latino Muslims. We can do this by showing our identity, praying, discussing Islam, etc.

Aisha: Education has a more significant impact. Preaching or the "Jehovah's Witness" mentality does not work, at least not for me. Being involved in the Latino community alone would have a significant impact on helping Latinos gain some interaction with Muslims as well as a greater understanding of Muslims. I think we need to start small. Look into your own community and its surround areas first. It is also vital to build a relationship with Spanish TV networks, radio stations, and newspapers.

Daniel: I believe in acting what you preach. This is the best dawah tool. We should also organize meetings with the community using Hispanic festivals as a possible outlet. It seems to me that anything would work at this point. Cities with large numbers of Latinos should be targeted first and then rural areas. Most other areas are exposed to larger metropolitan areas so you would hope that the trickle effect would occur. Still, Islam should not be limited to any geographical regions.

Yolanda: We have to distribute free literature. We also need to place ads.

Ricardo: Word-of-mouth is the best. Individual attention is most effective. Everyone has their own perspective on religion, life after death, the soul, the origin of man, etc. Because everyone has a different view, it requires that the message of Islam be delivered to him or her in a unique way. You can't expect to deliver the message in one direction and hope to reach everybody. That is impossible. Individual attention must take place. To do that on a mass scale is extremely difficult. That is why Muslims must not be so isolated from their neighbors. As an ummah, we must interact with non-Muslims in a positive fashion delivering the message verbally and by example. There are many things that don't work and many things that do work but it really depends on the individual who's receiving the message and the way the person delivers the message. Some people will be offended when you say, "We don't believe Jesus is the Son of God" while others won't be offended at all. Generally, one must be very patient, tolerant, and careful not to step on their beliefs. We must present Islam as something we believe because of such and such rather than presenting Islam as we're right and you're wrong because of such and such. There are many do's and don'ts.

10. What are your hopes and aspirations for Islam and Latino Muslims in America?

Daniel: InshAllah, we will be growing.

Getsa: I would like Islam to grow because I would like to meet more Muslimahs that are a good influence and role models.

Omar: I hope that there is more work done for Hispanic people in the Spanish language.

Farheed: I hope to see LADO become a dominant force when it comes to representing the Latino Muslim population. May Allah guide LADO.

Yolanda: My hopes are to organize and create a group that assists all new Muslims, not only Latino Muslims. There is a need for this in my own city. Many people who convert like me need guidance. This needs to be in place before dawah work can be done.

Aisha: I simply hope Islam will be recognized and respected as a faith in our community. I firmly believe this will happen if Muslims improve their actions individually. They must consider themselves part of the American society by being active in it and build bridges of understanding with other communities. The outcome of our efforts to educate people about Islam will be up to Allah (SWT), but we cannot think that things will happen without the work.

Ricardo: At the minimum, my hopes and aspirations are for people to understand Islam for what it is as opposed to evaluating Islam through a filter of lies, distortions, and misconceptions. At the maximum, I would hope for as many people to embrace Islam as possible.

Conclusion:

I want to thank the American Latino brothers and sisters who took time out to answer my questions. I hope you have benefited from the responses. The variety of perspectives among Latinos amazes me. Answers to questions were both inspiring and enlightening. Muslims will always disagree on a range of issues. Regardless of our differences, we all agree that calling people to Islam is essential.

This piece is based on the article initially published in The Latino Muslim Voice, January-March 2003, Online.

Jesus and The Virgin Mary In Islam

Juan Galvan

Many people may be surprised that Muslims love Mary, the mother of Jesus. In the Quran, no woman is given more attention than Mary. Mary receives the most attention of any woman mentioned in the Quran even though all the Prophets with the exception of Adam had mothers. Of the Quran's 114 chapters, she is among the eight people who have a chapter named after them. The nineteenth chapter of the Quran is named after her, Mariam. Mariam means Mary in Arabic. The third chapter in the Quran is named after her father, Imran. Chapters Mariam and Imran are among the most beautiful chapters in the Quran. Mary (peace be upon her) is the only woman named explicitly in the Quran. An authentic Haddith states that the Prophet said, "The superiority of 'Aisha to other ladies is like the superiority of Tharid (i.e. meat and bread dish) to other meals. Many men reached the level of perfection, but no woman reached such a level except Mary, the daughter of Imran and Asia, the wife of Pharaoh." (Bukhari 4.643). Indeed, both Mary and Pharaoh's wife are an example (Quran 66:11-12). The Virgin Mary plays a very significant role in Islam. She is an example and a sign for all people.

In the Quran, Mary's story begins while she is still in her mother's womb. The mother of Mary said: "O my Lord! I do dedicate into Thee what is in my womb for Thy special service: So accept this of me: For Thou hearest and knowest all things." (Quran 3:35). She wanted the baby in her womb to serve only the Creator. When Mary was delivered, she said: "O my Lord! Behold! I am delivered of a female child!" (Quran 3:36). She had expected her baby to be a male child who would grow up to be a scholar or religious leader. However, God had a better plan. God is the best of planners. Quran 3:36 continues "...and God knew best what she brought forth- 'And no wise is the male like the female. I have named her Mariam, and I commend her and her offspring to Thy protection from Satan, the Rejected.'" Mariam literally means "maidservant of God."

In Quran 3:37, God states that He accepted Mary as her mother had asked. He made Mary grow in purity and beauty. She was assigned to the care of a priest named Zacharias. This is interesting considering few women were given this opportunity.

"Every time that he entered (her) chamber to see her, he found her supplied with sustenance. He said: 'O Mary! Whence (comes) this to you?' She said: 'From God. For God provides sustenance to whom He pleases without measure.'" (Quran 3:37). Upon hearing Mary's answer, "There did Zakariya pray to his Lord, saying: 'O my Lord! Grant unto me from Thee a progeny that is pure: for Thou art He that heareth prayer!'" (Quran 3:38).

Although his wife was barren and he was very old, God blesses Zacharias and his wife Elizabeth with John. John is known as "John the Baptist" in the Bible. Zacharias was skeptical after the angels announced John's birth. The response to his skepticism was "Doth God accomplish what He willeth" (Quran 3:40). John would become a noble and chaste Prophet as the angels had stated (Quran 3:39).

The Quran discusses Mary's miraculous conception as well. "Relate in the Book (the story of) Mary, when she withdrew from her family to a place in the East. She placed a screen (to screen herself) from them; then We sent her Our angel, and he appeared before her as a man in all respects." (Quran 19:16-17). After seeing the angel, she said: "I seek refuge from thee to (God) Most Gracious: (come not near) if thou dost fear God." (Quran 19:18). The angel Gabriel responded: "Nay, I am only a messenger from thy Lord, (to announce) to thee the gift of a pure son." (Quran 19:19). Her next response is expected. She asked: "How shall I have a son, seeing that no man has touched me, and I am not unchaste?" (Quran 19:20). The Angel Gabriel said: "So (it will be): thy Lord saith, 'That is easy for Me: and (We wish) to appoint him as a Sign unto men and a Mercy from Us.' It is a matter (so) decreed." (Quran 19:21). Mary then becomes pregnant.

Jesus is a Prophet and a Messenger. A Messenger is a Prophet who is given revelation from God. Whereas the Torah was revealed to Moses, the Gospel was revealed to Jesus. Messengers are a mercy, guidance, and sign from God. "And God will teach him (Jesus) the Book and Wisdom, the Torah and the Gospel, and (appoint him) as a messenger to the Children of Israel, (with this message):

'I have come to you, with a Sign from your Lord, in that I make for you out of clay, as it were, the figure of a bird, and breathe into it, and it becomes a bird by God's leave. And I heal those born blind, and the lepers, and I bring the dead into life, by God's leave; and I declare to you what ye eat, and what ye store in your houses. Surely therein is a Sign for you if ye did believe. (I have come to you) to attest the Torah which was before me. And to make lawful to you part of what was (before) forbidden to you. I have come to you with a Sign from your Lord. So fear God, and obey me. It is God Who is my Lord and your Lord; then worship Him. This is a Way that is straight.'" (Quran 3:48-51).

God appointed messengers to help us answer questions such as: What happens after I die? What's right and wrong? Does a supernatural world exist? What's the purpose of my creation? Jesus was calling people to the worship of only God. Only by God's leave was Jesus able to perform miracles.

"When Jesus found unbelief on their (the disciples) part he said: 'Who will be my helpers to (the work of) God?'" Said the disciples: "We are God's helpers: We believe in God, and do thou bear witness that we are Muslims.'" (Quran 3:52).

After conceiving Jesus, Mary went away with the baby to a distant place (Quran 19:22). "And the pains of childbirth drove her to the trunk of a palm-tree. She cried (in her anguish): 'Ah! Would that I had died before this! Would that I had been a thing forgotten!'" (Quran 19:23). "But (a voice) cried to her from beneath the (palm-tree): 'Grieve not! For thy Lord hath provided a rivulet beneath thee; And shake towards thyself the trunk of the palm-tree: It will let fall fresh ripe dates upon thee. So eat and drink and cool (thine) eye. And if thou dost see any man, say, 'I have vowed a fast to (God) Most Gracious, and this day will I enter into no talk with any human being.'" (Quran 19:24-26).

Joseph, the magi, and manger are not mentioned in the Quran. God was Mary's only Provider. Muslims do not accept the virgin birth of Jesus as evidence of Jesus' divinity. "The similitude of Jesus before God is as that of Adam; He created him from dust, then said to him: 'Be.' And he was." (Quran 3:59). Adam's creation was even more miraculous because he was born without father and mother. When she brings the baby to her people, they said: "O Mary! Truly a strange thing has thou brought! O sister of Aaron! Thy father was not a man of evil, nor thy mother a woman unchaste!" (Quran 19:27-8). Mary then points to the baby. They said: "How can we talk to one who is a child in the cradle?" (Quran 19:29). Then a miracle occurs that is not mentioned in the Bible. In defense of his mother, Jesus said: "I am indeed a servant of God. He hath given me revelation and made me a prophet; And He hath made me blessed wheresoever I be, and hath enjoined on me Prayer and Charity as long as I live; (He hath made me) kind to my mother, and not overbearing or unblest; So peace is on me the day I was born, the day that I die, and the day that I shall be raised up to life (again)!" (Quran 19:30-33).

The virgin birth of Jesus was a sign. "And (remember) her who guarded her chastity: We breathed into her of Our spirit, and We made her and her son a sign for all peoples." (Quran 21:91). All previous Prophets confirmed the oneness of God (tawheed). Whereas the Holy Trinity is the fundamental concept of God in Christianity, tawheed is the fundamental concept of God in Islam. God exists independent of religion. Muslims do not believe in the concept of Holy Trinity (Quran 5:73). God is not Jesus (Quran 5:72). On the Day of Judgment, when Jesus is asked if he had called people to worship him and his mother as two gods, Jesus will say: "Glory to Thee! Never could I say what I had no right (to say). Had I said such a thing, Thou wouldst indeed have known it. Thou knowest what is in my heart, Thou I know not what is in Thine. For Thou knowest in full all that is hidden." (Quran 5:116).

People should not worship any of God's creation, including Jesus and Mary. We must not assign any of God's creation His divine attributes and characteristics. "He is God the Creator, the Maker, the Shaper. To Him belong the Names Most Beautiful. All that is in the heavens and the earth magnifies Him; He is the All-Mighty, the All-Wise." (Quran 59:24).

Although God can do all things, He only does things that are consistent with His fundamental nature. Begetting a son is not compatible with God's magnificent nature (Quran 19:92, Quran 19:35). Consistent with His fundamental nature is forgiveness. Although Adam and Eve could no longer live in the Paradise, God forgave Adam and Eve for their sin after they sincerely repented (Quran 2:35-37). We are responsible for our own deeds and will not be punished for the acts of another person (Quran 53:38-42). Therefore, Muslims reject the doctrine of original sin. Although Adam and Eve were punished, God would still be merciful by sending Guidance to mankind. "We said: 'Get down all of you from this place (the Paradise), then whenever there comes to you Guidance from Me, and whoever follows My Guidance, there shall be no fear on them, nor shall they grieve.'" (Quran 2:38).

When people hear the term Islam, they naturally tend to think of the organized religion of Islam which started in the 7th century CE with Prophet Muhammad. However, in Arabic, the word Islam comes from the root "salema" which means peace, purity, submission, and obedience. In the religious sense, Islam means peace and purity achieved by submitting to the will of God and obedience to His law. Muslims are those who submit. Muslims believe that all those who submitted to the will of God in line with divine revelation received before the advent of formal Islam with Prophet Muhammad, were themselves also Muslim. So coming from this understanding, Muslims believe that we are part of one continuing faith community with Jesus and Mary. Mary, Jesus, and the disciples were all "Muslims" because they submitted to God.

"Behold! The angels said: 'O Mary! God hath chosen thee and purified thee - chosen thee above the women of all nations. O Mary! Worship thy Lord devoutly: Prostrate thyself, and bow down (in prayer) with those who bow down.'" (Quran 3:42-43).

Another Prophet with a message similar to Jesus' would later be born in Arabia in the sixth century. He also called people to the worship of only God. Although unable to read and write, Muhammad (peace be upon him) would recite beautiful verses of the Quran as they were revealed to him. The Quran is a beautiful miracle, a sign, a mercy, a warner, and guidance for all people. Muhammad is the last Prophet from a line of Prophets that included Noah, Abraham, Moses, and Jesus (peace be upon them). All Prophets were models for righteous living. Muhammad's Sunnah, his sayings, example, and traditions, is also considered revelation. His Sunnah is expressed in various books of Haddiths.

It is through a Haddith that we learn about the five pillars of Islam. In an authentic Haddith, Ibn Umar reported: The Messenger of Allah, peace and blessings be upon him, said, "Islam is built upon five [pillars]: to worship Allah and to disbelieve in what is worshiped besides him, to

establish prayer, to give charity, to perform Ḥajj pilgrimage to the house, and to fast the month of Ramadan." Source: Sahih al-Bukhari 8, Sahih Muslim 16. The five pillars are the foundation of the Islamic faith.

"Indeed in the Messenger of God you have a good example to follow for him who hopes for (the Meeting with) God and the Last Day, and remembers God much." (Quran 33:21).

God created all people to worship Him and to live life-based on His teachings and guidance. "And hold fast, all together, by the Rope which God (stretches out for you), and be not divided among yourselves; and remember with gratitude God's favor on you; for ye were enemies and He joined your hearts in love, so that by His Grace, ye became brethren; and ye were on the brink of the pit of Fire, and He saved you from it. Thus doth God make His Signs clear to you that ye may be guided." (Quran 3:103).

"If anyone desires a religion other than Islam (submission to God), never will it be accepted of him; and in the Hereafter He will be in the ranks of those who have lost." (Quran 3:85). We accomplish this by bearing witness to God's oneness and accepting His final revelation in our daily lives. "O ye who believe! Fear God as He should be feared, and die not except in a state of Islam." (Quran 3:102). There is none worthy of worship but God, and Muhammad is His messenger.

End Note: While writing about the Virgin Mary, I wanted to avoid as much confusion as possible among non-Muslims. My article was written with a non-Muslim audience in mind. Consequently, I used English terms and figures familiar to Christians rather than those in Arabic. For example, "Isa" means Jesus in Arabic, and "Yahya" means John in Arabic. I also avoided using terms of respectability commonly used among Muslims such as SWT, PBUH, SAWS, RA, and AS. I apologize if I have offended anyone.

This piece is based on the article originally published in The Latino Muslim Voice, April-June 2004, Online.

Why Did I Accept Islam?

Abdallah Yusuf de La Plata

Why did I accept Islam? On more than one occasion, I have tried to be elusive about answering this question as I find it difficult to explain even to myself. Most brothers and sisters have had the good fortune to be born into a Muslim family. They have been liberated by the anxious necessity to find a satisfactory answer to the question why they would separate themselves from the culture they were born into, the education received from their parents, and family, their environment, their society, etc. in order to adopt a religion and a belief far removed and strange to the way one had known. Separation and conflict with parents, siblings, extended family, friends and those around us are familiar fears.

I come from an atheist family. My name is Nestor Daniel Pagano, and my last name might be an indication that the atheism and abandonment of religion has been deeply entrenched within my family, an ancestral tradition perhaps. Usually, last names are not just a coincidence. I figure in my family, my ancestors must have had confrontations with the church in order to change their names appropriately.

Even if this is just an assumption and some paid linguist can find some sort of connection with "Pagan" and "farmer." My father was really an atheist and frankly an enemy of all religion. Since my father was a socialist, his enmity came from his own ideas and political tendencies. Even if socialism does not necessarily equal atheism, socialists, in general, cannot separate the real message of religion from those whom they have witnessed corrupt religious institutions, leaders, and guides. This promotes an abandonment of all faith, felt to be a justified rejection, but commonly is an exaggerated generalization.

My father, in spite of what some people may think about atheists, was a very good person and he stressed the importance of three things, which were the basis of my education. First, love the poor with all that it implies. Help the needy, respect the humble and fight politically for fair wages that would allow them to have a good life, with health and dignity. Secondly, always be honorable. Don't lie, fulfill your promises, and act decently so that you may walk with your head up and never feel you the need to hide from anyone nor feel ashamed in front of anyone. Thirdly, abandon all that is religious. He considered that all bad came from religion and that it was the "opium of the people."

He thought that if the Church and its priests were the official representatives of the religion who were supposed to know and apply it better than anyone, then based on all their adverse actions he had witnessed, and then the doctrine must be inherently dangerous. He had seen that over time in history religion had acted like a tool of oppression and that there were no exceptions.

I accepted the first two of his teachings, but not the last one. I was able to distinguish something that he could not grasp. Evil comes from the men who manipulate religions, not the religion itself. If religion is used as a tool of oppression, it happens via manipulation from oppressive and tyrannous men. If it was applied as it should, religion is a tool to liberate people.

I always had an inclination towards searching for a religion despite my atheist education. I still believed in God, even the opposite was taught in my house. When I was about 14 years old I made a pilgrimage to Lujan. This city about 100 km from Buenos Aires was the center of an annual pilgrimage by thousands of Christians who gathered yearning to be close to other believers. I mention this pilgrimage not to suggest that it changed my life or left a lasting impression, but to demonstrate that I had an interest in faith and believers, not the church itself and other religious institutions. These were never approached by me - most likely because of what I had been instilled in.

Now in university, I am a veterinarian. I was left fascinated by cellular research, microorganisms and all the marvels of creation. I was surprised and dazzled especially with the smallest details and structures of biology, the complex operation of every part of a living creature. I became overwhelmed when I studied the nervous system. I marveled at how the neurons of animals are essentially equal to those of humans. How nervous impulses consist of electrical pulses, which are basically moving atoms of different charges crossing over a membrane. This led me to question the difference between man and animals. What permits a man to have high and complex thoughts above the levels of creatures?

Perhaps for some of you, this may appear quite rudimentary. However, I spent months pondering this question until one day, almost by inspiration, I obtained the answer: Man had a soul, something that was not perceptible by the elements of science. What may appear very elementary to others was a huge discovery. After this, I began my spiritual quest, which allowed for the development of my soul and finally the fulfillment of my purpose in life. My search led me to different faiths one could be. I began by reading books, from the Bible to Zen

Buddhism, coming across Hinduism and a little of Islam. I also looked at philosophers such as Gurdieff and others whose names I do not remember. Finally, I decided that I needed to learn something of the languages in order to read the original religious books and I approached an Islamic Center where they were teaching Arabic.

Why did I start with Arabic and Islam rather than another language or religion, I do not know. I cannot explain it. All I know is that I just decided to start my search with Islam. The Islamic Center I approached was located in the city of La Plata in a rented area maintained by a small group of converted citizens of La Plata with their own effort and finances. It was under the direction of Imam Mahmud Hussein from Buenos Aires who was tasked many years back to spread Islam when there were no Muslims in Argentina. In this Center, both Arabic and religion classes were offered along with periodic Islamic conferences.

I did not go with the intention to learn religion. I thought with the haughtiness and overconfidence of a well-read person, that they were not going to teach me anything. The brother who welcomed me, a convert from La Plata, was very kind and attentive. This highlights how important first impressions are when one approaches Islam. He showed me with very few words my error. In fact, he shows me I really did not know anything at all. I always give the same example: I approached with a glass looking for a little bit of water and I was shown an ocean full of treasures after which I was left stunned. They gave me a few pamphlets and I started to attend the Arabic and religion classes, they offered. A few weeks after that I accepted Islam, it was a well-examined decision made with serious consideration, one which I have committed to for the rest of my life.

Fifteen years have now passed since I accepted Islam. Indeed, Islam has profoundly changed my life. It is everything I had been looking for all my life and has fulfilled my needs much more than I had ever anticipated. It gave me direction and meaning to my existence, and completely filled all of my voids. Now, after having examined my position thousands of times, I still cannot explain everything. How many people have been told about Islam for more extended periods of time and have not accepted Islam? How many seekers have passed by Islamic Centers, attended conferences and read many more books than I have read, even more, profound and complete, and have not accepted Islam? What is it that makes some people accept the message of Islam versus others who may find it very interesting, but do not commit?

A sheik who I met on a trip to Iran brought me closer to an answer. The essence of being a human, when pure, free of prejudices and other similar defects that may impede one to see reality, and to be sincere, and recognizes and accepts the message of God. In this case, the soul of a person is Muslim even before accepting Islam, because his heart acknowledges before he speaks it that there is no god except God ("La ilaha illa Allah"). This being the root of Islam. In this state, the man who is looking for a way of life is taking a step towards God, and like the hadith says, God then takes ten towards you.

In essence, this is what happened to me. I got closer to the Islamic Center thinking I would learn a bit about Islam and go on my way. I didn't have the intention to become Muslim, but I was looking to get closer to God with sincerity and without prejudice. I have no doubt that God guides those who search in this manner and who take the first step towards Him. Like I said, I had no intention to become a Muslim, but I found for myself an ocean of knowledge and all the answer to my worries. With a message that my heart recognized as authentic, I accepted it immediately. I accepted Islam and since then God has given me the strength I have needed to stay firm on this path. A path that has even led me to the House of God, the Kaaba. All praise is to Allah! Lord of the worlds!

For this reason, I give testimony that there is no god but Allah, The one without partners and that Muhammad (Peace be Upon Him) is His servant and His messenger. Ash hadu an la ilaha illa Allah. Ash hadu anna Muhammad rasulul Lah.

Towards My Destination

Ali Melena

I am a 27 year old Mexican American or as some would say a Chicano. I have been asked to write my story of how I became a Muslim. I think it will Insha'Allah, God-willing, help people understand Islam and why it attracted me. People have a wrong perception of Islam and Muslims. What little they know is usually from movies and television, which is almost all the time false. I think that Islam is the answer to the problems of the youth and society in general. I hope my story Insha'Allah will attract more Latinos and people of all races to the light of Islam.

My life before was terrible. I had no direction. I was wasting my life away by dropping out of school in the 11th grade. I would hang out on the streets with my friends "partying," getting high, drinking, and selling marijuana. Despite most of my friends were gang members, I was never in a gang. I knew most of them before they were criminals and drug dealers. I felt it was not a problem. I slowly began to use harder drugs. I had dreams and aspirations but they seemed too far away to make a reality. The more I became depressed, the more I turned to drugs as a temporary escape.

One day a friend of mine told me that he knew where to get some good marijuana. I was eager to sample and buy some, so I agreed to go check it out. We arrived and went inside this apartment. There were a couple of people inside. We sat around and talked for a while and "sampled" the weed. My friend and I bought some, and as we were getting ready to leave one of the guys present invited us to his apartment to give my friend a book.

When we arrived at his apartment, he gave my friend a book and asked him to read it. He said that it might help him out with his problems in life. On the way home, I asked my friend to show me the book he was given. It was the Quran. I had never in my life heard of "The Holy Quran." I began to briefly read some pages. While I was reading, I knew what I was reading was true. It was like a slap in the face - a wakeup call. The Quran is so clear and easy to understand. I was really impressed and wanted to know more about Islam and Muslims.

The strangest thing is I was not looking for a new religion. I used to laugh at people who went to church. I would sometimes say that there was no God although deep down, I knew there was. I decided to go to the library a couple of days later and check out the Quran. I began to read it and study it. I learned about Prophet Muhammad (Peace be upon him) and the true story of Jesus, son of Mary (Peace be upon him). The Quran stressed the fact that God was one and had no partners or a son. This was most interesting to me because I never understood the concept of the Trinity. The Quran describes the birth of Prophet Jesus (PBUH) and his mission. There is also a Surah, or Chapter, called Mary and tells her story as well.

As a child, I always went to church. My mother was a Seventh Day Adventist and took my sister and me every Saturday. I never was really religious and stopped going to church when I was about 14 or 15. The rest of my family is Catholic. I always wondered why we were Seventh Day Adventist, but the rest of my family was Catholic. When we would go visit my family back in Mexico, we went to a Catholic Church for weddings and Quinceañeras, a sweet 15 celebration.

Muhammad (PBUH) is the last Messenger of God sent to all mankind. The Quran tells the stories of all the Prophets such as Adam, Abraham, Noah, Isaac, David, Moses, Jesus (Peace be upon them all) in a clear and understandable manner. I did months of research on Islam. I bought a Holy Quran at a bookstore and studied about World History and Islam's contributions to Medicine and Science.

I learned that Spain was a Muslim country for about 800 years and that Muslims were expelled from Spain by the Christian King and Queen Ferdinand and Isabella. Later, Christian Spaniards came to Mexico and forced the Aztecs and others to become Catholic. History and my Islamic roots were all becoming clear to me.

After months of study and research, I could not deny the truth anymore. I had put it off too long but was still living the life I was before. And, I knew that if I became Muslim I would have to give all that up. One day while reading the Quran, I began to cry and fell to my knees and thanked Allah for guiding me to the truth. I found out that there was a mosque by my house, and so I went one Friday to see how Muslims prayed and conducted their service. I saw that people from all races and colors attended the mosque. I saw that they took off their shoes when entering and sat on the carpeted floor. A man got up and began to call the athan, or call to prayer. When I heard it my eyes filled up with tears. It sounded so beautiful. It was all bizarre at first but seemed so right at the same time. Islam is not just a religion but a way of life.

After attending the mosque for a couple of Fridays, I was ready to be a Muslim and say my shahadah, or declaration of faith. I told the khateeb, the person giving the lecture, that I wanted to be a Muslim. The following Friday in front of the community, I said my shahadah first in Arabic then in English. I bear witness that there is no other God but Allah, and I bear witness that Muhammad (PBUH) is His Messenger.

When I finished, a brother shouted, "Takbir!" Then, all the community said, "Allahu Akbar!" a few times, and then all the brothers came and hugged me. I never received so many hugs in one day. I will always remember that day; it was great. I'm at peace with myself and clear in religion. Being Muslim has really changed my life for the better thanks to Almighty God. I have received my G.E.D. and work in the computer field. I had the blessing of being able to perform Hajj, or Pilgrimage, to the Holy City of Mecca. It was an experience of a lifetime. About three million people from every race and color in one place worshiping one God. Islam is amazing!

No Compulsion Made My Conversion

Ana Morales

My name is Ana Morales, and I am Puerto Rican. I come from a family of 14 children, and I was the youngest of them. I was practically raised as an only child because my brothers (8 of them) and my sisters (5 of them) were all much older than me. Although my family was not very religious, to say the least, I remember that in my early years I attended a Catholic school. And, if I remember correctly, the first time I went to the church was my graduation day from kindergarten. Hahaha.

At 9 years old, we moved to the United States. At that time my father had been living separately from me for some time. During this period, my sister suffered from some strange attacks that my mom tried to cure with Santeria. Though very small, I knew that Santeria was bad. When I was 11 we returned to Puerto Rico and at 13 years old I performed my first communion (a bit late, don't you think). I found it strange to have to admit to things that were embarrassing to me. I thought of the priest who would be seeing us every Sunday after confession. So I confessed that I lied a lot. After all who does not lie? I did my confirmation shortly after. In this ceremony, young people confirm their affiliation with the church and belief in the Trinity and that Jesus is the son of God. Looking back, the Catholic Church asks a lot of young inexperienced folk to hold this ceremony. By then my sister who used to have the attacks announced that she had become part of the Pentecostal church. This news came as a blow to me.

As a teenager, I belonged to a church youth group, attempting to fill the gaps in my life. In one of the churches that I belonged to, I felt no sense to continue with them after a fellow group member slandered me. In another church I belonged to, I told the priest that the girls in the choir were dressed inappropriately to be at the altar and he responded, "Better that way than if they do not come to church. Don't you think?" That's some logic but wearing a miniskirt near the altar was not something I was going to agree with. I attended the church because I liked it and that was my duty as a Catholic, but I did not agree with the rules and laws I found there.

Like many teens, I was exposed to drugs, alcohol, and sex, but I was mature and never resorted to any of them. Alhamdulillah (Praise be to God). I finished high school in 1989 and went to college, but I was unable to complete it for economic reasons. I completed a bilingual secretarial course and began working as a part-time telemarketer to help with expenses. In 1991 my father was diagnosed with a brain tumor. He died a few months later in July leaving me and my mother alone. I left my job and started looking for a new one. After applying to different jobs, one of them called me. Subhan'Allah (Glory be to God). Allah's plan for me began. The day of my interview in September 1991 would be the first time I would meet an Arab-Palestinian and Muslim. He was to become my boss and future husband. Alhamdulillah!! When I told my mom that my boss wanted to ask for my hand in marriage, she said, "You're crazy! An Arab, Muslim? How old is he?" That was another issue. He was 36 and I was 20, but I was determined. That December we got engaged and seven months later we were married.

I remember the first Ramadan that we shared. I prepared his suhoor (breakfast before the fast) and everything without any interest in why he fasted. I would watch him doing his prayers, and he did not speak to me about Islam. I had no interest in that. I rarely asked him questions. I do remember asking him, "Why is it that the Quran is the last and only book that one should follow?" He answered, "In a company, if a new boss comes and passes a memorandum with new and improved work rules, would you still go by what the old boss had stipulated? No. Right?"

After five years of marriage, we moved to Palestine. The change was drastic for me – the people, the food, and the language. Mostly, it was the language. Gradually I got used it and learned the basics of the language. In 2004, I began to feel overwhelmed. I had abandoned my religious life. I was neither Catholic nor a Muslim. I then began to ask God to guide me on the right track. After a while, I started rebelling and I claimed that God had forgotten me. Astaghfirullah (I ask Allah's forgiveness). That summer of 2004, I sent my girls to a religious camp. I met the camp director who invited me to speak about spiritual matters, which I, of course, did not attend. Then my sister-in-law gave me a Spanish interpretation of the Quran, which took me most of the year to read. As I read it, I came to understand that he who knows the truth and does not follow it, is undoubtedly wrong. I started attending the talks as I had a misconception about the Prophet (Peace be upon him). I began to read about his life and what I read began to interest me. I started looking for more information and continued with the talks. The sisters were kind, patient, and sincere. No one ever forced me to be a Muslim. The conversations helped to grow a love of Islam and the Prophet (PBUH) within me.

At home, I discussed the talks with my family. My husband told me that sometimes there were things that I knew that he did not know. Soon I began to feel changes within me. Before starting any task, I would say "bismillah" (In the name of God). I would wear long sleeves. On one occasion, I looked for a dress to attend the wedding of my husband's daughter. I did not find anything I liked. One was low cut and the other was too short. Soon after, I purchased an abaya (a long, loose overgarment), which would be the first of my new wardrobe.

On July 12, 2005, I declared my shahadah in front of my husband and did my first salat (the Muslim prayer). Ever since, I have worn the hijab (headscarf), fulfilled my prayers, fasted during Ramadan, and performed other religious duties.

The peace and tolerance that I have gained today from being Muslim would have never been achieved outside of Islam.

A Very Islamic Christmas Present

Anghela Calvo

My memories of Christmas were not about presents, shiny decorations, or the materialism that often leaves Muslim reverts with a bitter taste from their memories. It wasn't even about the retracing of Prophet Jesus' (PBUH) birth or the profound importance of this event for my mostly Catholic family. Christmas was a day when all my family gathered together and forgot about all the disagreements they had during the year. It was a chance to start over and express the love that sometimes the natural human emotions of pride and resentment don't let us communicate. It was a time for every one of us to shine.

My aunt would take a whole week off from work to bake the most delicious concoctions that we have ever tasted. From gingerbread men made from scratch to cream puffs so delicate it would take her twice as long to make; praying that the mighty sweet filling could hold them together. It was a time when my uncle could make his famous hot chocolate that would warm the whole air and turn the house into a place Hansel and Gretel would most likely wander into. It was the time for each one of the men in my family to draw straws to see who would dress as Santa Claus or Papa Noel as he is known in the Spanish-speaking world. This kept happening even when my cousins were old enough to remember that Santa's belly had too much of a "pillowy" consistency.

As the young ones grew up, they did not only realize that Santa was one more of the fictional characters that filled their childhood. Living in one of the most multicultural cities in the world, they also realized that the religious history of their parents would probably not follow them throughout their whole lives.

During my late teenage years, I also decided to choose the path less traveled and maybe the least understood. Being raised in Bolivia, I was instructed in the Catholic religion early in life. Coming from a lineage where many of my family members were interested in religion and even joined the clergy, religion was always an essential part of my life. At the same time, I still felt the need to not let emotional or cultural baggage affect my choice in the path of spirituality.

After jumping from Catholicism to just Christianity to being a self-proclaimed agnostic, I became a Muslim. Having moved permanently to New York, I was able to study faiths under a different light that was not through the lens of what the majority practiced or what I had learned from my early religion classes - which only served to expand my knowledge of the Catholic religion.

Defying stereotypes that many people have, I didn't convert because of a Muslim man nor was I brainwashed by a group of Muslims. My decision to become a Muslim was a long journey of methodical studying about the religion. The first person who taught me about Islam was a devout Christian professor at the college who specialized in Eastern religions. Part curiosity, part challenge, and the rest a feeling that I was not able to comprehend led me to beg the distinguished looking old man to let me over tally into his course on Islam.

After warning me that no one in his class gets more than a B and that I should get ready for some intensive learning, I ended up sitting in a packed classroom full of students who after 9/11 needed some answers to their questions. My professor taught me about the religion in a totally impartial way. Full of theory and anecdotes, he gave me facts and sparked my interest without sugarcoating anything. He used a simple, no more than a 30-page book on the essentials of Islam paired with a more in-depth book that made my head turn trying to understand complicated Arabic terms and their meanings. His sincere respect didn't seem to affect his beliefs but his clear message was efficiently conveyed, at least to me. Not sure how it all happened but I found myself reciting the declaration of faith or shahadah.

I spent a year after that being a closet Muslim. I didn't know a Muslim other than myself. My knowledge came from books and documentaries. Without ever putting a foot in a mosque, I found myself secretly watching Muslims from afar impressed by their sense of piety, or taqwa.

The year that I spent learning about my new religion and about myself gave me the strength to adjust to the new life I had chosen. I was rejoicing at what I learned every day and impatient to start this new spiritual journey. Little did I know that I could not keep myself in a little bubble all the time. I couldn't just live with my religion especially if there were people around me that started peeking through my transparent shield.

I have always considered myself a strong woman. I would never even allow myself to be seen as a weak person. After all, I was raised by one of the strongest women I have known. But "coming out" to my family entirely broke me down. I did not have the tools to teach them or even express what I was going through and as many families that see their relatives slip away, they were not yet ready to understand. The only possible solution I could find was distance. To justify my fear and helplessness, I started labeling them and their actions as incorrect. I loved them so much that I needed to shield them and myself from any possible battle of beliefs. I no longer shared the baked goods or the hot chocolate or the laughs or the hugs. My heart became bitter and theirs confused.

"Whosever desires to have expansion in his sustenance and a prolonged life should treat his relatives with kindness." (Bukhari & Muslim). It took learning rather than reading and it took practicing rather than judging to become humble and realize that my own actions contradicted what I mistakenly thought I was professing. With time I learned that as I submitted to one God, I freed myself from pride and I embraced compassion and love.

Love and understanding were nourished with time between me and my family. The smallest act is weighed higher on my scale now. One year my younger cousin offered to accompany me to the mosque during Eid-ul-Fitr. And, I ended up having a feast with her and my uncle and our family ties were strengthened. Heart moving gifts like a rock that had "Insha'Allah" (If God wills) inscribed into it made my heart melt. My cousin's final speech at her college debate class was against Islamophobia in which I was mentioned several times. I felt moved by how love breaks down barriers in this often harsh society.

The ultimate token of peace was given to me this past Christmas. I usually don't participate in Christmas celebrations but I make an effort to visit my family at the end of year vacation so as to show my love and appreciation for them. The morning after Christmas I received a present sent from my aunt and cousin. It was a white, amira hijab (princess hijab) neatly packed with a picture of a hijabi woman in front. I was moved just picturing my family taking the trouble to go to a store to ask for a Muslim garb that they didn't even know had a name. They took the trouble to get out of their comfort zone and instead of a gift card, they gave me something that maybe without their knowledge was an essential part of my identity. Not only was I acknowledged as someone deserving of their love but also as a Muslim woman.

My journey to regain my family is still a work in process but I could not find a more worthy cause. From my experience, the closer I get to my Creator the easier it is for me to deal with everyone and everything in life.

Alhamdulillah. Praise be to God.

I Embraced Islam In Texas

Cesar Velazquez

I embraced Islam at the age of twenty-one, during my sophomore year of college. My story is not one of struggle or conflict, and there was no internal battle that I had to fight in order to accept the truth. I was not on a path of reflection or one of self-discovery, nor was I one of those college students just testing the waters of any lifestyle and philosophy, trying to find something real in this world. I merely found a translation of the Quran, read it, and knew that it was the truth. In fact, my vague memories of hearing about Islam do not include any moments of conflict or disbelief despite never having seen the religion practiced, nor was I attracted to it.

Also, from the lines that I recall from textbooks or the meandering discussion on the meaning of life with old friends, whenever I heard the name of the Prophet Muhammad, upon him be peace, I do not remember questioning the authenticity of his prophethood. Similar to the stories that I heard about Abraham, Jesus, and Moses, upon them be peace, I recognized the Prophet Muhammad, upon him be peace, for who he was. However, I never did believe everything that I was told. I never accepted the prophethood of Joseph Smith, for example, nor of the dozens of preachers claiming to have access to divine inspirations. I believed then, before Islam, much as I believe now. And the Quran provides an explanation that I cannot do better than:

"When it is recited to them they say, 'We believe in it; it is the truth from our Lord. We were already Muslims before it came.'" (Quran 28:53).

"Those We have given the Book recognize it as they recognize their own children. As for those who have lost their own selves, they have no faith." (Quran 6:20).

So in that way, I believe that Islam was destined for me, and I was destined for Islam. I look back at my upbringing and realize that it was none other than God Himself protecting my belief from what people told me, whereas others believed as they were told.

I remember growing up, my family did they best they knew to provide for my religious upbringing. For me, this meant that one Wednesday evening per week I would go to the local Catholic Church and learn about the religion. I enjoyed those days because it was a calmer and friendlier way of socializing with other youths and teachers than school. Everyone was personable, and it was a place where we could be ourselves. Class instruction was by one teacher per week, usually volunteers, although I remember one nun also did teach. The content of the class was the same as other Sunday schools across the country: the several sacraments such as communion, marriage, and last rites, the stories of the Prophets, upon them be peace, and memorization of prayers. Concerning the latter, for us Catholics, this meant memorizing the Our Father and Hail Mary.

Now at this time, I loved school and books. Every week I would walk to the library and check out my favorite stories. I would check out whatever I could from my school library. My favorite author was Shel Silverstein, and my favorite genre was martial arts narratives. However, I was interested in every subject and to this day, I can recall the names of all of my elementary school teachers, and most of my middle school teachers. In other words, I loved to learn, and my grades reflected it. I was in the advanced class for everything—and eventually moved to a class entirely for those the teachers considered gifted. That being said, in Catholic school, I sat in the back of the class where one would find the special education students or children who rebelled against every command. In the back of the class, crowded around a large cafeteria-style table in a dimly lit section of the room, sharing dried out markers. This was the particular reason that I could not remember one prayer—the Hail Mary.

I tried and tried, but I could never find the beginning of the prayer by the time the quiz started. I tried to recite and write, but I could not see it. So for this, I was sent to the back of the class, where I was deprived, or as I like to look at it now, protected from the lecture. Yes, I view that inability to learn the Hail Mary as one of the many times that God had protected me from praying to others besides Him. See, in Islam, we reject that God has any intermediaries, in His being, His attributes, or His rights. I loved Mary Mother of Jesus, without a doubt, and my reverence for her personality has only increased. However, I did not need to ask Mary to pray for my sins. Only God Himself could forgive my sins, and my prayer to Him is the least that He required of me. Indeed, God warns us in the Quran:

"If you call on them, they hear not your call; and if they heard, they could not answer you. And on the day of Resurrection, they will deny your associating them (with Allah). And none can inform thee like the All-Aware one." (Quran 35:14).

While concerning Himself, He lets us know that:

"When my servants ask you concerning Me, I am indeed close (to them). I listen to the prayer of every supplicant when he calls on Me..." (Quran 2:186).

And so it proceeded. I had no problems with the religion of Catholicism throughout my formative years and went from first communion to first confession to confirmation. Though I enjoyed the friendships that I made at the church, my understanding of these Catholic rites was that they were standard operating procedures that man created - nothing mandatory from my Lord. Did I accept that the bread and wine that I consumed was literally the flesh of another man? Of course not. And I was in doubt as to the sincerity of those that claimed such belief. Who gave them this authority? I would ask. Confession? Did this man's counsel truly forgive my sins? Of course not. This is what we do, I explained to myself, similar to the style of clothes *we* wear or the food that *we* eat. It is just what we do. And of course, the penance that I was prescribed was a mere opinion. And lastly, confirmation. For weeks and weeks, we were told to choose a name of a saint from the Bible to serve as our name for confirmation. In the end, my exchange with the priest at confirmation went as follows: *And your name? Jesus. Make sure you live up to your name.* Although I could never live up to the name of any of God's Messengers, today I find that command to have foretold much.

As I continued to mature, I never had loyalty to the Catholic Church. I would often go to the churches of the smaller sects. But nor did I have any commitment to any other branches of Christianity. My loyalty, as I often said vocally, was to the truth. As the dubious facts made themselves apparent, such as the many contradictions found in the Bible or the majority of the Bible not even purported to be from the Prophets, upon them be peace, this did not lead me to atheism or agnosticism as was the case with so many former churchgoers. How could I have said such a thing when I believe in the truth? Truth apparent to me was that God was real, manifest, and all-knowing and that He sent prophets. Those prophets that I learned about were undoubtedly from among them. But my loyalty was to the truth only, which I saw to be free from contradiction or fallacy. So I recall my immediate resistance when I first was told that Jesus, upon him be peace, was God Himself. This was wrong and I made it known as such. How could God sleep? How could

God eat? How could God be born? And furthermore, this made the concept of revelation absurd.

As I discussed with one fellow churchgoer: *God is all-knowing, correct? Yes. And God gave the Holy Spirit the Gospel to deliver to Jesus, correct? Yes. And we are to believe that God is God, the Holy Spirit is God, and Jesus is God? Yes. Then because God is all-knowing, then God is all-knowing, and the Holy Spirit is all-knowing, and Jesus is all-knowing? Yes. Then we say that God, who is all-knowing, gave the Gospel to Himself, to deliver to Himself, even though he already knew what it contained? Yes. But that would be ridiculous; Jesus was a prophet-like the prophets that came before him! Well, I don't care what you say; I'm not going to believe it.*

Another problem I had was with the intermediation of Jesus, upon him be peace. When a friend and I were talking about praying, he said that he would begin by saying "in the name of Jesus." I said that this is not the right way to pray, that we should rather say "in the name of God" as Jesus prayed. Even stranger to me was to find out that people were praying to Jesus, upon him be peace. *But that is not how Jesus taught us to pray,* I would say.

As I went to college, I took note that the Trinitarian and god-man ideology was an official theology of every prominent church, and the smaller ones that did not accept these concepts had other beliefs and practices that Jesus, upon him be peace, did not teach us either. At the same time, I was reasonably content with my beliefs. I believed in the God that no one else was like, and His Prophets and that the truth was unchangeable and not subject to our fancies. At the same time, thinking back towards that time, I know now that I desired more.

When I wanted to pray, I wanted to pray without necessarily asking for anything. I knew God was worthy of me remembering Him even when I did not have any problem on my mind or any reason to rush to Him out of gratitude. He was worthy of my prayers just because of who He is. To be fair, many Christians and Jews praise God often, saying words like "thanks be to God" and "God is good." But, I was a person in a religion of one, and even feeling that I knew the truth, I was aware that what I knew was only a small portion. So my prayer was short and alone. But, then, God brought me what I knew had to have always existed in the form of His last and final revelation—The Quran.

It was really a simple story of how I accepted Islam, which should not be surprising. I was not an exceptional Christian in terms of my beliefs. Throughout history, millions of people had a Unitarian theology concerning God and Jesus the Messiah, Son of Mary. Although many of them were slaughtered wholesale by other sects, where are the millions of people now? To be sure, in every church there are people that are always praising God, and trust their fellow Christians, and try their best to hold fast to the Bible, but reject the thought of a tripartite deity. It goes against their hearts, but they did not follow the path that I took by vocalizing this belief. But what about the large Unitarian sects in the eastern world - in Europe and the Middle East?

History teaches us that many of them, particularly in Spain and the Levant, accepted Islam. I was not aware of this history when I accepted Islam; I was not even aware of the meaning of Unitarian theology. I thought that all mainstream Christians accepted the Trinitarian version. But understanding what I know now, concerning the rapid growth of Islam in the Iberian Peninsula and Greater Arabia by thousands of people converting without hesitation, I know those people experienced what I had. They were already Muslim; they just needed to see Islam to understand it. I did not see it so much as I knew it when one day I saw a translation of the Quran at a friend's house. I asked for a copy, just to read out of interest. And when I sat to read it, I began with a foreword consisting of a short biography of the Prophet Muhammad, upon him be peace. I recognized him as a prophet without issue - it was apparent. Then turning page by page, I realized that this was the final revelation. That God did not leave us with a mystery but perfected religion for all of us and for the rest of time. It was apparent.

I know many people find validation in their religious affiliation by finding Islamic roots in their culture or lineage. I never engaged in this. Although, being Puerto Rican, this is not a difficult task. Between the Spanish, Moriscos, and Africans, I can easily find Muslim roots because the Island is terribly small. Tens of thousands of Spanish Muslims, Moorish sailors, and captive African Muslims are enough to give everyone in the Antilles a Muslim ancestor. First, I always identified with my indigenous heritage, because they were wronged. And there is no serious proof that they were Muslims following the same Prophet and laws as I do.

Secondly, I could not and still don't today care less if every ancestor of mine was the first to disbelieve. The truth is not subject to culture and lineage. If I found out that my Spanish ancestors were those that imprisoned Galileo for saying that the world was round, should I then say that the world is pancake-shaped? That is absurd. But there are facts concerning Allah, His books, His Angels, and His Prophets, just as there are facts concerning geometry. So if you accept that you cannot change the shape of the world to suit your fancy, why would anyone maintain a religion out of love for his culture? I will not deny reality. Many Muslims follow their culture leading to changes in clothes or name not in order to conform to Islam, but rather because he likes the style. Because he associates, for example, African-ness and Eastern-ness with Islam.

I never went through this phase. So my game's changed, but the name stays the same. I love Islam, and God has been good to me. There is not a significant change for a Christian or a Jew that accepts Islam to go through in terms of belief or culture. This is not by coincidence, but because all of the prophets conveyed the same essential message concerning God, prophethood, and the afterlife. This message never changed. Although there are different details concerning the fast, prayer, and charity, these are also familiar elements to any Christian or Jew that practices his religion. So this is my invitation to you to come back home to the religion of all the prophets, upon them all be peace.

My Journey To Islam

Daniel Saravia

I was born in Bolivia and came to the United States when I was six years old. Since arriving in the United States, I have lived in Northern Virginia. I was born into Catholicism, though I never honestly did consider myself a Catholic and was not religious growing up. I believed in God and that was about it. The same can be said for my family - two older sisters, a younger brother, and sister. I am now married with two beautiful daughters and a wonderful son. The following is a short story based on my journey back to Islam.

In early 2001, I "thought" I was living a happy life. I had a good paying job, a car and "best of all" I was "21." After work, I would love to go workout at the gym and then see what I could get myself into later that night. I would meet up with some friends and we would go bar hopping, clubbing or start a "little get-together." This was a daily routine that lasted nearly a year.

Then in March of 2001, things began to not go too well. I was having some family issues. My family did not agree with the way I was living my life an there was always tension when I was home. At the same time, I was having financial issues. I would waste my money on "having a good time" and not on what I should have used it for. My bills were always late and resulting in late charges every month. Needless to say, all this was very stressful. It all finally caught up with me and I felt like I was going crazy. I didn't know what to do.

I had made up my mind; I was going to go out and "release" some steam. Before leaving, I decided to check my e-mail, for what reason I do not know. Once I logged on I saw a friend of mine was online. He greeted me hello. All I responded was a "hi." My friend noticed I didn't say much after that so he asked if everything was ok. I said "No." I then told him no, that I wasn't feeling well and I didn't know what I was going to do. All he said to me was "Go Pray." Go pray? I refused. I said, "I don't know how to pray." He told me again "Go Pray." I refused again then I told him that I had to go. I turned off my PC and headed upstairs. Once I got near the door, something held me back. I stopped in front of my door and froze. I started to tremble a bit. After a few minutes, I went to my room and sincerely prayed for the first time in my life. I had an "experience." I felt God's presence. It was very beautiful and emotional and hard to put into words.

The next day I woke up as a new man. I was very motivated and decided to get on the right path and change my ways. I began to read the Bible and go to Church on Sundays. At the beginning of April 2001, I decided to make a sacrifice for God. I stopped eating beef, chicken, seafood, and pork until God assured me I was on the right path. After a couple of months, I had made tremendous strides in bettering myself, but I still felt that I was missing something. I always felt incomplete.

Then one day, while at work, I happened to walk by a coworker's desk and noticed a screensaver with a nature theme. It had what appeared to be verses from the Bible. I had never read anything so deep in my life. When the co-worker returned, I asked him where I could find that verse in the Bible. My coworker said to me that the verse was not from the Bible but from the Quran. He explained he was a Muslim and his religion was Islam. This was the first time in my life I heard any of these three words. I thanked him, returned to my desk and decided to find out what Islam was about. The more I read, the more I wanted to learn. Shortly afterward, I purchased my first Quran and began to read even more. Everything that I read, I felt I already knew. It was as if I was just refreshing my memory. After learning the basics of Islam, I came to the conclusion that I essentially was already Muslim, but didn't know it.

At this point, there was one more, for lack of a better word, an obstacle to overcome: the role of Jesus (peace be upon him). I was taught growing up, that Jesus was God, the Son of God. I know now that Jesus (peace be upon him) is a hugely respected and loved Prophet, but not God in Islam. To become a Muslim, I would need to agree to this and know this like I know my name. I would have to believe in it. I began to pray a lot more asking God to guide me to the right path. I did a lot of research, and I continued reading both the Bible and the Quran.

During the week of August 31, 2001, I felt God point me back to Islam. Everything felt perfect. I believed that Jesus (peace be upon him) was/is a messenger of God and that he is the Messiah. I proceeded to search for local Mosques and Islamic Centers. That's when I found A.D.A.M.S. (All Dulles Area Muslim Society). I met with Br Mushfiqur on August 31, 2001, the day I declared my shahadah and completed my return to Islam.

Life has been very good. Alhamdulillah (Praise be to God). Since I reverted, Allah has blessed me immensely. He has multiplied my happiness. He has surrounded me with loving, caring and understanding people. My family has been very supportive and understanding.

Alhamdulillah. Since then, my younger brother, older sister, and brother-in-law have also accepted Islam as their way of life. Insha'Allah (If God wills), one day Allah will guide the rest of my family back to the right path of Islam.

The Quran Saved Me

Daoud Ali

Although born in Los Angeles, I spent the first 8 years of my life in Mexico. Following my parents' divorce, my mother brought my brother and me back to the United States and we settled in Los Angeles.

I had a very modest upbringing. As a single parent, my mother did her best to provide for us. She worked as a seamstress in a sweatshop making minimum wage for 13 years. Like many Mexican-Americans, I was raised as Roman Catholic but was not particularly devout. By the time I entered college, religion was the furthest thing from my mind.

In my first year in college, I read critiques of Christianity by Nietzsche, Feuerbach, and others. This moved me further away from faith. Then during my senior year, I met a beautiful young lady I found irresistible. She was Muslim and answered some of my questions about Islam. I fell in love with her; however, she told me the only way we could marry was if I accepted Islam. At this point, I was more familiar with Islam and the idea of converting did not frighten me.

We married in 1994 following my college graduation. For the next four years, I was a nominal Muslim and not practicing as I should be. I was consumed by a high-paying, high-stress job at an IT firm and made little time, if any, for worship.

This all changed one night while driving home from work after a 36-hour shift. I began to feel dizzy, my heart was pounding, and my chest constricted, such that I couldn't breathe. I pulled over to the nearest exit and miraculously a hospital was there, right across the street.

That night began my battle with panic attacks and anxiety. At the beginning, there were days when I could not imagine how I'd live until the next morning. During the darkest moments, it was the Quran and Allah's mercy that pulled me through. I could not sleep and could barely eat for weeks on end. As I lay awake every night, I would read the Quran. I read it cover to cover several times, each time seeing something new that touched my heart and made me reflect. Since then I have not abandoned prayer. While the panic attacks are gone, my love of the Islam remains.

My Sister Stuck By Me

Denise Padilla

I was born in La Habra, CA and raised in San Francisco, CA. I loved growing up in the city with my four siblings because we were surrounded by so much diversity and were able to learn from other cultures. My best friend growing up was a Vietnamese Muslim named Aminah, and I had friends from many different backgrounds - Black, Asian, and Latino. Growing up, I participated in many sports like track, soccer, and basketball. After high school, I attended City College of San Francisco (CCSF) and later Las Positas College in Livermore. Years later, I moved to San Mateo and attended Foothill College and recently transferred to San Jose State University last fall to major in Social Work.

I began to wonder about Catholicism before I converted. I wondered why we considered Jesus (PBUH) as God (SWT). Why do women not cover up before entering the church? Why do they eat pork? In other words, there were a lot of inconsistencies that made me look into another religion. Islam made more sense to me. The more I learned, the more fascinated I became. I was surprised when I discovered that the Virgin Mary was held highly in Islam and learned why women wear hijab and dress modestly. I came to understand why Muslims don't eat pork how Jesus (PBUH) will return, and how women are regarded as equals of men. I also loved the history of Muslims in Spain, but how devastating it was at the same time. I thought to myself, "You mean to tell me that I have Muslim blood?" I later realized that my mother's last name is Arabic so I changed it to its original form, Al-Qala, rather than Alcalá.

The most challenging thing about embracing Islam was not knowing how people would react to my conversion. I often have to step back and realize that I cannot control people's thoughts about my converting. If people were to leave my life because of this change, then they were never present, to begin with. I remember at work I wore my headscarf and many of the parents looked at me funny while others asked questions. I even had one mother approach me abruptly asking me if I believed in Jesus (PBUH). I smiled at her and said, "Of course I do." I have to remind myself to remain patient and continue to be myself.

I am currently in a serious relationship and will be married soon. In the future, I plan on having a family, but not until I graduate from San Jose State. I want to give my full attention to my kids and balancing a full-time job, college, and raising my kids would be much too difficult to balance.

I converted on September 12th, 2010 in Philadelphia, PA with my fiancé's family. Before I converted, I had already made significant changes in my life. I no longer ate pork. I attended workshops on Islam to learn more. I no longer waste my nights at clubs. And, I no longer drank alcohol - not even a sip for about seven years. I began to be more conscious of what I consumed and how it could potentially affect me in a negative manner.

My family, especially my mother, began to notice these changes and started questioning me. I remember one day she was making breakfast with pork, which I inquired about. After her confirmation that it was pork, I decided not to eat it. She asked, "Why don't you eat pork? Are going to be Muslim?" I looked at her and said, "Possibly." She was speechless and said nothing to me afterward. When I converted, I decided not to tell my family except one of my sisters because she was the only one who seemed supportive at that time. I remember texting her when I was on my way to the mosque telling her that I was about to do it. After my conversion, I called my sister and told her that it was official. She asked me, "Are you happy?" I replied that I was very happy and then she responded, "Well, that's all that matters." I began to cry because it meant so much to me that she was there when I needed her the most. My mother seems to be the only one who has a hard time accepting my conversion, but I've learned all I can do is be patient and love her more than ever.

I have been the administrative assistant at the Boys & Girls Clubs of the Peninsula in Redwood City, CA for almost seven years. I love my job because I get to interact with youth, parents, and the community. As soon as I graduate, I plan on gaining experience outside the organization and hopefully returning to the Club to offer my services as a social worker. My overall goals in Islam are to continue to learn so that I can teach others. Once I learn, I will be able to be more at peace with my family.

To My Mother, In Memory

Diana Cruz

Allah (SWT) and my mother are a significant part of my life. My mother, who passed away from breast cancer in April of 2000, taught me about God and how important it is to always keep God in mind in everything I do in life. She told me that I don't need to go to church or talk to a priest in order for God to forgive my sins or to seek refuge. She said, "God listens to you when you pray to him so look for him." I could tell when I was growing up, my mother was very strict with me. In order to go to the corner store, I needed to take my brother.

I thank Allah that my mother was very strict when it came to my friends I had. The best advice that I received from my mom regarding friends was, "Friends at school stay at school." The friends that my mother approved of were the ones I hung out with the most. I can say they are still my friends to this day and are outstanding people.

I enjoyed being involved in school activities during high school and college. I graduated in 1991 from Curie High School on the south side of Chicago and received my Bachelors in Business Administration from Robert Morris College. I was born in Chicago, IL and grew up mostly on the south side. I lived in Eagle Pass, Texas for about three years from 5th through 7th grade. I enjoy what I do for a living although the most important part of what I do is taking care of my family.

My family and friends are very supportive of my conversion and accepted me with open arms. My conversion did not change their love for me, Subhan'Allah (Glory be to God) and my experience has been very positive with my family. My mother, may she rest in peace, said as long you believe and pray to God I am happy for you. My stepfather who raised me gives me compliments every time he sees me in hijab. He says, "You look so beautiful with the scarf covering your head." My goal is to increase the strength of my faith. I want to expand me and my children's knowledge about Islam. Insha'Allah (If God wills), I will start learning Arabic in order to understand the Quran in the beautiful language that Allah has chosen.

What prompted me to reconsider my former religion was that my mother had cancer. She was the kindest person, and I couldn't understand why this would happen to her. I asked God why he was doing this to my mother. Why would God do this to my family including my 9 old sister, who is now 11 years old? I could not find answers in Christianity. I was depressed and started researching other religions. I remember telling my mom I am going back to my born religion, Mormonism. That's how it all started. I read very little about Islam, but somehow I always came back to Islam in pieces. Then I met Ricky who would become my future husband. My girlfriend, who is a devout Christian, introduced me to him. She had known him for years.

At this time I was attending college, working full time, and helping my mother as much as possible, plus taking care of my children. Ricky, who saw my hardships, became my best friend and comforter. When Ricky told me that he's a Muslim, at first I thought he was kidding. My bigger question was, "You are a Latino Muslim?" I was interested immediately. We started talking about Islam every day. Then, I started doing my own research on Islam. I embraced Islam in an instant; Allah knew that I was ready. Being a Latino Muslim gives me the opportunity to provide the dawah (the call to Islam), especially when I go to a Mexican restaurant or store and I respond in Spanish. They look at me puzzled and usually, the cashier starts laughing because she thinks I am Arab. Most of the time they ask me questions about how I came to Islam.

Islam answered many questions. When I asked why this was happening to my mom?" Islam responded. I found solace and understood that Allah will take you when you have done your time on Earth. Insha'Allah, my mother is at peace. Being a Muslim brought me closer to God and made me a better person. Islam made me understand why I am here on Earth. It made me understand the importance of being a mother. People can benefit from Islam because Islam is the truth about God, the prophets, and how to live your life.

Finding Inner Peace Through Islam

Eddie Yusuf Sencion

I remember being in high school in Cambridge, MA in early 1990 and being introduced to the "Autobiography of Malcolm X" by Alex Haley. This book was the beginning of my self-examination in regards to my Christianity and led to many questions. I remember never fully believing the Christmas stories about how Jesus was born on the 25th of December, or how Jesus was GOD and part of a "Triune Godhead." I always thought to myself that these teachings had an air of falseness, and I later learned that these were all man-made teachings.

I was a young Dominican kid with three younger brothers, and parents who divorced when I was about 11 or 12 years old. My mother gave us a great upbringing but as with most young male youth, the vices of the inner city streets proved to be alluring. By 16, I became involved with drugs and guns. I supplemented my work income by selling drugs and engaging in other rackets my cronies and I came up with. I recall getting out of my college classes and going right to the streets, where my other education awaited me. Robbing others of drugs and money was one of my favorite past times in addition to selling them.

I was arrested several times but was never convicted for reasons I cannot comprehend. As a result, I continued with this fast lifestyle: cars, drugs, women, and alcohol. You name it; I had a hand in it. In 2000, I had received a job with a great company in Boston where I worked as Air Operations Manager for a very successful tour company. During my time there, I met some really great people, one of whom would die on September 11th when the airplane he was on left from Boston's Logan Airport and crashed into the NYC World Trade Center. It was a sorrowful time in my office, affecting us all differently. Some of my colleagues lost their jobs. Others had nervous breakdowns. I was in shock and deeply saddened at the turn of events in our country.

I remember discovering that the majority of those who committed the attacks were from Saudi Arabia and Muslims. These facts worried me very much. I thought to myself, that if all Muslims are taught to be this way by their religious affiliation, then we Americans are in considerable trouble. So, as a concerned American, I decided to take action and find out if Islam really taught their followers to commit these atrocities. I did not want to hear any lectures from people who were anti-Islamic or racists. I had learned early on that "The News" is not always accurate in reporting facts. I decided to buy a Quran and see for myself if there were any teachings that mirrored the act of killing thousands of innocent people.

A couple of days after September 11th, I stopped by a Barnes and Nobles after my shift was over to purchase my first copy of a translation of the Quran in English. I brought it home but did not begin to read it until the next day during my lunch break. I read that at my own desk because I did not want to alarm others around me in case they saw what I was reading. I recall reading about Adam, Abraham, Noah, Moses, Aaron, Lot, Job, David, Zachariah, Jesus, and Muhammad (may peace and blessings be upon them all). I was entirely taken aback by the beauty of how the Quran told the stories of these amazing prophets, free of the negative stories found in the Bible.

While I was reading, one of my coworkers came by my desk and asked me in a very excited voice if I was Muslim. I replied that I was not and that I was just interested in learning more about the religion. He was very excited and asked me if I had ever been to a mosque. My response was simply "What? Mosque? What is that?" And he proceeded to explain that mosques are a place where Muslims worship and he invited to take me to a local mosque in Cambridge, MA, the city where I grew up. I agreed to go because I wanted to see with my very own eyes what this group of people was all about.

I remember my coworker being a very polite and happy person who was always concerned with everyone's well-being. He was always in a good mood and never showed he could even think about being violent, much less carry out anything like September 11th. When we got to the mosque, we took off our shoes and made our way to the bathroom where he proceeded to ask me if I had used the bathroom that day and I said yes! He then continued to instruct me that Muslims in a place of worship they must cleanse themselves with water in a process known as wudu. I remember thinking; this is amazing because for years I approached God after answering the call of nature, and never cleansing myself. I did this "wudu" and afterward felt refreshed.

Next would come to the most indelible mark left on my psyche, one which partially convinced me that someday I would be a Muslim. I was in complete amazement as we approached the prayer hall to see Muslims kneel and prostrate in worship of our Creator. I remember thinking about how Jesus prayed face down and that Moses and many other prophets did the same. The internal peace I felt that day was one I would come back to years later. I continued to read on and off but I was too caught up in my life to actually become a Muslim. I had to stop smoking, drinking, and carousing. I was neither willing nor ready to give all this up.

A year later I moved to Florida. The first thing I did was seek out a mosque. I recall the Muslims being very friendly and inviting when I visited the local mosque in Hollywood, FL. I stopped visiting the mosque soon after I discovered that Jose Padilla used to attend that place of worship. I did not want any problems or to be associated with any "terrorists," so I stayed away despite no one there being a terrorist. For the next seven years, I continued to live my life, occasionally reading the Quran but never committing myself to Islam. I had a spectacular job, a great apartment, money, vacations, luxury cars, and women. I had everything that a man in our society dreams about but through it all there was this increasing feeling of guilt, sadness, and remorse.

Despite all of these material things, I was depressed like I had lost everything. I would come home from nightclubs and strip bars feeling guilty. Finally, one morning I awoke and realized why I felt this way about my life. It was because I was not serving GOD, and I was doing all the things God detests. I called my friend from Egypt, whom I had met in Florida, and told him over the phone that today I was going to take my shahadah, the Islamic declaration of faith. He was very excited because he had never seen anyone take shahadah. He immediately drove over to my house and brought with him my first piece of Islamic clothing, a thobe.

Because it was a Friday, we drove down to the Miami Gardens Masjid. After sitting through what became my first Friday congregational prayer, my friend approached an elder Muslim man and explained to him my intention for that day. The man became overjoyed and recruited several other witnesses and right there in front of my friend and several other men who would soon become my first brothers I took my shahadah by repeated after him the following words: *lā 'ilāha 'illallāh, Muḥammad rasūlu-llāh. There is no god but God, and Muhammad is the messenger of God.* My life that day changed forever, and I have been overjoyed ever since. I finally realized that Allah (SWT) had been calling me all of my life, but I had not chosen to listen until that day!

The Seeds And The Sprouts

Gabriel Martinez

Bismillahi Rahmanir Raheem

I bear witness to the fact that there is no deity worthy of worship but Allah and I bear witness to the fact that Muhammad is his Prophet and messenger. With love, I share with you my wonderful journey to Islam.

The seeds of Islam were planted long ago by Allah (SWT) through my oldest brother Louis "Ali" Martinez, who was the first and only Muslim for many years in our family. He converted to Islam while imprisoned in 1977, and was my first Muslim influence. He shared his belief in stages with me, which I have now come to know as *dawah*. Alhamdulillah (Thank God).

The second in our family to convert was my nephew "Hakim Malik" Toro. He was introduced to Islam by members of the 5% Nation, a movement founded by a former member of the Nation of Islam. Later when he was incarcerated, he learned about the fundamental beliefs of Islam after reading the Quran. He took shahadah in 1987 and accepted the real Islam as was taught by the Prophet Muhammad (PBUH) 1400 years ago. Like my brother, he also shared his knowledge of Islam with me in stages. Despite this, I found it very difficult to let go of the strongly instilled belief of Jesus as God in the flesh as the sole means of obtaining salvation. I viewed all other beliefs and religions as deception: to believe otherwise would mean hellfire for eternity.

I was not open-minded in the least about the matter and continued on living the life Allah had given me to - deaf, dumb and blind to the simple truth. Allah, throughout all history, sent every single prophet of The One and Only God of all Creation to proclaim to all humanity the same message, "La Ilaha Il Allah."

I first became a father in 1997, and I named my first born Imanuel Jabril Martinez out of respect for Christianity, Islam, and my family. My second was born in 2001 and named Issac Ali Martinez. Tragedy struck when my brother Ali was killed in 1992 in the Bronx New York. Many of the Christian members of our family blamed Islam for his downfall and ultimate death, and also for my nephew's incarceration. Then came 9/11. The view for most of my family was that of most Americans at the time - Islam was a dangerous religion and its followers were deceived.

During this time, I continued my careless, hate-filled lifestyle-drinking heavily, doing drugs of all kinds, and glorifying the gangster lifestyle at every opportunity. If not for the strong faith of my dear God-fearing mother Teodora, who taught us early on that the faith, trust, salvation, and the never-ending merciful love of God is ever so real and available if we just reach out to Him, I would have been completely lost. She taught us that if we only worship and love Him, God will, in turn, love you and show you love. However, even when I tried to live a Christian lifestyle in the late 1980's and early 1990's, I found that there were so many unanswered questions and contradictions with the teachings vs. the practices of Christians.

I felt something was terribly wrong with the fruit of Christianity, and its awful hate-filled violent history against people deemed infidels or not in agreement with what they perpetrated to humanity to be the only world order and decree of God. I could not understand the events that transpired throughout history in the name of Christianity, filled with the incomprehensible treatment of indigenous people of color in the name of Christianity. When I committed myself to study of the entire Bible, I found the ultimate message of peace, reverence, surrender and uncompromising self-beneficial worship to the one God of all creation. I learned of the message and warnings to the world by the Prophets, warning of God's wrath against those who worship, glorify, or idolize anything in any shape, form, or fashion before or in place of Him, I learned of His never-ending mercy and love for humanity. I found that there was equal goodwill for men and women.

I found myself ever so confused, so I just quit trying to live righteously. I was on law's wrong side and joined others in their sinful actions. I refused to practice either of the faiths, but ironically at the end of each day before I lay down to sleep, I prayed for God's mercy and protection--often times with guilt so overwhelming I wanted to die by numbing myself with dope. However, what I feared more than anything else was that one day I would wake up and not feel His presence. That is what I feared even more than death. I feared His wrath and disapproval. I feared He would turn away from me one day.

After I became a father for the first time, I was so grateful to God for the gift of a son that I decided to leave the lawless life for good and earn an honest living. For the sake of my child, I vowed to never jeopardize my freedom again, but. I never stopped abusing drugs. This led to the decline of my marriage. In July 2006, we separated and shortly afterward I was in a horrible motorcycle accident that left me without a spleen and threatened the loss of a leg. Following my recovery from surgery, I found myself looking to God and not asking "why me", but uttering, "Oh God, I thank you." I began thanking the Almighty for all. The moment I thanked God, I felt an overwhelming understanding of why the events that had led up to that moment had occurred. I felt as if the Lord was assuring me that it is necessary for me to suffer today in order to see tomorrow. "That you may see that I love thee and my mercy knows no bounds."

I went back home to my ex-wife's for a while after spending nearly two weeks in the hospital. I was not able to work or do much on the account of my leg needed to be cast for several weeks. One day, I was sitting down just talking to my 9-year-olds on Imanuel, and I inquired about school. I asked him what he liked about it, what was he learning, and if he was enjoying his vacation. I assured him I was ok, and not to worry, that I would heal. All the while, he would giggle whenever I jokingly tickled him. We both laughed about my tickling him for a good while, and then he looked me in my eyes and said something to me that changed my whole life. He put his hand undermine, kissed me on the arm and said, "Daddy, I'm really sad that this happened to you but I'm glad you're sitting here talking with me." My heart just dropped immediately. I kissed my son on his head hiding the tears that started to well up in my eyes. I excused myself and went to the bathroom and cried uncontrollably. I realized then, that truly the best things in life are free. My son just wanted to spend time with me. Playing and laughing with him didn't cost a dime. I thought about how I would 70 to 80 hours a week, buy him toys, and tell him to "run along and play" so I could spend my time drinking or worse. I realized that I was losing my sons. I was not caring enough for the gift God had granted me.

I made a decision then that I would no longer chase a dollar before playing and chasing my children around the house. No more would I put my job in front of my family. I called my job and told them that when I was fully recovered, I no longer wished to manage the business. I told them that I wanted to work 40 to 50 hours a week, and no matter how much I lost financially, what I gained was priceless. I vowed to call the children every day I was away from them and spend a lot more time with them.

After a while, I approached my ex-wife and apologized. I expressed regret for not sharing nearly enough religion with her during our years together, despite knowing how little knowledge she had of God being raised in Cuba. I shared my desire to live a righteous life and raise the children in the knowledge of God. I asked if she would aid me. She had no interest. I acknowledged her decision but asked her to not interfere with my goal to teach my sons. I went home that night and wept and prayed. I demanded that God show me once and for all, "Am I a Christian, Muslim, Buddhist, Jew, Jedi, or what?" I prayed hard on this because I did not want my children to suffer in this life or the afterlife because of my ignorance.

In order to teach them, I needed to gain knowledge for myself. I typed into my Netflix account searches on Islam, God, Christianity, Judaism, etc. I researched online and read or watched all I could find. Most importantly, I prayed. I visited the local mosque and got literature on Islam. I started to see the truth. That the culture and practice of Islam were not at all like it was portrayed in the media. It was beautiful, peaceful, powerful, and oh so inspiring, but all that had been instilled in me about Christ and the divinity held me back. I felt like I needed to know and understand more. Then "it" happened.

I watched a video on the History Channel titled, "A History of God," that talked in depth about the major monotheistic religions of the world. It addressed the myths surrounding Christ, the divinity, and the "Trinity." It discussed how the Trinity and divinity of Christ came at the Council of Nicea in 325 AD. That was it. Having cleared much of my confusion and relieving much of my misgivings about turning my back on much of my childhood teachings about Christianity, I took shahadah shortly afterward. I believed in the One True God of all Creation and in all of the Prophets. I still loved Jesus as a great Prophet of God but believed that Muhammad is the seal of the Prophets. By divine inspiration and revelation, he was chosen to bring it to mankind.

I have learned that God's mercy knows no ends. I believe that he can forgive without the aid of any acts by man or beast and, and that nothing and no one can disturb His plan. I went to the mosque the following Friday on March 30, 2007, after calling my nephew and sharing what I had learned and asked him to go with me. After taking shahadah, I took the Quran and Islam and ran with it and have been running ever since. Alhamdulillah. That's my story. I bid you all in the Arabic *Assalamu 'Alaikum* (Peace be upon you). Thanks for your time.

When A Curtain Was Lifted

Grysell Fabaro

I was born in the Bronx and raised in Queens, New York. Despite being baptized Catholic, my family was never religious. I went to public and Catholic schools until my family moved to Arizona when I was 16. My parents are from Argentina and the majority of my family is in Argentina except for one aunt and cousin in California. I live in Phoenix, Arizona.

I met my Muslim husband four years ago who introduced me to Islam. We married shortly afterward, and one year later we had a son. For three years, I never turned to Islam, but I also never denounced it. My husband always talked about it but was adamant that I did not have to take his religion. He was content with my curiosity to know more; to change was to be my decision, and not to be done for him. I never felt any pressure from him. From what I learned from him, I felt that Islam could be something that finally answered all my questions.

After getting married and shortly afterward pregnant, I attended Jummah, Friday congregational prayer, whenever possible with my husband. I felt Islam could be my home, but I was not ready. After the birth of my son, I took three months off from work that allowed me to attend Jummah every Friday. I felt closer to Islam, but was still not ready or was too stubborn. Finally, three years after we met, I became a Muslim. Ironically, he already considered me a Muslim because I was regularly attending Jummah, started wearing a khimar (a type of head covering), was reading the Quran, and had already begun praying.

One year after converting, I should be further in Islam, but sadly this is not true primarily due to my multiple barriers: laziness, fulltime employment, being a mother to a two-year-old son, etc. I want to further my spiritual growth and knowledge by regularly reading the Quran and praying because when doing so, I feel –peacefulness and happiness. I also notice the change in my behavior, and others did, too.

In this world, it is easy to stray or become complacent when you lack motivation or support from the people around you, which I require. There are several mosques in Phoenix, but the most popular where my friends attend are at least 30 minutes away. I do not know many sisters, and at times feel like an outcast because I'm still learning and not as knowledgeable. I long to find the right, supportive friends who can assist me.

When I converted last year, my parents just could not understand. They still do not understand. I suspect that most of this resistance originates from my father. My parents are not religious people ironically, which adds to my confusion about their discontent. They view the conservative way I dress and the way we, my husband and I, live our lives as "stupid." My father is the type of person who ridicules what he does not understand. I do not know what my family in Argentina thinks. My husband and I went to visit my family in California recently and my aunt surprised me with Assalamualaikum. She watches the telenovela "El Clon," which as shallow as it may be in my opinion, does give knowledge of Islam.

At this time, I feel like I am starting fresh. I have returned to my readings and am attempting to keep to my prayer schedule by installing a prayer alert on my computer. I also have tried to adopt an increasing halal diet and continue to wear my khimar. Most people cannot discern that I am Latina, but when they hear me speak Spanish, there is a natural curiosity. I currently am struggling with my decision to wear a khimar; I am seeking another job and fear its impact on my success. Should I mention it before the interview or only after I have secured the job?

Breaking The Windows Of Ignorance

Hamza Perez

I was born Jason John Perez on February 14, 1977, in Brooklyn, New York. My mother was from Santurce, Puerto Rico and my father was from Moca, Puerto Rico. In Brooklyn, my family came from a well-known gang/street tribe in the Sunset Park area called "The Turban Saints." In Brooklyn, my mother would take me shopping with her to Fifth Avenue in Bay Ridge and to Fulton St. downtown Brooklyn. I really enjoyed going to Fulton while my mother would go shopping in a store called "Woolworth." I would hang out outside listening to an old man play music in front of the store and watch these strange but beautiful looking people dressed all in white who smelled good and had the smell of incense flowing through the wind. At that time, I had no idea that they were Muslims.

In the mid-eighties, my mother and father got divorced so we moved from Brooklyn to Canovanas, Puerto Rico. Then when I was about nine years old, my family moved from Puerto Rico to Worcester, Massachusetts. We moved into a housing project called Plumley Village that consisted of Hispanics and Blacks with a small population of Vietnamese. In these housing projects, there was a man named "Brother Lump." He would put his speaker in the window and play Malcolm X and Farrakhan speeches. Every time I would run by his house as a kid I would listen to the voice of Malcolm and it sounded so powerful to me.

We enjoyed playing sports, basketball, and football in particular, but the basketball court was at the top of the hill from where we lived, entering the white boys' neighborhood. We would take a shortcut to the court through a masjid parking lot. We always liked playing basketball but the court was pretty far but that shortcut through the masjid parking lot was nice and it saved a little time. We were scared of the masjid and the Muslims. There was a rumor that they killed goats in the mosque. So we called the Muslims 'goat killers.' The rumors in the housing projects were that the masjid was also a Satanic church that sacrificed animals in the temple. We had given it the name "The Goat Killing Church" and we would sometimes throw rocks at the windows of the masjid when we would pass by it.

As we got older, we began falling to the negative influences that surrounded us. We began experimenting with drugs, looking and searching for some type of happiness. I first started getting really high in

Loiza Aldea, Puerto Rico when I got kicked out of school in Massachusetts. I was only fifteen and my friend in Loiza was giving me laced marijuana that was mixed with heroin. We called it Diablitos. I got in so much trouble I was sent me back to the states, and I took all of my bad habits with me and started putting on my friends in Mass on to a new way of getting high. I was only sixteen years old and I was the first one from my crew to start selling drugs in the projects. I received my first package from a Jamaican who saw some potential in me and fronted me my first package. Soon enough we all started selling drugs. It was mostly weed but then in Burncoat High School a friend of mine invited me to a block called Piedmont St. and introduced me to the crack game. That's when the hustling got really serious and the money got real serious as well as the risk.

I sold a lot of crack but was never really a big-time dealer. We were just on the block Bichotes. I started living on my own at the age of 17 in a crack infested area called Preston St. Later on some friends and I were all selling crack together on a different block called Chandler. One night in the garage of my house, we were getting high sitting in a car and I convinced them to turn the block into a form of corporation and to put all the money in one pot and pay everyone at the end of the week. The plan worked and we were now officially organized and getting money but deep down I was still not happy. I would buy a couple of Dutch Masters cigars, a small bottle of Henny, and go to the steps of a church called Mt. Carmel and smoke weed and talk to God. I would say to God "What's up God? What's going to happen to me? What do you have planned for me?" Even though I was jacked up and in the streets, I always believed in God.

My roommate and a longtime friend, who was a Latin King, became very frustrated with the false happiness that our lives on the street brought us. One day I believe he went to smoke some weed by the masjid. A Muslim brother invited him in and my roommate had learned about Islam and had taken his shahadah and from Luis he became Luqman. Brother Luqman was missing for some time. The rumor on the streets was that he was wearing a dress and had become Muslim and ran off with a bunch of locos (crazies) or Arabs and Pakistanis. At that time I didn't even know what a Pakistani was. One day I finally saw Luqman and he looked really happy and he was listening to something absolutely amazing in the car. I had no idea what it was and I said to him "Yo, I have to have this." And, he let me take it. It was a yellow cassette that had some Surahs (chapters) from the Quran. I couldn't wait to get back home and listen to it while I smoked because it made me feel relaxed and it sounded so beautiful.

Some time passed and one night I was smoking weed and drinking a 22 ounce of Heineken in front of my house when I saw my friend Luqman get out of a car and walk towards me. He was walking with this old man from Pakistan. I automatically stopped smoking out of respect and he introduced me to this man. The man asked me straight up, "Do you believe that there is only one God?" I stood in shock as you could hear in the background my other friends rolling dice, smoking, and being loud but I felt so calm and I replied, "Yes." The elderly man whose name is Shayhk Iqbal (Abu Hassan) then asked me if I believed that Muhammad (Peace be upon him) was his messenger and I replied, "Yes." I did not know much about the Prophet (Peace and blessings be upon him) but something told me to believe. Shaykh Iqbal then told me to take his hand and I told him, "Hold up." I told the man that I wanted to take my shahadah but that I was a man of corruption and that I do things that are not good as the smell of weed surrounded us and I could smell the Heineken on my breath. Shaykh Iqbal told me that little by little Allah would change me. I took my shahadah right then and there on Grosvenor St. on the sidewalk.

They took me straight to the masjid smelling like weed and beer and showed me how to make wudu and put me right in the salat line. It was the Ramadan of 1998 and my first salat was a 20 rakat taraweeh. I took my shahadah. After my friend and I had come to the call of Islam, Allah brought over 50 people that were affiliated with us to take shahadah over the course of three years. It was completely amazing. Drug dealers and criminals and even college students that we knew embraced Islam. A few months ago an old Palestinian named Abu Ayman came to me in the masjid complaining about some kids who had broken some windows in the masjid the previous day with rocks. I stood silent not knowing what to say to him, but in my heart, I was chanting 'Allahu Akbar,' thinking that maybe they might be the next generation.

Enough Is Enough - My Decision

Holly Garza

How I made the hardest and yet easiest decision of my life.

To make a long story short, a few years ago I started reading the Quran, believed it, accepted it as the truth, then I got distracted by thinking Islam was about a scarf and being told what to do rather than about the truth, and by wanting to "be free," or so I incorrectly assumed. I then denied I was Muslim and decided to chicken out, curse, and party my life away while being vengeful, sad, and angry at what trials and struggles life gave me instead of being a practicing Muslim. What's that old saying though??? "To make God laugh tell him what you will plan to do" is what they say...Oh so true! I planned to not be Muslim, astaghfirullah, or so I thought.

Islam encourages us to think, question, be nice, be conscious of life, be respectful, and be loving. Islam is my birthright and way of life. I deserve it. It's a remarkable thing you just have to feel to get. To think I was denying myself Islam is horrendous and unthinkable to me. The promises of Heaven and of no death in Paradise are great - to think I kept that from me! So I continued "living." In reality, I was imprisoned, shackled by my anger and hurt feelings. I was so misguided on my own. When God guides someone, they are guided. Boy, did I get reminders, blessings, notices, and the urge in my heart! I kept feeling the call in my heart. Some reminders were easy to recognize, others weren't obvious that they were little crumbs on my road to Islam. It took years to catch what my calling in life was - Islam.

Ever since I was a child the concept of praying to God through God and not a statue, or person was a familiar concept. I always wanted to know things and questioned everything, never settling for "you just have to have faith" as an answer. I was always uncomfortable with someone killing the son of God. It did not make sense to me. Later in my older childhood years, we became Jehovah Witnesses, which answered many questions, as they also believe in the oneness of God and being kind amongst other things. However, there were things I questioned as I got older in that religion, but that is another matter.

I tried to flee Islam, after all. Hatred, anger, and vices are easier to live with than actually working to be a better person. I was a good person all my life and I felt that it was abused and stripped from me through the tests of life. I had this whole screw-this-I-don't-give-a-crap phony mentality that is so popular right now. It is so easy to let others' stupidity bring us to their level of anger as well.

One day waiting to go home in the parking lot of yet another bar in the freezing cold of winter I decided I had enough. I had had enough of the hangovers, enough of the dried out, head throbbing half a day feeling crappy the morning after. It did not matter if it was only a few times a month or just one time. I was done with it. I had enough of the hurt, anger, and depression rotting away at my heart. It's hard to explain. The empty unreligious God is not close to me feeling and that I'm religious by name, I believe in God by just saying it. That is not true belief. You don't feel whole.

I have the utmost respect for all religious followers. The genuinely God-fearing Christians, Catholics, and Jews. Those of you who strive for the good, respect yourselves and others and try to live by God as you know and understand. However, most people proclaim to believe but do not know anything or follow it.

I was truly lost. Anyhow, I started rereading the Quran last year, here and there, but not taking heed of what it said. God in his mercy was storing all this away in my brain though, while I kept living how I was.

Eventually, on February 9, I was running ten ways to Sunday. Depressed, angry, hateful, hurt - just lost. I had lived through my mother's, my daughter's, and sister's deaths and was going through my father's long losing battle with life. I was lost in depression, sin, and vices even though I denied it. I am not angry with myself; my daughter's death was not my fault I said emptily. I do not have a problem. It's not an everyday thing. My old mentality is. I was getting tired and it was getting old. I started crying over sad and angry thoughts and listened to angry and sad music. I started going out a little less, drinking less. I quit drinking little by little. My Dad lost his battle but not before begging us through his pain to not turn into drunks. I won't and I didn't, Dad.

I read the Quran that whole week and started talking to a brother on campus about hooking me up with some Muslimahs (Muslim women) for knowledge on Islam. By this point, I was actively seeking Islam out. Boy did he! The brother from campus told a group of sisters who told others, which in turn e-mailed and Facebooked me. During this time, I also started receiving online support from Spanish speaking Muslims and groups that I had inquired to over the months. I thought it was too much too soon that day, and then, alhamdulillah, I changed my mind within a week. What changed my mind?

I started praying more and felt God's love, closeness, and help. Anger would turn to calmness, hurt and sadness into hope, and the lost sensation turned into ease. I prayed more and more as time went on and I gained peace in my heart, and now I pray all the time I can. Five times a day plus dua (supplication). All I can say is that it is impossible to put into words. That loved, calm inside, closeness to God feeling. I felt an intense sensation like a magnet calling me to pray, to read, and to all things Islamic. It would not go away.

I was getting very close to a sister named Sadaf who told me, "Let's take you to say shahadah. God does not need you to change to go to him, just go to him." What a beautiful thing! We made plans to go on a Wednesday but I could not make it. I kept praying. The next Friday we were on our way. It was beautiful. It was Jummah (Friday for us in Islam; it's almost like our Sunday).

I prayed at the mosque side by side with other sisters. Sisters of many races standing side-by-side saying the same thing shoulder to shoulder. It was such a beautiful experience. I prayed to be able to do it. I prayed for things that shall remain with me and my Lord, and I prayed the prayers as everyone else.

When I said my shahadah, I cried. I did not mean to do that. The day I took it the sheikh (like our Muslim preacher guy) said, "Wow! A new Muslim! All the hardships, all the sins, all the hurts before Islam, God will help you heal and get through and all sins are erased by Allah."

It is true. You honestly do feel a huge change. I cried. Life has been somewhat hard, to put it mildly so thank God. I have not regretted becoming a Muslimah once! The things I thought would be hard like wearing a scarf, praying five times a day, and explaining why I follow Islam have all become very easy. Thank God for that. Alhamdulillah. This is not to say there are no hardships like people's rude manners, my trying to be nice when faced with ignorance, and the all-around offensive comments about my religion due to the lack of knowledge and rudeness.

Life goes on, but for me and my way, I am a Muslimah forever.

"I'm Going To Be A Muslim"

Israel Interiano

My conversion was a lifelong process when looking back. It started when I was in about 2nd grade. I almost drowned to the point I blacked out. I had given up trying to stay above water and believed I was going to die. At the last second, my friend's dad pulled me out. This made me a very devout Catholic as a child growing up. I was an altar boy, and I loved going to church on Sundays. Time passed and I was in high school with a car. I was doing an errand for my job one day when I got into a horrible car accident. My Jeep Cherokee did a 180-degree turn across two lanes in a major freeway in Wichita. So many different outcomes could have occurred but I came out unscathed.

While my first near-death experience led me to become religious, this experience gave me a more inquisitive mind. During the wreck as my car was swerving before it spun, I remember thinking, "This is it. God, if you want me to live, let me live." The first conscious decision of relinquishing any power I thought I had to God. I remember saying that out loud as I took my hands off the steering wheel. Afterwards, I started thinking, "This is twice now that I could have died unexpectedly. I can really die at any moment by some freak accident. If that's the case then I need to make sure I'm prepared." I thought that good deeds weren't enough and that I really needed to understand as much about religion as possible. I remember asking myself, "The Hindus say all non-Hindus are going to hell and the Christians say all non-Christians are going to hell...so who is actually correct?" Islam never even crossed my mind. I didn't really know any Muslims, and I never thought about Islam.

I lost everything after my wreck. I didn't look the same because I lost 20lbs in about two weeks from stress. I lost a lot of money, and my car was damaged. I thought, "Wow. How can I say I have anything in this world if it was all taken away in an instant?" I also remember my mom always told me that the only thing that lasts forever is the love you have for God. If that's the case then I might as well just live my life for God. I just realized how everything you think you have is only temporary and actually belongs to God. God took everything away from me in a second that gave me pride...things I would have never wanted to give up. So, I felt that it was pointless to have a severe attachment to anything too material because at the end of the day it does not belong to you.

I started doing more research and soon came across information about some of the corruption and atrocities that the church has committed. At this point, I still didn't know anything about Islam but I understood that most religions have parts in history that may be dark. But Catholicism is institutionalized. Anything institutionalized will become corrupt because of human nature. Therefore, the Catholic Church must be corrupt. This was my opinion at the time. I thought that I didn't know what the ideal religion should be like but I knew what it shouldn't be like. At about this time, I read a book about Islam that I found on my sister's bookshelf. She's not a Muslim but she took a class on religion in college. I read it and became enveloped. Everything made so much sense, and there was an explanation for the various questions I had.

I finished the book in about two days. Immediately afterward I heard a little voice inside my head say: "I'm going to be a Muslim." I really had no idea what had just happened. I thought, "Wow. I'm not going to be a Catholic anymore." I knew no Muslims so I had no idea how this was going to happen. I went to college and my cousin was living with Saudis. I thought this was a good time to learn from them to see how they can balance prayer and fasting. One, in particular, made extra effort to talk to me and answer any questions I might have had. I knew immediately I wanted to convert but I still needed to be entirely sure it was something I could handle. If I was going to be a Muslim, I wanted to make sure I would never miss a prayer, always fast during Ramadan, etc. I didn't feel I was mentally ready at the time for many reasons.

A few years later, I took a trip to Europe to study abroad and took a short vacation around Europe after school was over. It was the best time of my life. I remember on my last day in Europe that I sat there thinking about how I just had the best time of my life and now it's all over. I thought I would feel melancholic upon my return knowing that what I had just lived would never return. This is when I felt that everything in life is only fleeting happiness. Everything is just a moment of time that will soon be over. And if that's the case then what's the point of vain pursuits if the pleasure they provide will not last forever. At the end of the day, all those frivolities can even become detrimental. This is when I thought again about what my mother always told me, "The only thing that lasts forever is the love you have for God." So again, I thought that I should place my focus on that.

A couple of years later before starting graduate school, I was hanging out with a Muslim friend. He knew I was going to convert one day, and he knew I always realized Islam was the truth. One day he just said, "Look, you know Islam is the truth and you're still not following it. God will not forgive you for that. You'll go to Hell forever for that." I became scared. I mean really scared. It reminded me of when I almost drowned as a kid. Because I was so afraid of dying, it was hard for me to sleep a couple of nights. I had never read the Quran so I picked it up and read it. I was immediately amazed by it.

I was thinking in bed one morning. I thought, "I have to go to work today...I can die on my way to work...If I die then I would die a non-Muslim knowing that Islam is the truth." I thought, "If I were on my deathbed would I want to convert?" Yes. "If I knew judgment day was tomorrow would I want to convert?" Yes. "But I'm still not a Muslim so I would die a disbeliever. I can't let that happen." So, I shot out of bed and ran to a book I had that explained how to convert. I put my head down and thanks be to God - I became a Muslim.

From Mexico To Saudi Arabia

Jehan Sanchez

I was born in a small village called "La Cruz Balleza" in Chihuahua, Mexico. My parents were wonderful but my father was my world. Sadly, my father died by a bolt of lightning, killing him instantly. My young mother became widowed with me and three of my sisters, one who was not yet born. I was five years old, and I was the oldest.

My sisters, my mom, and I moved to my grandmother's farm. I lived with my grandmother until age 11. My childhood was not a happy one. My mother had to work wherever she could in order to provide for me and my sisters, which meant that she had to leave us. My sisters and I encountered many hardships and trauma in our childhood. Sometimes we did not have anything to eat, but we survived with the will of Allah and His protection.

When my mother found work in the city, my sisters and I moved with her. My mother worked during the day while I and my sisters sat at a relative's home. My relative did not keep us in her home. Instead, we had to spend the day in a cold or hot shack, depending on the weather. We were hungry and lonely all day long as we waited for our mother. In the evening, when our mother returned from work, we would devour the food that her boss had kindly provided for her. My mother asked us one day why we were always hungry. The truth was that our relative was buying groceries with my mother's money but was not feeding us. Instead, she would feed herself and her grown-up son.

Shortly after, my mother remarried. My sisters and I moved in with our stepfather. He was a loving and caring man who would always come home with some sort of fruit, a box of cornflakes, or a box of cookies but he never came back empty-handed. My stepfather would always give me advice. When I was almost 12 years old, he would always tell me that I was a good person and to not let anyone put me down whenever the kids from school or the neighborhood were mean to me and my sisters. He was always there for us, advising us, encouraging us, and ever by our side. He too died leaving my mother a widow and leaving my stepbrothers and sisters orphans. Nevertheless, he left a mark in my heart and I have always remembered him as the kind man that he was.

When my aunt who lived in the United States came to visit my family, I saw how well-dressed and how well educated she seemed. I felt that if I moved to America with her I could also have a better life. I did not understand my motives at the time. I did not understand why I wanted to leave my family. I loved my mother and sisters, but I felt I needed to go. Today I know perfectly well. It was Allah, the Most-Wise, who was calling me. I had this feeling that there was something better over there. I moved to the United States to live and work with my aunt in the winter of 1981. As a 13-year-old, I felt that living in America would improve my life and it so happened that it also improved my family's life. Every month my aunt would send my mother the $100 that I earned working for her.

Life at my aunt's house was not what I expected. Her husband was an alcoholic and an abusive man, both physically and mentally. It was tough living there at times. Many times, I ran away to get away from the problems but soon I had to return home. I felt so alone that I cried myself to sleep. I often regretted the move but my heart would tell me that life would get better and so I decided to stay. Time passed and my sister, Aisha, joined me in America. Later, my aunt was ordered by social services to put me in school.

I wanted to be an astronaut or a pilot, but because I was so young, I also wanted to be a singer. I even entered a singing competition one day but I never showed up. Alhamdulillah. One day my social worker came to see me at school and asked me if I wanted to return to Mexico or stay and go live in a foster home in Boulder. She explained to me what a foster home was but I had already chosen. I chose to stay in America but my sister decided to go back to Mexico. For me, America was the place where I needed to stay. Where I knew life would be better and I completely believed that by staying in America I could help my family, too. Allah, the Exalted, was telling me that indeed my life, someday, would be better. It would be better than anything I ever imagined it would be.

My foster parents were very supportive and understanding. I was the only Mexican living there but everyone made sure that I knew that I was welcome and that I was an extraordinary person just like everyone else. My social worker and my therapist would give me money from their own pockets and were always caring and great people. I also earned money by doing my chores, having proper conduct, and by following the house rules. I was always deemed on "Contract" (the highest level), which meant that I was a responsible person. I started high school that fall.

When I was 17, I got a job. One tiring day at school, during my last class, I was about to fall asleep. Having to work and go to school was a little bit of a challenge. One day, our teacher decided to give us a glance at the map of the Middle East. It was there that I learned about the Arabs, their traditions, and their strange religion. Our teacher gave us a bird's view of the Islamic faith. We were told by our teacher that Muslims pray five times a day. Hearing this, I said to myself "I don't even remember when the last time was that I prayed." How can I pray five times a day?

Then he told us about fasting. I had no idea what that word meant. Therefore, I asked my teacher. He kindly informed us that Muslims fast from sunrise until sunset and it was called Ramadan. Now wait a minute, I thought! I can't even go an hour without food much less a whole day! The teacher told us about how once in a lifetime a Muslim should perform a pilgrimage, or Hajj, if able to financially and healthy. I listened attentively to my teacher speak about things that were utterly beyond my wildest dreams.

My teacher then told us about how Muslim men can have up to four wives. Now that really woke me up! I sat up straight listening in disbelief. What, women sharing their husbands? No way! I had never had a boyfriend; much less a husband, but I could not digest the word "sharing." "How can women do that?" I thought by now. The whole class was laughing—especially the boys. They were intrigued by the idea of men having four wives. Well, not me. I was a civilized woman.

Later in the school year, I met my first husband. We dated and then got married and had a son. My marriage didn't last very long and we divorced. High school finished and I forgot about the Muslims and their odd religion.

One day while at work, I met my "husband-to-be." He was a quiet person and extremely shy. He was young but looked so mature and was well-mannered and polite. I fell in love with him instantly. He, on the other hand, would hardly look at me. I thought to myself, "I have to know him a little better! What are his habits? When does he come to eat at the restaurant?" I could not get over how shy and polite he was. He was not like other boys—nowhere close to the others.

I would notice that he did not drink alcohol. One day he introduced me to one of his friends and his wife. His friend's wife was not a Muslim but my "soon-to-be" husband and his friend would pray together. They looked like they were in another world—so peaceful and so calm. There was so much serenity around them that it was completely beautiful. I was not sure why they prayed the way they did, so I asked him. He said he was a Muslim. Finally, I had seen a Muslim pray and I was hypnotized.

Whenever I saw my future husband, I could not help myself; I wanted to talk to him. I tried to get to know him better. Alhamdulillah. I have always been a good person with morals and manners but seeing him so quiet and respectful made me feel ashamed because I was the one who asked too many questions about him and his life.

One lovely summer day as I was waiting for my bus to take me to work, I noticed a lady who was getting out of a car with whom I believed was her husband. She was covered in black—from head to toe—and I wondered why she was covered that way. I knew she was a Muslim lady but her attire was new to me.

When I saw her, I wanted to talk to her but I was scared. I felt that she would not speak to me once she saw what I was wearing. To me it was normal: shorts and a tank top. That's how everyone dressed but I felt embarrassed by my appearance. I desperately wanted to talk to her but I could not overcome my fears. I looked forward to my sunny afternoons at the bus stop so I could see that mysterious lady. Then one day I asked about her. I was told that she was Muslim, which I already knew.

Strange thing is that although I was not a Muslim yet, I considered myself one of them. I don't know why. My knowledge about Muslims was still weak. Yet I felt I was one of them. The wife of my husband's friend later became a Muslim. I saw changes—good changes—she dressed differently now. There were no more shorts or miniskirts, tight jeans, or revealing blouses. We became friends but she did not speak to me about Islam. In fact, no one did.

As time passed by, I asked my husband-to-be for a Holy Quran, the last revealed book of Allah, the Majestic. He gave me one. I loved that book so much. I carried it with me wherever I went.

On a cold and terrible evening, someone decided to attack me in my own home. The only thing I recall was that at that very moment, I grabbed my Holy Quran and held onto it as if my life depended on it. It was as if it was a dear, lost friend who could save me from execution. I cried and cried and held onto my Book desperate for relief. The next day my Muslim friend who happened to be there during that argument told me that he was shocked at how I held onto the Holy Quran. Yes, I was not a Muslim but I believed in that Book so much and I found comfort in it.

"Verily with every hardship, there is relief." (Quran 94: 5-6). This is one of my favorite verses from the Holy Quran.

One beautiful, warm and splendid summer day, the birds were chirping, the sky was so blue, and the day was like a dream. I was walking home, and then suddenly a thought came to me that said, "If Jesus died for my sins then why am I still sinning?" I have asked myself so many times… "What does that mean?" I have no idea. It made perfect sense a couple of months later. I was sitting on my sofa and suddenly I felt this energy. There was this push and I got up and went to the house of my husband-to-be. My friend's husband was there, too. I walked up to them and told them I wanted to become a Muslim.

I said my shahadah (testimony of faith) on December 1988. I was 20 years old. I felt so free and so light. I was now part of the strange religion that I had heard about while in high school.

Abû Hurayrah relates that Allah's Messenger (peace be upon him) said: "Islam began strange, and it will become strange again just like it was at the beginning, so blessed are the strangers." [Sahîh Muslim (1/130)].

I was on cloud nine. I was now one of those blissful strangers. I was a Muslim lady. Finally, I felt that my heart had been mended. Islam restored my broken heart and gave me such peace that it was overwhelming. I was so proud of myself. I had accomplished something so extraordinary but of course, it was Allah, the Most Compassionate, who showed me the light. He was the One who made my life perfect. He gave me the understanding. He opened my eyes and my heart and guided my lost soul to tranquility.

My life before this had been so extremely painful. The loss of my father had clouded my heart and mind but Islam took all of that away. I still cried for my father but now I understood why Allah took him from me. It was clear. I still could not accept it but I understood it. Islam somehow makes you aware that our Creator is capable of everything and that everything happens for a reason.

I went on with my new and precious religion, learning, although not much. I was so busy with work and had no time to see my Muslim friends. However, I tried to pray and I tried to fast. My first Ramadan was a little bit hard but I tried my best. I decided to wear my veil but was unsuccessful. It was difficult because I had no one to help me—no moral support. Islamic material was scarce back then. There weren't many Muslims at the time, at least not in my city. But, I went on. Life was so good. I now felt protected and loved—loved by the Almighty.

My husband and I got married July 1989. We had a small ceremony at the Islamic Center. My dear husband taught me how to pray correctly. He bought me my first real headscarf (hijab) and we fasted together my second Ramadan (the fasting month). It was amazing. I read the Holy Quran from beginning to end. I would fast and pray during the day then pray and read the Quran at night. What seemed so strange when I was a 17 year old in high school was now the reason for my existence. It was my world, my joy.

After a couple of years passed by, my husband and I decided that I should move to Saudi Arabia to live with his parents while he finished his education. I was not working anymore and life was a bit expensive. I was thrilled by the idea of moving to a foreign land. The paperwork did not take very long and things were going very smoothly. I was soon leaving America for a better life.

Saudi Arabia at last! The land where Prophets (peace and blessings be upon them) were born, where Islam was born, where Mecca and Medina—the homes where our beloved Prophet (peace and blessings be upon him) lived and struggled day and night delivering the Message that Allah, the Exalted, had entrusted upon him. It was the Message that billions of people including myself believed in with all their might. I was finally here.

My in-laws were very good to me. Even though I had met them before, I had never actually lived with them, especially without my husband to support and comfort me. However, for some reason, I felt right at home. I did not speak or understand the language but Saudi Arabia was my home away from home.

After about a week in Saudi Arabia, my dear mother-in-law made plans for me to perform Umrah (the lesser Hajj). Oh Allah! I could not believe it. Was I dreaming? I was going to stand and pray where Prophet Muhammad, Abraham, Ishmael and many other Prophets prayed (peace and blessings be upon them). I was anxious and at the same time worried. I had no idea what to say or do. Some members of my new family had gladly given me some pointers but still, I was nervous. I did not know what to do—cry or laugh from excitement.

The trip to Mecca was so lovely. Everything was new to me. I was taking it all in. I was without words. We arrived in Mecca. As we were getting closer to the Holy Mosque (Al-Haraam), the excitement was unreal. I was going to perform Umrah—me the village girl!

Once inside the Haraam, I could not see straight because I was crying. I still could not see the Kaaba (the black cube that Muslims face when praying). At last, I saw the Kaaba. I was totally speechless. By this time, I was not crying anymore—I was bawling. It was an indescribable feeling. All I could think of was that I was loved. Allah had showered me with His mercy and compassion and had chosen me out of billions of human beings to be His slave. I performed tawaf (circumambulating the Kaaba) and then I went on to Safa and Marwa (two small mountains). I was standing where Hajar, Ishmael's mother, once stood (peace and blessings be upon them). This was where she had looked and sought food for her young baby, running from mountain to mountain until finally, the Spring of Zamzam erupted under Ishmael's feet. I was surrounded by hundreds of people who believed in the One True God. People save up money throughout all their lives to come and perform the acts that Prophets like Abraham and his son, Ishmael (peace be upon them both) had performed and who restored the Kaaba by the will of Allah.

I considered myself a Muslim even before I accepted Islam but I never imagined myself living in Saudi Arabia. After a few months, my husband joined us in Saudi Arabia and we started to build a family. Ten years ago, my husband and I performed the Hajj (greater pilgrimage). It was my first Hajj and it was the trip of a lifetime.

As we set out for Hajj, I could not help but cry from the joy. I was, with the will of Allah, answering His call. I was completing my religion. Islam is based on five pillars.

The first pillar is the testimony of faith, or *shahadah*, as we say in Arabic. The second one is prayer or *salah*. The third is almsgiving or charity (*zakat*). The fourth is fasting the whole month of *Ramadan*, which is the ninth month of the Islamic calendar. The fifth pillar is the pilgrimage or *Hajj*. I was on my way to completing all five.

We arrived in Mecca, performed our religious obligations there and then we headed for Mina. Mina is where all the Muslims camp during the Hajj. As I entered my beautiful, gigantic, air-conditioned, and well-lit tent, I thought back to the time when Prophet Abraham and his beloved son went to perform their Hajj. Of course, the props were much, much different but the religion, the duties were the same. The day of Arafat was a day to remember. I was surrounded by all my sisters in the faith… The men were in one tent and women in another. I recall that day very well. It was a beautiful sunny day, not too hot—it was perfect. I remember feeling so warm. I felt so much peace. I truly felt clean and I felt no worries. It was a feeling of being born free of sin, hatred, and rancor. It was a marvelous feeling. I honestly hoped to die at that very moment. I prayed and asked for forgiveness for mercy and compassion, everyone there had one goal in mind… forgiveness from the All-Merciful.

On our last day of pilgrimage, as thousands of pilgrims from all over the world, rich and poor, white and black stood side by side, we waited in the scorching heat to perform our religious rites and waited for the sun to hit its zenith. I could not help but think of Judgment Day when everyone will stand before Allah and give account for their deeds. May Allah, the Most Merciful, have mercy on all of us.

Six years ago, my sister—now renamed Aisha—and one of her young teenage daughters paid me a visit here in Saudi Arabia. I have always spoken to my family about Islam and especially to my sister Aisha. We have always been in communication and she always listened to my comments about Islam. A couple of weeks after her arrival she announced her shahadah. What a unique experience! I was able to witness my lovely sister become a Muslim—a new era had begun. Four days later, my beautiful niece announced her shahadah.

"Our Lord! Pour out on us patience and constancy, and make us die as those who have surrendered themselves unto You." (Quran 7:126).

Islam is the religion that all of the Prophets brought. It was revealed to them by Allah, the All-Mighty. It is not just for the rich. It is not just for the Arabs—it is for all humankind. It is for those who genuinely believe that there is only One God. Jesus (peace and blessings be upon him) was a Prophet and a Messenger; Muhammad (peace and blessings be upon him) was the last Messenger of Allah.

"This day, I have perfected your religion for you, completed My Favor upon you, and have chosen for you Islam as your religion." (Quran 5:3).

Glory be to Allah, the Lord of the worlds, and everything that exists.

When God Reached Out To Me

Jessica Nadia

I am 18 years old. I come from an Italian and Latino background, and I live in Sydney, Australia. I hope by sharing my story, it will help you through your journey that you may be facing or have already faced, and I hope it inspires you to take that leap of faith, just as it has helped me.

When the truth is revealed to you and you stand face to face with it, how long can you refuse to accept it? How long would you run away denying it? There comes a point in your life when you have to break free from all the chains that hold you back, from answering the True Call. It is a moment where nothing else seems significant and equivalent to the call of the Almighty Allah and His path of freedom, bliss, and satisfaction. All the lies with which you have been living with start fading and your beliefs as a disbeliever fall like a pack of cards, and what you witness is a Eureka! moment, a moment when you realize the truth, a moment when you understand the beauty of Islam.

The moment a Muslim revert declares their faith to Islam they undergo a great struggle. Many will lose friends along the way who refuse to accept their new religion and lifestyle and also family members who are unable to digest the fact that they have embraced Islam. My life before Islam had no meaning and no direction. I was baptized as a Catholic, but never really learned the religion. As a child and younger teen, I grew up in a family environment surrounded by drugs, alcohol, abuse, and emotional, physical, and sexual abuse. My parents split up when I was 11 years old. I do not remember much of my father because he was never around. When he was, it was only for the wrong reasons. My father lived on alcohol. He was violent and suicidal and tried many attempts to end his life. Life at that time was a constant struggle, but it all has made me the person I am today. I do not blame or victimize myself according to the events that took place in my life, instead, I feel blessed for who I have become.

My spiritual journey all began when I was about 11 years old. I came across something that will never be erased from my mind. I witnessed my uncle commit suicide - right before my very eyes. My uncle drenched himself in gasoline and lit himself in the backyard. At that very moment, I was terrified of death itself. I witnessed someone take away his life in just a split second, but I did not understand what lies ahead, what happens after you die. I suddenly realized, my father, my uncle, almost my entire family had nothing to live for, no reason holding us back. I realized that I had no belief myself. I claimed to be a Christian but what more could an 11-year-old child know, growing up in an environment where everything we claimed to be was entirely different behind closed doors. All I knew was that I was a Christian, Jesus is the Son of God, and he died for all of our sins. For the first time in my life, I got down on my knees and prayed with all my heart and soul. I asked God to make me a stronger person, to guide me through life and to show me the truth when the time was right.

When I started high school, I was at an all-girls' private Catholic school. I hung out with the wrong crowd on the streets. I was up to no good for most of my teen years, but I was still able to walk away from and refuse many things. When I was in my sophomore year, I began searching for answers again. I wanted to not only consider myself as a Catholic but also understand and truly believe in it. I found myself attending church every week and regular youth groups. It seemed the more and more I learned about it the more I did not understand it and most of all did not believe in it. My questions were unanswered, and most of all I felt empty, lost, and confused. All through my childhood I would pray to God and ask him to help me, even though I wasn't practicing my religion completely. My curiosity led me to research online other beliefs and faiths, including Islam. I had no intention of converting to Islam. I saw things that seemed weird or strange, and out of ignorance one day I just said, "I'm going to stay a Christian because Islam it too strange and different."

At this stage, I was confused, upset, and I did not have a clue what to do. I also kept this all to myself so no one else knew what I was doing. One night I remember I was in my room about to go to bed and I felt so confused and lost. I was quite emotional and I remember calling out to God to help me, "Please make this decision for me, because I don't know what to do." I asked God, if Christianity is the right religion, then I'll stay a Christian, but if Islam is the right religion then make me a Muslim. I guess I was looking for a sign of some sort - the same sign I asked for all those years ago. After that, I was still quite emotional and decided to just go to sleep. Then things started to get really weird.

The next few days all I could think about was Islam. It consumed my mind. The Quran, Muhammad, Allah, the religion. All of it. I couldn't explain it. All I was interested in looking up on the Internet was Islam. When I did research I found out the truth. Islam just made much sense.

I would listen to the Quran and start crying out of nowhere, and I couldn't understand why. I just loved everything about it and wanted to know more. At that point, I did not know any Muslims. I told a few of my closest friends at that time and expressed what I was going through and that I wanted to convert. I wanted their support, their opinions not once did it ever cross my mind that I could actually lose some of them along the way. All they could say to me was how extreme Islam was and that Muslim women are oppressed. They would basically say why you would want to be like that, don't you want to be free and live. Not soon afterward I had no choice but to change schools and finish my last years elsewhere. I met some fantastic friends who I can now call family. Their support has been truly amazing.

I began to get very close to a guy named Murad that a family friend was seeing. When they would come over, we would often debate about religion and Islam was always the main subject. At that point, I had no intention whatsoever of telling my mother what I was going through due to the fact of her hate and resentment towards the religion. Murad and I began talking almost every week about Islam. Then on the night of June 17, 2008, out of nowhere he said to me, "You know, you could die tomorrow, and not be a Muslim."

At that point I had this immediate sense of emotion overtake me and all I knew was that I had to become a Muslim - on this night, at this hour, right at this moment. I began making wudu in the downstairs bathroom, everyone in my family was all asleep upstairs. After I was done, I got down on my knees and said my shahadah. It seems like yesterday. The feeling was beyond words. Right at that moment, I could not get up; I couldn't even move. Murad kept calling out to me on the phone, saying, "You're a Muslim, you're a Muslim," but I could not stop crying. I was filled with joy and had a sense of feeling of being reborn. I walked up to my bed, laid down, and gazed out my window. There was a full moon that night. I gazed up at the sky and remember knowing in my heart that Allah was looking down on me. And, all I could feel was unconditional love and happiness that my life as a Muslim had just begun.

For just over two years, I kept my faith a secret from my family. I did so not only for fear of rejection or of hurting them, but because of my age, I would not be taken seriously. I needed to become stronger as a person. I fasted during Ramadan, learned how to pray via the Internet and tried my very best to read the Quran every night. By the time I turned 18, I decided it was time to let my family know. I couldn't handle living a double life anymore, fearing they would walk into my room while I was praying, reading my Quran, etc. My mother did realize a change in me for a long time by then and suspected I was interested in the religion, but never did it cross her mind that I was already a Muslim. When my mother and certain family members realized I was Muslim, everything came crashing down. I would live in and out of my home for weeks at a time, and a number of times I would go home to find most of my belongings scattered everywhere, and some things even were thrown out.

After I began wearing the hijab, things really started to get messed up. I was threatened with a knife and went through months and months of constant battles with family members. I was told I was no longer welcome to visit certain family members, attend family functions and celebrations, and so on. I always knew when the time came to them knowing it would be very hard, but never until I actually went through that chapter in my life did I realize just how hard it would really be. It tore me to pieces to have my own mother, who was very proud of me and thought the world of me to suddenly resent me and look at me as if I were nothing.

The hardest part of becoming a Muslim was hurting my family and losing my relationship with some of them along the way. This whole process hasn't been natural, but I must say it was worth it. I still managed to keep myself together with the help and guidance of Allah. We all get tested in life and this was mine. I was pushed to the very edge - the breaking point. And, yet when I look back, this was all proof to me about just how serious I am and how strongly I feel about Islam. At the end of the day, I have changed my religion, not my culture. Things simply take time in life and we just have to stay strong and be patient. And, the ones who are left are those who indeed matter.

Islam has given me peace, and my life finally has meaning. Not once have I ever looked back or even considered changing back to my old religion. My family situation is getting better, day-by-day, one step at a time. I have a wonderful group of friends who are like family to me, and I have met an amazing guy, who means the world to me. Satan is failing because I was able to join the Religion of God and see through the rubbish of the media. That is why Islam is the fasting growing religion and no one is able to put out the light of God. I pray that all of you who enter Islam will feel as blessed as I do and continue to stay strong and true to yourself. Take that first step; trust me you won't look back.

"You never know how strong you are, till being strong is the only choice you have." – Bob Marley.

Where The Floor Meets The Carpet

Jesus Villareal

First some background information. Growing up, my mother, younger sister, and I (my parents got divorced when I was six) were together all the time. My mother worked two and sometimes three jobs at a time to support and feed us. The times that we were not at school and she was not at work were usually spent at church. To us, church was a time when we could get away from the dangerous neighborhoods that we used to live in (the projects or ghetto to some people) and immerse ourselves in a wholesome, positive environment full of fellowship and good things.

I was baptized Roman Catholic but we used to visit other Christian churches and settings. You name it: Pentecostal, Jehovah's Witnesses, Baptist, etc. My family and I went all over the place! I figured that my Mom was searching for the one Christian church that had it all. I mean the Jehovah's Witnesses were awesome people! They were very upright, moral, and educated. They impressed us with their excellent morals and nice dress attire. They would often come to our home in the projects to talk to us. However, they did not have several of the beliefs that my mother was ingrained with when she was growing up, like Christmas for instance. The Catholics did not really leave a godly impression on us. I figured that the only reason that my mother attended the Catholic Church was that was the religion that she was brought up with.

High school rolls around and I take four years of the Latin language. There I learned about the gods and goddesses of ancient Rome. It was interesting to find out that they also had a god that was born on December 25th (imagine that!). So, of course, I asked my questions to the various preachers, priests, and pastors that we usually visited on a monthly basis. Questions such as "Was Jesus really born on December 25th?" and "Since when do rabbits lay eggs?" (Referring to the Easter holiday). These questions were often countered with "I will have your answer by next Sunday" and "Don't meddle with God's business!" Of course, next Sunday would come by and I would get the same "I will have your answer by next Sunday." That got old really quick. So I did not go to church anymore and questioned everything that was presented to me.

By this time, I was about to graduate from high school and join the Marines, which I did. I left for San Diego, California (Marine Corps boot camp) on June 17, 1996. Boot camp was a breeze. There I met people of all faiths: some Muslims, a Buddhist, Christians, and my bunkmate who just happened to be a Mormon. None of these guys made any sense to me. Of course, the only one that really attempted to present their religion was my bunkmate Van Hecke, the Mormon. The only way that I knew that the other two guys were Muslims was because they got food that contained pork and they asked for something else because it was against the Muslim religion to eat swine. They did not pray (that I saw), nor talk to anyone that I was aware of about their faith.

So this whole time I am in the Marines and I only believe in God, just one God. Not this confusing belief of "the father, the son, and the holy spirit" - three in one God idea. And not the "if you are not with me you are going to hell" style that evangelical Christians attempt to crown people with. I mean, I did not see myself as an idiot, rabbits don't lay eggs, there are differences in opinion amongst Christians concerning Jesus' birth, and there are several types of the Bible. (Depending on your flavor). None of that made any sense to me! So I do my time in the boot camp and get out of the Marine Corps active duty and begin college on June 17, 2000. Although I was out of the active component of the Marine Corps, I still was active in the Marine Corps Reserve component, one weekend a month and two weeks in the summer.

So time goes by and then September the 11th happens. It was a Tuesday morning just like any other Tuesday morning and I was on my way to my history class in college. I turned on the radio as I usually did and was searching for a good station to listen to some rap. I switched to one channel and they were talking about some plane that hit one of the towers. All of the radio stations that I turned to were talking about the same thing. An airplane had crashed into one of the towers. I turned off the radio and turned on my CD player to the tune of "Sippin' On Some Syrup" by Three 6 Mafia.

When I got to school, I parked and headed towards a cafeteria to get some of those nasty-tasting potato and egg tacos with the paper-thin flour tortillas. (What can I say, I'm Mexican, and I can critique tacos.) As I entered the cafeteria, I saw several students huddled together looking up at the TV. They were looking at the same thing that I was trying to avoid listening to on the radio, the airplane that hit the tower. Suddenly, a second plane hit the second tower. Some people yelled out, some cried, but me, I let out an expletive. I was thinking to myself "What is going on?" So as a member of the Marine Corps Reserve, I called my Platoon Sergeant and asked what was going on. He said that he did not know but to call up the rest of the Marines and tell them to have their gear ready. So I did.

That weekend just so happened to be the drill weekend. I had never seen so many Marines at that station at any time! Marines that had been AWOL (left without letting anybody know) for a long time showed up! Old men who used to be Marines also showed up! America was united for once! You could smell the testosterone in the air! These Marines were pumped up and ready to take care of business! There was no way that you could stop these Marines from accomplishing anything at that point in time! The motivation of these guys including myself had never been seen before. My buddy Carlos and I told our Platoon Sergeant that if there was any list going around to fight overseas we wanted to be the first ones on it!

Weeks passed by and my buddy Carlos and I wanted to learn about our enemy so that we could exploit every weakness that we could. So we decided to sign up for an Arabic class at Berlitz Language Center. That did not happen. Why? Because it was a rip off! They were offering a three-month "immersion course" in which classes were three times a week for an hour and a half each session. How much you ask? A whopping $5,000! And this did not even guarantee any type of proficiency! It was definitely out of the question. So we began learning the Arabic alphabet (little did we know that Arabic is not the primary language of Afghanistan) and educate ourselves on the religion of our enemy, Islam. We also worked out and kept ourselves fit, so when the call came to go fight those creeps (for lack of a better word) in their homeland, we would be ready. February 2002 rolled around and I told my friends that I needed to learn Arabic so that I could go and kill those Muslims!

I told them that I was going to go to a mosque so that I could say to them that I wanted to learn about their religion, but in fact, I wanted to learn Arabic so that I could kill them! My friends and family thought that I was nuts! So the time came and I called the place that my enemies worshipped at the local mosque. I told them that I wanted to learn about Islam and what time I could come over. I went over there around the Asr (afternoon) prayer time. Before I went, my mom told me to call her when I got there and when I left to make sure that I was okay. I mean, she had every right to be scared and afraid for me. CNN and the rest of the media outlets were quoting the Quran in Sura Baqara verse 191 which stated, "Kill them wherever you find them." I laughed to myself, "I am going to kill them wherever I find them."

I got to the mosque and there was only one other car there. I found that somewhat suspicious. I must admit that I was nervous. I had to reassure myself that I could do this, go inside an abode that was infested with the enemy. I thought to myself "You're a Marine, you grew up in a bad neighborhood, you study Jiu Jitsu, and you carry a beautiful 45 caliber handgun complete with a concealed handgun permit." I could do this! So I wiped the sweat from my forehead that was due to my nervousness, and I marched inside the mosque. When I went in, I was expecting someone to jump from behind a corner or a wall or something and beat me down.

But instead, I got to the part where the floor meets the carpet and I saw a shoe rack nearby. That is when I saw my very first Muslim in person. At least it felt like that. His name was Abu Khalid. I told him that I came here to learn about Islam and he told me to take off my shoes and wait in the library. I did and as soon as I saw that the room that I was being escorted into did not have any deranged Muslims trying to kill me, my nervousness subsided. A few minutes later another Muslim came in. His name was Abdullah Muhammad. I thought to myself "What a name. At least it's not Osama."

To be honest with you, I really don't remember all of the questions or in what order they were asked. But I can assure you that I barraged him with a slew of questions about suicide bombers, killing innocent civilians, and of course, how could I forget that lovely little verse in the Quran, Baqara verse 191. He explained to me that suicide was forbidden in Islam and that the killing of innocent civilians was forbidden. He also opened up the Quran and showed me verse 191 of Sura Baqara. It indeed says "Kill them where ever you find them," but the Quran also said, "But if they desist, then there should be no hostility except against the oppressors." I was shocked! The (expletive) media was not being totally honest about what the Quran said! I was appalled, and I felt ignorant and stupid!

I came all the way over here wanting to bring an end to these people and I did not once look up anything in the Quran. For the next 14 days, I went to the mosque at around the same time (Asr time) and I sat with Abdullah. I would ask him question after question about Islam and what they thought about Jesus Christ, his mother Mary, and various other issues. The 14th day was a Saturday. I remember I got out of my car, walked into the mosque, and took off my shoes. I was a regular there and I acted as if I belonged there. I walked into the library and I saw some Muslims reading. And, I just sat down and began reading some Islamic literature that I had been given.

At the table, there was this Black guy who asks me how I was doing and if I was Muslim. So I exchange niceties with this Muslim at the mosque and then he asks me a question that has changed my life. "Are you ready to become a Muslim?" he asked. At that time, it seems as if my entire life flashed before my eyes in a split second. I had never been asked to accept anything even remotely related to my enemy or any group of people that I despised.

Everything that Abdullah taught me about the Islamic teachings of Jesus Christ, the Virgin Mary, and Islam as a whole made sense to me. Without any hesitation, I said, "Hell no! Are you crazy?! What's the matter with you?! Quit imposing your religion on me!" (Just playing, that last sentence was a joke… so here I go once again). Without any hesitation, I said, "Yes." He told me to repeat after him and I did. "Ashadu anla ilahah illa lah, wa ashadu anna Muhammadan abduhu wa rasululah" "I testify that there is no god but God, and I testify that Muhammad is the slave and final messenger of God." There! I was a Muslim! I finally came to believe in a way of life that I could logically understand.

I hope I have given justice to the way that Allah (SWT) brought me to Islam. Can I get a "takbir," anybody?

Like Everyone Else...Not!

Joanna Sigaran

My family is from El Salvador, and I basically was born here in Canada, in Kingston, three hours from Toronto. I can write and speak Spanish; I try my best. Alhamdulillah, I am thrilled at the interaction and the faith that every one is sharing and that there are Latino Muslims here in Canada.

I accepted Islam the summer of 2001. I myself had some exposure to Islam, my first time while at the university. I remember meeting a brother who was Muslim, and we once had a discussion over Islam and Christianity. I thoroughly enjoyed talking about it, but as I was "busy" with school, I barely followed my curiosity to discover more at that time.

While in the university, I married a fellow classmate, who was apparently Muslim, although not practicing, but as I was Catholic we had our marriage under the Church and had one son baptized. Our family lived like most people do, where religion is just something you do on the side and sometimes even not. I knew that I had a stronger faith as a younger girl, but through my teenage years, I lived the life as I was shown. I went to parties; I just lived to the fullest.

It is strange that although your heart craves to know about psychology, sociology, and religion and have faith in one God, I still held back on my curiosities. It was only when I and my husband eventually separated that I had free time and followed my heart.

And alhamdulillah, by the Grace of Allah, I came to know Islam. I felt there were many steps in my life that were leading me in this direction. Even the realization of what I was saying in Mass to what I never felt comfortable about "Jesus like God." Astaghfirullah! I give credit to another brother who was stronger in his religious persuasion. His personal qualities showed faith. I then wanted to know more about Islam. And, I started reading the English version of the Quran. After finishing the book almost a year later, I made my shahadah, in my heart. Since then I continue learning and hope, insha'Allah, that God allows me to keep learning and understanding the deen (religion).

It had been difficult with my family and there are still its difficulties. But Allah is the Greatest; a lot has changed since the beginning. My family is closer now, and we express our feelings more. We are trying to respect each other, and we say we love each other more.

Some ideas of some challenges for my family:

- On wearing of hijab their response: "How can you subjugate yourself? Do you not think you are beautiful?"
- On not going to parties or drinking: "You have to have some fun sometimes?"
- On not eating pork: "You don't know what you're missing!" or my mom feeling like I disrespected her for not eating her food. It's like I am saying her food is not good, not tasty, and she lives for the happiness of her children so not being able to satisfy you does not feel right.
- Fighting the constant stereotypes of Muslims.
- Making fun of Arabic words in Spanish: "Oh your food hasn't been ...jallado" ("hasn't been pulled").
- My sister stealing my first Quran, hijab, prayer mats and books and hiding them in her home and my sisters crying about what I am doing to myself.

I love them all, and it has been hard. And now by the grace of Allah, well, they are still not Muslims but my family especially my mom sees the connection of Islam. They know it brings a message of peace. My mom makes halal meals for me on occasion, and she respects me and my son and our eating differences. My dad and mom came out to a Ramadan iftar this past Ramadan. Subhan'Allah! I can share more knowledge about Islam and not feel like I am saying "I am better than you" because I think that is how they feel when you are saying you choose your way rather than theirs. My family is really open to hearing about the messages, especially my younger 18-year-old sister. She just openly told me and my dad that she does have some questions as to the meaning of the act of eating the bread and drinking wine at Mass, and my other sister too is realizing what are her own beliefs.

My dad is the tough "cookie" who is just as tough in his words, a very hard worker who "works hard", "plays hard" and constantly makes up Latino puns on the English language and anything else. Quick to joke. Quick to anger. And the one who loves me dearly, and who was, I believe, "the one who hurt the most" about my conversion. He is still dealing with it. They are all, but even he is becoming softer, more tolerant. I thank Allah. All is possible with Allah!! It truly is. My one suggestion to everyone is to keep praying for your family, for their forgiveness, for their hearts to be illuminated by the message of Islam.

Insha'Allah, everything is possible. Remember to be patient and to respect them as best as we can. Allah is most forgiving.

With salaams and duas for every one of you. Please forgive me for taking so much of your time. I am just so happy to hear of everyone's stories and wanted to share with you what time, patience and prayer can do in the toughest of situations. May Allah continue to guide each one of us and keep us on the straight path, and may our difficulties and burdens become lightened.

Twice Brothers

Jorge Salinas

Among Latino Muslims, we are brothers twice. On one hand, we are brothers because of Islam. On the other, we are brothers because we are Latino. According to my family history, my great-grandparents and grandparents left Syria and went to Saudi Arabia or vice versa. From there they continued their journey to Spain. They landed precisely in Jaén in Andalucia. Back then, the government of that country made life impossible. They changed their names to avoid problems. The social issues they faced made my great-grandfather continue to move. Only he was able to arrive in Cuba, though. Although he had already obtained a Spanish name, habits die-hard. They discovered that he was Muslim. And, let us not forget the dictatorships of Machado, Prio Socarras, and Batista. They made life impossible for most Cubans. My great-grandfather, seeing as he was faced with various social needs and hunger had no choice but to accept Catholicism outwardly.

When my grandfather was born, my great-grandfather had made many sacrifices in order to survive. It seemed like a gamble just to make ends meet. He lost everything: his surname, religion, and customs. We never talked about it until I started growing and started craving knowledge. I wanted to know all about the Arab world - its language and customs. It became somewhat of an obsession.

Being a doctor by profession, I went to the Islamic Republic of Pakistan some years ago with a medical brigade because of the devastating earthquake that occurred in the highest mountains of the world in Rawalakot, Kashmir. The experience was a very great surprise and joy for me. There, when it came time for prayers, the call to prayer was recited. My eyes would fill up with tears and my heart felt something very strange. I was not scared but it was as if something was happening to me. I felt sadness, joy, nostalgia, curiosity, and security. Something incredible was happening. It was true. I had a sense of familiarity as if I had heard that call, the Adhan, before. I was stunned by how beautiful everything in Islam was. Then, that's when the most wonderful, loving, and hospitable people opened their hearts. This opened the door very wide for me to embrace Islam.

But my story does not end there. Arriving in Cuba, I incorporated into my life all these habits known to you, and I practiced Islam with some patients who had come to Cuba to continue their treatment.

However, when they left, I was alone and did not know that there were more Muslims in Cuba. I always thought that the Arabs in Cuba were Catholics and they are. The information I gave to others was that in Cuba there are no Muslims. I thought I was the only Muslim in Cuba and that gave me joy in itself until one day I started feeling much need to be among other Muslims.

My wife told me, "Look to see if there are more here." I got very sad thinking I was the only one. One day in my living room I began crying like a child, tears streaming down my face, because of the feeling of sadness that invaded me again. I felt alone. I wanted my brothers there because you never have people who respect and want to be near without being blood brothers unless they are Muslims. At that very moment, I turned my head to the side of the house where I now pray in the direction of the Kaaba and I saw an Arab smiling at me.

It was enough for me to pick up the phone immediately and call all Arab embassies in Cuba. The Egyptian Embassy told me that in Cuba there was an Islamic legal and official league-licensed to practice Islam. I called their main speaker and there were indeed Cuban Muslims living in Cuba since the '80s. The Islamic League of Cuba actually existed since the '60s.

Last year, with help from a friend in the United States, I was able to obtain a scholarship to study Islam in Lebanon. Unfortunately, due to the extreme conditions that we find ourselves within Cuba, I was not able to take advantage of the opportunity. I needed a passport and could not afford one. My dream is to study Islam abroad and bring the beauty of Islam back to Cuba to open the eyes of other Cubans to Islam. This is my story.

A Marine Who Embraced Islam In Japan

Jose R. Valle

I was born in Mexico and brought to the United States at a very young age. My family settled in South Central Los Angeles. Our neighborhood had mostly African Americans, few Latinos, and even fewer Whites. Growing up in a primarily Black area, I would hear about the Nation of Islam every so often but nothing to catch my interest, maybe because of my age or naiveté. I joined the Marine Corps when I was 19 and actually heard much more about the Nation of Islam. I remember thinking that some of their ideas were excellent but not all. Even though I grew up in a prejudicial and racist society, I found it hard to believe that all Whites are devils and our enemy.

In 1991, I went to Operation Desert Storm. I remember hearing the athan, asking about it, and vaguely recall being told that it was the Islamic call to prayer. I said to myself, "Five times a day!" May Allah forgive me. Then in 1993 while I was in Japan, after reading about Islam, its pillars, and whatever I could get my hands on, I made my shahadah by myself in my room. I was raised Catholic but never agreed with confessing to a man or believing that a man could forgive my sins. Learning about Islam was like a light bulb coming on. As I read, I would say to myself, "Yes, of course, did someone read my mind?" Mind you, I had never met a Muslim before.

Afterward, I regret to say that I called myself a Muslim but I was not following the deen (religion) but al-dunya (the world). I can easily say that I had no guidance but the truth is that Satan tempted me and I was not strong enough to resist. Allah did not give up on me and for the past three years now I am proud to say that I am living the deen. I have my shortcomings but Allah is my witness that I am worshipping Him the best way I can.

My family is Catholic because that is what their parents told them they are and they are genuinely unaware that there are other religions other than the ones in Mexico. And, religion is not a subject mentioned at my family gatherings. My friends respected my decision and have been supportive. I have to say that none of them are Muslim. The most challenging thing for me about Islam is my lack of understanding of the Arabic language.

I get very frustrated during conversations with other Muslims when a translation of an ayat (verse of the Quran) is explained and the translator has to "settle" for an English word because there is no equivalent word or phrase to accurately express the message. I can totally understand the inability to translate the message because it happens in translations from Spanish to English and vice versa. Insha'Allah, I will continue to improve my understanding of the Arabic language so that I too can understand the message as it is meant to be.

Islam has made me more patient, more aware of the blessings bestowed on us every day, and much more aware of our Creator and Sustainer.

What makes me ecstatic is that I played a part in showing them that not all of us are misled as some of our brothers. The Nation of Islam has a saying, "Each one teaches one." If all of us could do that, what a difference it could make on our planet. Masha'Allah (Whatever Allah wills). I am married with two daughters. My wife is not Muslim; she is Catholic. I would not be truthful if I said it has been easy. Allah (SWT) has brought this wonderful woman and children in my life for reasons Allah knows. And, I thank Him every day for my family and blessings, which are too many to count, and if we are together, it is for the sake of Allah.

May Allah (SWT) be pleased with us, our efforts, and accept our duas.

From Juan To Shafiq

Juan Alvarado

My parents came to the United States from the Dominican Republic in the 60's, an era of repression, persecution, and uncertainty. They came looking for better opportunities. They landed in the South Bronx at a time when there was lots of work available. I was later born in the Bronx, New York. Typical of most other Latinos, I was born into the Roman Catholic faith. My parents were faithful Catholics, who went to church every Sunday. Likewise, I learned to be a faithful Catholic.

My childhood memories include catechism classes, public school education, and lots of family. My immediate family gave refuge to friends and other family members who were also immigrants from the Dominican Republic. Hence, I learned early on to look out for others less fortunate.

Ever since childhood I always noticed that I was "spiritual" to say the least. For some reason, I found myself unlike the other children around me and because of it sometimes felt alienated. At age ten, I even had a vision of what at the time I thought was the Virgin Mary. However, looking back I now think the vision I had was a lady in hijab – the traditional covering of a Muslim lady. Could it be a sign?

As a youngster, I went through the motions of what it means to be Catholic. I was baptized, did my communion and confirmation. I was even an altar boy at one point. But by the time I was a teen, I was growing impatient with Catholicism and started exploring different forms of spirituality. Specifically, I felt strongly against the concept of Catholic sainthood and that there is so much written in the Bible that is not followed by that church. By 16, I can confidently say that I renounced Catholicism, although I still considered myself "Christian." I visited different churches of different denominations but just could not feel that sense of belonging. Also, one of the things that I did not like was the interdenominational bickering. Another thing was the complexity of Christianity, or so it seemed to me. I considered myself "Christian" but I had renounced some of its pagan roots – specifically its practices of Christmas and Easter.

During my search, I found an interest in other religions. Specifically, I looked into Judaism, Buddhism, Hinduism, Santeria, and various New Age or Occult movements. I liked Judaism but could not deal with life without Jesus. Buddhism seemed too esoteric and even too bland.

Hinduism's caste system and a vast number of gods/goddesses just repelled me. Both of these religions, however, influenced me to become a vegetarian for many years. Santeria was interesting in a historical sense but its secrecy and concept of gods repelled me. The many New Age movements just seemed too complicated and did not get a hold of my full interest.

By the time I was 19, I renounced Christianity once and for all and continued my search. This search led me to read on a non-stop basis, something that I still do. At 20, a friend of mine gave me a book on Islam or what I thought was Islam. He gave me a book that the Ansar Cult published. To sum up their ideas, I would say that they mix authentic Islam with Black Nationalism. It has gone by different names: Ansaru Allah Community and Nuwaubian Nation, among others. After reading up on them, I decided to become "Muslim" at 23. As a matter of fact, I do consider that I was Muslim then but that I was astray. I believed wholeheartedly in the absolute unity of God (tawheed) but had some other ideas that were not on a par with authentic Islam. Because of my intense reading background, I always noted the many mistakes in the Ansar doctrine but I guess I just put up with it because there was something there that I related to. I always noted too that the leader of this movement always changed his beliefs and doctrines every so often, which I found to be strange.

My parents did not like the idea that I became Muslim. I don't think they had the impression I was interested in it. My father thought that having gone to college influenced me in some way. My mother did not mind so much but was afraid I would become the victim of a crime or discrimination. Alhamdulillah, they gradually have come to accept my choice. Unfortunately, their acceptance is merely an acceptance of convenience – as they still cling to their old ways, some of which is haram (prohibited).

After about two years of going to the Ansar mosque, I started going to mainstream mosques as well and noted the differences. One day, while at the Islamic Cultural Center of NY on 96th Street and 3rd Ave., I met a Hispanic brother who noticed that I was 'into' the Ansar movement (he saw that I wore their insignia) and cared enough to give me a book called "The Ansar Cult in America" which set my mind free once and for all.

He introduced me to some brothers in a Hispanic Islamic movement called Alianza Islamica. They were located on Lexington Ave. at the time in the Barrio part of Manhattan. I realized my mistaken ideas and took shahadah with Alianza Islamica. I was 25 then. By God's grace, this only happened because of my habit of reading and because of a brother that cared. I always noted that there were some very dramatic differences between what was written on Islam and what the Ansars wrote and did. In the end, like I said, I pronounced the testimony of faith among the Sunni and so far that is the end of my spiritual story.

It is hard to say precisely what it is that I liked about Islam that attracted me to it because I like it all. If I had to say what initially drew me to Islam, I'd say that Islam's insistence on God's unity would be on the top of the list. I'd also say that Islam's golden history made a lasting impression. This history made me aware that I may possibly have had ancestors that were Muslim because of the Islamic empire within Spain.

Lastly, with regards to my quest, I still love to read but I am no longer searching. I have found what the truth is.

How Allah Found Me In Texas

Juan Galvan

I always wish there existed a way to tell Muslims I encounter that I made the decision to embrace Islam. I want them to understand how much I appreciate my faith and do not take for granted all the blessings *Allah* (SWT) has bestowed. All the people I have encountered in my life and my ultimate choice to revert to Islam are a part of my journey that has led me to where I am today.

I am a Texan-born, Mexican-American from modest roots. I was born in 1974 to migrant workers and had seven siblings. I spent most of my youth in small, rural towns in the Texas Panhandle with such unique names like Quitaque and Turkey. None had a mall, a movie theater, or even a fast-food restaurant. These towns were so small that a fire truck or police car siren meant either a neighbor's house was on fire or a neighbor was being arrested. Growing up in small communities gave me a significant amount of appreciation for the simplicity of God's creations.

I was raised in the Roman Catholic Church and completed many of its sacraments such as first communion and confirmation. I recall the first time I received a jolt to my long-held religious beliefs. While in high school, a Christian friend told me that the Holy Trinity was not true and that Jesus was not God. "He is wrong, Jesus had to be God." I thought to myself. I argued that God and humanity were disconnected by Adam and Eve's sin. God sent His only "begotten" son to die for us because of His love for mankind. I believed that logically because only God forgives, Jesus had to be God. I even had Bible quotes to prove it; indeed, being a devout Roman Catholic I had read almost the entirety of the Bible. In high school, I was a lecturer, usher, Eucharistic minister, and religious education teacher at my church. The idea that Jesus was God just made so much sense.

Despite my strong faith, I always respected and sought out knowledge of other religions. I often attended other Christian churches and joined interfaith Bible study groups. During one of these study groups, I introduced myself to another participant as Catholic. He immediately responded that the Catholic Church was a "false doctrine". He accused me of worshipping Mary, the saints, and the Pope. I argued that we as Catholics only revere these individuals, especially someone as important as the mother of God! Despite my vocal protests, this encounter once again made me question my religious beliefs.

In 1998, I began to attend The University of Texas in Austin and eventually graduated with a Bachelor of Business Administration in Management Information Systems in 2001--not bad for a kid who had to hoe cotton to pay for clothing and school supplies! While at UT, I continued learning about other faiths. It was during this time that I happened upon a man praying in the park. He was barefoot and was prostrated. As I had never seen a person pray in this manner, it piqued my interest. I approached him once he completed his prayer and introduced myself. He said his name was Armando and that he was a Muslim. Like many others who have never met a Latino Muslim, I thought this was odd. How could a Latino be a Muslim and pray to Allah? He spoke to me about Islam and shared so much knowledge. He taught me that Spain was ruled by Muslims for over 700 years and thousands of Spanish words have Arabic roots. Armando said that Jesus was a prophet and that nothing and no one is worthy of worship but Allah. I learned that Allah means God in Arabic, just like Dios does in Spanish. During this brief conversation, I began to realize that my "reverence" for Mary and the saints was much more than mere reverence.

The more I studied Islam, the more my questions about religion were answered. How can the Father be the Son? Why can't God just forgive anyone He wants? What happens to babies who die before baptism? I came upon a verse in the Quran that greatly affected me to the point of tears:

"And when they (who call themselves Christian) listen to what has been sent down to the Messenger, you see their eyes overflowing with tears because of the truth they have recognized. They say: 'Our Lord! We believe; so write us down among the witnesses.'" (Quran 5:83).

Despite this emotional experience, I remained a Christian, but they left a mark on me. I thought frequently of Islam and studied it briefly, but like many other non-Muslims contemplating Islam, I had fears. Would my family and friends reject me? Would I be accepted by other Muslims? Mostly I feared change and what the existence of God and His prophets would mean for my future. For the next three years, I tried to live an ordinary life and convince myself of my happiness. At this point I had utterly rejected my Christian beliefs. Sometimes I thought I was an atheist, and other times I believed at minimum I was an agnostic. No matter how much I tried to deny it, I would always return to the belief in one God.

It was during this period I had a life altering experience. As I was driving one Saturday morning, a red truck moved into my lane. I had no time to react and I found myself hitting the truck. I nearly died. My left lung collapsed and I needed a chest tube to survive. I had multiple broken bones and was hospitalized for several days. Under these circumstances, my priorities shifted from the worldly to the spiritual. Along with a greater appreciation for the Creator, came an intense desire to embrace the truth. Three years before my accident, I was given several Islamic brochures with titles such as: Concept of God in Islam and Who Was Jesus. I revisited these brochures along with comments from a Quran that I had stowed away.

A few months later on a Friday afternoon, I stepped into a mosque for the first time. One of my college friends encouraged me to go to the mosque with her cousin. He was dressed in what looked like to me green pajamas and a small hat. I was perplexed by the lack of shoes and chairs in the prayer area and the different dress. I also wondered where all the women were, and learned they had their own prayer area. But, what left the great impression was the unity Muslims exhibited when praying together, side by side.

I visited this mosque regularly for about a month before embracing Islam during the summer of 2001. I recall that day vividly. Before *Maghrib* (sunset) prayer, I whispered to my friend Golam that there is a lot of peace in knowing that I only have to worship one God. I didn't need to worship money or wealth, nor did I have to please the world. I merely believed that Islam was true and I wanted to become a Muslim. I had a moment of uncertainty and wondered if I would be a good Muslim, but these fears instantly subsided. After *Maghrib* prayer, it was time to say *shahadah*, the declaration of faith and officially become a Muslim. Golam stood up and faced the crowd announcing, "There's someone who will take *shahadah*. He attends the University of Texas. He grew up in Texas. He's been coming to the mosque regularly."

Next thing I knew, I was sitting in front of all the mosque attendants going through a "Muslim baptism" as a Christian friend once put it. I was handed a microphone and the *Imam*, or spiritual leader, told me to repeat his words in English and Arabic: I testify that there is no God but *Allah*. I also testify that *Muhammad* is His servant and messenger. After I took my *shahadah*, the Imam stated, "Congratulations. God forgives the sins of those who turn towards Him. And He can turn your previous bad deeds into good deeds." Everyone clapped and stood up to shake my hand or hug me. I felt very much at home. I tried hard not to cry, but failed.

I fell further in love with Islam while listening to talks about brotherhood, prayer, and charity. I found myself intrigued by brothers who found time to pray five times a day. Many were college students like me who had figured out ways to complete their obligatory prayers. I was amazed by people who could fast from sunrise till sunset for an entire month. I was impressed by the self-discipline and comradery exhibited by these Muslims, and understood the importance of setting a good example and being a respectable Muslim. Where would I be if Armando had not been praying in the park that day, fulfilling his obligation to God?

Following my conversion, I began the arduous process of notifying my family. My father's first questions were, "¿Qué es éso?" (What is that) and "Como los Árabes?" (Like the Arabs). I explained that it is a religion and was for everyone, not just Arabs who make up less than 25 percent of the entire Muslim population. My sister incredulously asked if I still loved Jesus and inquired how I could do this to the Virgin Mary. Patiently, I told her that I still loved Jesus but believed he is a prophet. I also shared with her the chapter in the *Quran* called "Mary". After the attacks of 9/11, I found myself defending Islam to my family. Trying to reason with my sister who said my leader Osama bin Laden was calling for a holy war. Assuring my parents that I was okay and not a terrorist. Not surprisingly, converting to Islam can be viewed as a huge radical change. Family may not understand why you would leave something that they love so much. One spends a lot of time dispelling misconceptions and providing education. My family did come around and wholly respect my religious beliefs. When I visit with my family, they are conscience to the fact that we do not eat pork or drink alcohol. My mom even makes my beloved tamales lard free!

A struggle occurs within everyone, every day, and everywhere. One thing I wish I had been told prior to my conversion, is to first embrace Islam if you believe it to be true and then work on becoming a better Muslim. Expectations may be the ideal, but reality can be much different. Every Muslim is born knowing nothing about Islam; they learn over time, never becoming perfect. So, have patience. You do not know the happiness that your Creator has in store for you.

My conversion story made me reflect upon how much my life has changed since my humble beginnings in the Panhandle of Texas. Sure, it has had its ups and downs, but the thread that ties these life stages together is my love of God and family. Becoming a Muslim led me to my wife and ultimately my best and most important job, fatherhood. Teaching my three sons how to pray and taking them to the mosque brings me so much happiness. Recently, while helping my eldest son and namesake recite surah Al-Fatiha, I was overcome with emotion thinking about all of *Allah*'s (SWT) blessings. As I continue through my life's journey, I will remain cognizant of these blessings and use my knowledge and skill to help others come closer to Islam.

May *Allah* accept our efforts and good deeds and grant us forgiveness and guidance. All praise and thanks to *Allah*, the Majestic.

A Cuban Professor's Journey To Allah

Julio Cèsar Pino

Are there many Muslims in Cuba? Why would a Cuban want to become a Muslim? These are the two questions I am most frequently asked when introducing myself, or in the case of old friends, re-introduce myself by my Muslim name, Assad Jibril Pino. The answer to the first query is a simple yes. Several thousand Muslims reside in Cuba, most of them descendants of Lebanese immigrants. However, the second question always makes me pause and ponder before I reply, even though I have heard it hundreds of times. It is a loaded question of course because it presumes that religion is the product of ethnic identity and that Muslim and Cuban only belong together on the restaurant menu of a Miami luncheonette: "I'll have Moros y Cristianos, with a side of croquetas." Actually, I no longer eat this Islamophobic dish, because it contains pork. But, I have come to believe that there is a path, however crooked, that connects Cuba to Islam for me personally, beyond the Moorish heritage of my ancestors.

That I was born in Havana in 1960, "in the fist of the Revolution" to use the phraseology of the island Cubans (this "island Cuban" versus "Miami Cuban" business can lead to schizophrenia, unless one is agile at linguistic somersaults), had a decisive impact on my decision to revert to Islam in the summer of 2000. Fidel Castro often said that a revolution allows no neutrals. From the moment a child reaches school age in Cuba, he or she is confronted with problems of war and peace, justice, and oppression, and integration or marginalization from family, friends, neighbors, and the nation.

Was I for or against the Revolution of 1959? Where did I belong - with my parents who were officially dubbed "gusanos" (counterrevolutionary worms) or with my mother's side of the family, members of which belonged to the Communist Party? These were playground questions for me, not theoretical debates. The Revolution brought justice - I could see it in the improvement of the lives of my relatives - but also repression, the fear of speaking out that I registered whenever my parents conversed privately about politics.

My father made the decision to take our family out of Cuba in 1968. The experience was particularly traumatic for me, being an only child because I was leaving behind my cousins, who all belonged to the Castroite side of the clan. Moving to Los Angeles where my father's sister resided, my parents followed the usual Latin American Catholic practice when it comes to religion: walk the walk, just don't talk the talk. I was pushed into parochial school and sent to Sunday mass on special occasions like Epiphany or the Day of the Three Kings (I still remember, back in Cuba, putting out hay for their horses in order to receive presents on January 6). At the same time, Catholicism was never mentioned at home. There was no prayer, no invocation of God, no mention of Jesus (peace be upon him) for help and salvation.

Mercifully, the priests and nuns at the high school I attended during the 1970s deprogrammed me from Christianity. What can I possibly say about the supposed Christians who blessed the Vietnam War? After three years of this ridiculous situation, I screamed for a release and received my parents' consent to transfer to a public high school. I also became an agnostic, a view I maintained until finding Islam.

My release from parochial school and enrollment at the University of California at Los Angeles (UCLA) in 1980, majoring in history and specializing in Brazil, furthered my estrangement from organized religion. The 1980s posed terrible and challenging tasks for Latinos on campus. Our brothers and sisters in Central America were being butchered by American-trained death-squads daily. Poverty and unemployment inside the United States surged while the rich grew fatter under the presidency of the time.

I joined several organizations at UCLA, dedicated to ending this horror. Politics became a substitute religion for me, not just a way to fight back against oppression but a substance to fill the void I had felt ever since childhood - the unfulfilled need to bring social justice to the world. But, as anyone who has ever dived into politics can attest, the terrible irony is that the deeper the commitment, the greater the alienation. Petty squabbles inside an organization turn into political purges, and close friends become demons once they deviate from the party line. Quickly, I turned into a cynic, and like many burnt-out politicos, I took to drink.

1991: the USSR is gone, the Sandinistas in Nicaragua have been defeated at the polls, the Salvadoran rebels disarm, and Cuba enters the worst economic crisis in history, leaving my island relatives pleading with me and my mother to send back home anything and everything we can, even a bottle of aspirin. Personally, however, I had started walking the long road back to recovery, alhamdulillah (all thanks be to Allah). That year I gave up drinking for good, received my doctorate in History from UCLA, and headed into the job market.

The next year, I married a sweet Korean-American woman of my age and landed a tenure-track job at Kent State University (KSU) of Ohio, where I currently teach the History of Latin America and the History of Civilization. After seven years of research, I turned my manuscript on the shantytowns of Rio de Janeiro into a book, 'Family and Favela', published in 1997. Professionally, I never felt more satisfied, but over the horizon loomed a crisis that nearly wrecked my life. I was mad at my parents for not giving me a happier childhood, estranged from my wife, and numbing myself again, this time not through alcohol but by buying entertainment appliances to fill up my empty heart.

In the same manner of others who score victories in their careers, I had begun to take my family for granted. Without going into the sordid details, I will say that my emotional blindness almost cost me my marriage. For six agonizing months, after my wife left me, not a day went by that I did not cry and scream like an animal for her to return. I got down on my knees and prayed to whatever higher power might exist to grant me the courage of Jesus, Buddha, and Muhammad just to survive.

The only thing I knew for sure about these messengers is that they underwent and understood personal tragedy and yet came out victorious, charged with a mission to help others in distress. The supplication (today I would say dua') was answered. My wife came back, although I did not merit such mercy from Allah, and this miracle made me want to explore why the Divinity, which I was now sure existed, would want to help me.

I began reading in the Catholic canon, from *The Confessions of Saint Augustine* to *The Imitation of Christ* by Thomas á Kèmpis (my mother's favorite book, incidentally), but it was all too dry and abstruse. Next, I turned to the mystical tradition, covering the journals of Søren Kierkegaard, the notebooks of Simone Weil, and the "confessional" poetry of Anne Sexton. This was the great turning point. Stupid me, I'd been examining religion through the lens of reason. Yet, as these journeyers kept insisting, there is not a rational path to meeting Allah, only what Sexton called "the awful rowing towards God" that leads to embracing faith.

Still, even the unorthodox Christianity preached by the mystics seemed unrewarding. Surrendering myself blindly to Christ, even if he was the Son of God, took me back to parochial school. It provided no detailed answers on how to restructure my life so that the outside of me, the husband and successful professor, coincided with the inside-me - the insecure creature too frightened to taste life.

Sometime in the mid-90s, I purchased the famous Muhammad Pickthall translation of the meanings of the Holy Quran for the sake of augmenting my history lectures on Islam. I had never gotten around to reading it. Then, on a trip from Cleveland to Miami in 1999, for some reason, I decided to take it along on the plane. I recall the woman in the seat next to me asking what I was reading. "The Quran," I replied brusquely. She stared at me in perplexity. "The holy book of the Muslims," I added for her benefit.

She asked, "Is that what you are?"

I replied, "No, I'm just interested in world literature." I devoured roughly half the book during the plane ride of two hours and finished it during my stay at my parents' house. What amazed me is that the Quran addressed everything - from usury to divorce to women's rights. All religions claim they are more than just a religion but a complete way of life, but only in Islam is this vow fulfilled. Only Muslims, for example, arrange their day around prayer. I reflected on the lectures I gave in my History of Civilization course. What had I been teaching the students at Kent State about Islam? That it was the most democratic and egalitarian of all the world's religions because it recognized no distinction or merit based on race, social class, nationality or gender. Instead merit was based only on degrees of faith. But now, for the first time, the words hit home. All that was needed to make my conversion final was a triggering event.

Recife, Brazil: June 2000. I was attending a conference of scholars who specialize in Brazil. For reading material, I brought along a book of Sufi poetry and prayers, which I had perused during my "mystical" phase but had never finished. Up in my hotel room, between sessions of the conference, I finally reached the last page and tucked the book away in my luggage. Later, walking along the lovely beach, I flashed back to the book hidden inside my layers of clothes. A voice from inside says, "This is what I want to be, and will be from now onwards - a Muslim."

After returning to the United States, I tried to find some local Muslims. But how? Should I just look up "Islam" in the telephone book? Suddenly, I remembered that I once had a student in my Latin America class, an African-American young man named Musa. He was a quiet but very resourceful and devoted brother who, when not attending KSU, worked with troubled teens in Akron. He had told me that there was a small mosque in Akron and that I was welcome to visit anytime.

The Internet found the address for me. Knowing that Jummah services were held on Friday, I spent Thursday night on my knees praying to Allah to do the best thing for me. Was I worthy of joining the Ummah (Islamic community)? How would I be received, since there are relatively few Latino Muslims? As I prayed I felt tears flowing down my face, for the first time in many years. Something dramatic was about to happen in my life, I knew it.

That Friday, I drove from Kent to Akron to attend my first Jummah prayer. Walking upstairs of the modest two-tiered mosque, I was startled by the variety of faces: African-Americans, South Asians, one brother who "even looked European", as I said silently to myself, and several Arabs, including the Imam. He gave a fiery but controlled khutba (sermon). I do not remember the topic of the sermon, but will never forget the speaker's frequent incantation: "O, Slaves of Allah!" That phrase resonates with me to this day. Why would anyone want to be a "slave" of the Divinity? I found the answer surrounding me that day: men of resolution, at peace with themselves, because they had surrendered their lives to Allah to do as He willed.

The following week I came back, and after the sermon, I shyly asked one of the brothers if he would be witness to my conversion. Much to my surprise, he called the entire congregation to gather around me. The Imam administered the shahadah (public declaration of faith), and what I remember most was his promise, "All your previous sins are forgiven. On the Day Of Judgment, we shall be your witnesses that you took the shahadah in front of us." Julio Cèsar Pino died that day, and Assad Jibril Pino was born.

After the obligatory bath, my next step was to contact my parents. I knew no phone call could express my joy, nor encompass the teachings of Islam, a religion entirely unknown to them. Thus, I wrote them a long letter and included a Spanish translation of the Surah al-Fatiha (the opening chapter of the Quran). Almost three years later, I still think my parents "don't really get it" - they can't comprehend why and how Islam changed my life, but they are tolerant. I wish I could say the same for some of my colleagues at the university. Embracing Islam is one thing; practicing Islam and fulfilling its obligations is something else. When I wrote and spoke publicly concerning the genocide of the Palestinians in 2001, I was subject to defamation, harassment, and even death threats in my office. Nonetheless, that's fairly standard fare for most Muslims in America.

Nothing comes before my faith now. What I love most about Islam is precisely the discipline it requires of the believers - so that we may be one community. I always thought of myself as a disciplined person, but it took Islam to make me realize I was disciplining myself over the wrong things. In my days before Islam, I would say, "I have to be at that movie theater exactly at seven. I have to be first in line." Today, after performing my morning prayers, I ask myself what I can do to advance Islam, even in a small way. It might require phoning my congressman to obtain a visa for a student from overseas or perhaps sending money to a mosque somewhere in Africa.

Professionally, I have undergone conversion also. My current research project involves the lives of Muslim slaves in 19th-century Brazil and their continual connection to their African homelands. In my History of Civilization class, which made me interested in Islam in the first place, I now always include the contemporary Middle East and have had the pleasure of hosting Palestinian guest speakers. Almost all of my students enjoy this part of the course, and some have even asked me to teach a class exclusively about the history of Islam.

In my period of jahiliyya (days before Islam), depending on how I felt that day, I would tell those who asked that I was Cuban, Cuban-American, or even American (if I happened to be living in Brazil). Now, I just say Muslim, and leave it up to them to place me in a category. If they are pleased and curious, then by permission of Allah I tell them the astonishing story of how a Cubano became a Muslim.

Come To Success: The Islamic Call To Prayer

Julissa Fikri

I was born to my father who is from Puerto Rico and my mother who is from the Dominican Republic. They were both raised in the Christian religion. My parents divorced when I was age five. I was born in Spanish Harlem, New York City. I was raised there until the age of eight, but after a tragic death in the family, my mom moved us to New Jersey. Life growing up in the suburbs was good, and I had a great education. I was involved in my modern dance groups in high school and also took ballet at a private academy.

I was a much-focused student in high school and always maintained good friendships. My friends were mostly those girls that were in my dance group. I was very close to a very small circle of girls. I graduated high school and went to college. It was at this turning point that much started to change. I was ready to move out as I experienced lots of conflict with my mom at the time. She was going through many issues with my stepdad and was taking out her frustrations on me. I, in turn, got a job and saved up enough to move out. My grandmother was leaving to go back to the Dominican Republic. She left me her apartment located in Spanish Harlem. I decided to take a chance and become independent.

When I got older, I had a profound experience that made me realize that Allah had to exist. I was involved in a lot of alcohol and drug abuse at the time. I made very bad friends and wanted a way out. I did a lot of research and developed a growing desire to seek the truth. Although I was raised in the Christian faith, I had abandoned it when I was 14 years old. I just didn't understand its purpose at that time. It failed to reach me spiritually. And, it only felt as an obligation to my aunt and uncle. I remember studying a lot of different religions and found Islam to be the religion that connected all of the dots for me. Subhan'Allah! It was after my negative experience that I reached out to Allah in a supplication (dua).

After this, indeed I was shown the signs toward the true straight path. I had a dream that I heard the athan, the Islamic call to prayer. I followed a strong feeling in my heart that made me not want to stop finding the truth. A friend gave me the Quran in Spanish and since then I have embraced Islam. I will never forget how much this changed my life. In fact, it saved my life. Islam saved me from the street life, the drug patterns, and the deadly cycle that Shaytan (Satan) had me trapped in. What attracted me to Islam was the unity and peace that it brought to my life. I had lacked all feelings of love and peace during my dark stages that when I was studying the teachings of Prophet Muhammad (PBUH) it made me understand his compassion for humanity and his love for God.

I am now married to my wonderful husband whom I adore. I have two children and one on the way. I currently live in Spanish Harlem, NYC. My family gave a strong mixed reaction to my conversion as I had expected. My friends were more accepting of my conversion and gave me lots of support. I am a stay at home mom. One of my goals is to bring a better and more relatable understanding of Islam to the Latino community. I also want to raise my children in this deen and to grow in knowledge.

I hope that Latino and non-Latinos alike can learn from my story and not fall victim to the streets or the fast life. The destruction of it all is not beautiful for it can only bring you down even more. The end result is death. There is so much beauty in Islam that can help all of mankind follow the straight path. I have had many interesting things happen to me. In fact, I share a lot of the experiences through my YouTube channel. I developed the channel as a way to chronicle my challenges and experiences as a Latina Muslim.

Islam has benefited me tremendously. I am free of all vices and negative energy. I used to be so angry before and now I feel so liberated. I love the peace and unity that has come to me and my family since embracing Islam. It really does bring us together. Islam can benefit others in that they can see you become part of one big family and you can find that the oneness of Allah is indeed worth worshipping. If you can look all around you, it seems clear that One Divine Creator is responsible for the earth, humans, and all other creation alike. It only makes perfect sense.

Back To One's Roots

Justin Benavidez

I remember vividly the day it happened. It was a sunny California day and I was walking out of a store with my Portuguese grandfather when, suddenly, he turned, pointed to his forearm, and said: "Arab blood runs through our veins." Immediately to my mind appeared a swarthy Arab wearing a black turban and robe holding a scimitar. The image terrified me—and the thought of being related to *that* was even more terrifying. "We're one of those?" I thought. The news was a bombshell that rocked my world. "Where did my grandfather's comment come from?" I was confused. It was so out of context and I was completely caught off guard. Then I became embarrassed by the possibility of having Arab ancestry. "If the kids at school find out that I'm one of those," I thought, "that'll be the end of me."

I was about ten years old. I didn't know anything about Arabs or Islam, yet somehow I associated Arabs with savagery from some far away land—and I wanted nothing to do with them. Even as a child, identity and culture played essential roles in my perception of things. I identified with my Mexican-American heritage and consciously ignored my Portuguese roots. To me Mexican-American culture was cool. To me it meant wearing khakis and a button-down flannel, rooting for the Oakland Raiders, and eating tacos. Who doesn't like tacos? But being Arab? That wasn't cool. There was no way I was going to share with my friends the news that I had turban-wearing grandfathers. My idea of ridding the problem from my life was to bury it in the back of my mind and hope it would eventually disappear... And it almost did. Never did I think that being a Muslim would ever become part of my identity, let alone be the core of my ethos.

I am often asked why I converted. First of all, it was never my intention to be a Muslim. It just happened. Secondly, in the beginning, it wasn't easy being a Muslim. I was initially interested in Islam only after learning that its prophet and law defended the poor and oppressed. I heard a lot about Islam being a religion of social justice from Malcolm X and Louis Farrakhan, two influential African American leaders. Social justice was a deep concern of mine and I was open to looking at different methods and philosophies to deal with the problem. I wanted to know what Islam had to say on the issue. I wasn't too interested in anything else about Islam—I wasn't Black or Arab, so I just assumed Islam was irrelevant to me.

I've been a Muslim for almost fifteen years, a period filled with many experiences, too many to include every detail for this anthology project. Since the anthology is concerned with the conversion stories of Latino Muslims, my story will primarily focus on the period leading up to my conversion and the challenges I faced along the journey. Many aspects of my life will not be mentioned, including my wife's critical role in the latter half of my life as a Muslim. God willing, I'll have the opportunity at some point in the future to write a complete account of my story.

One of the most pivotal periods in my life was my days as a student at Ohlone College. And, it was there that the road to Islam began. But before I crossed that path, I had become involved in the Chicano movement—a cause in which I became totally immersed. Everything in this period of my life was about *la causa* (the cause) and *la lucha* (the struggle). I was focused on improving the living conditions of Latino immigrants and farm workers—an issue that was personal to me given that my Mexican grandfather, Manuel Soto, was a migrant farm worker who picked fruits and vegetables in the fields from Texas to California. I worked with MALDEF (Mexican American Legal Defense Fund) and La Raza Centro Legal in San Francisco in organizing to defeat the anti-immigration law Proposition 187. I marched with the UFW (United Farm Workers) in San Jose, and I attended Cesar Chavez's funeral in Delano.

Much of my activism was carried out through MEChA, a national Chicano student organization, and I served as president for one year. In terms of who I was, I had never before felt a sense of meaning and self-assured identity like I did during my time with MEChA. Our motto proudly proclaimed, *"No Se Venden"* (No Selling Out). To be a Chicano meant staying true to the "struggle" against the white man's system and resisting assimilation and European hegemony. The dream was to rebuild what had been taken from us: our ancestors' land, ancient wisdom, identity, and an indigenous language. The plan was to create in America an Aztlan, the mythical homeland of the Aztecs, if not within each of us. We were idealists, and we were young, confused, and full of rage. We were not, however, exclusive; we worked with anyone who shared a similar struggle.

MEChA began working with an African American club on campus. I became close friends with one of the members, Lenny Sullivan. Later that year, he converted to Islam and began telling everyone he ran into on campus about Islam and what it was all about. I was intrigued. He had grown a short beard and changed his name to Bilal, the name of the first African convert to Islam. My ego, however, prevented me from approaching him. So I waited until he came to me, which took some time. It took so long in fact that I worried he'd forgotten about me. I wanted to know Islam's view of social justice. I was looking to see how the struggle of the Prophet Muhammad might parallel that of Mexican-Americans. I believe that I was receptive to Islam and its social justice aspect because it came from a convert. Had an immigrant Muslim approached me, I would have perceived it as a foreign religion with a foreign message. Bilal finally caught up with me and the preaching began. He reminded me of Malcolm X. He was articulate, passionate, and sincere. I had just started reading the *Autobiography of Malcolm X*. This is one of my favorite books. But in terms of my conversion to Islam, it didn't quite have the impact on me like it had on others. The impact of Islam would happen by another means.

Bilal invited me to his home for dinner to talk about Islam and his experience thus far as a Muslim. I looked forward to our evening together primarily because it had become difficult to have a meaningful discussion with him like we used to before he became a Muslim. He had been so busy with studies and preaching that it was difficult to get even a moment with him. Bilal was a serious person and, like me, he was interested in issues concerning spirituality, intellectual questions, and community engagement. He was the only person I felt truly comfortable with.

When I arrived at his father's place, a small, cozy apartment in Fremont, Mr. Ansari, Bilal's father, answered the door. His stocky frame and baritone voice added to his presence. Mr. Ansari was an O.G. (ol' timer). He had also converted to Islam, starting out with the Nation of Islam and then became a follower of Warith Deen Muhammad, may God's mercy be upon him. Bilal told me stories of his father's experiences in the Nation and the impact of Malcolm X on his father's life. On the table was a book and inside it there was an old black and white photograph of his father standing on a street corner in New York City listening to Malcolm give a talk to a large crowd. I was impressed. "Now that's some history!" I thought. Being in the company of Mr. Ansari was being in the presence of history.

We had dinner and he talked while I listened to stories about the Prophet Muhammad: his character, how he was with his family and neighbors, and how he exhibited kindness and patience with those who disparaged him. I was fascinated with Muhammad's character but at the same time defensive. While listening to Bilal tell me stories, I'd compare and contrast Muhammad's character to Jesus', who was to me *the* spiritual master and the archetype of selfless-servitude to humanity. To me, no one surpassed Jesus, particularly in the realm of service. We had dinner again and he told me about the stories of the Prophet Muhammad's life. I don't remember the stories per se, but I do remember that after one or two stories, my heart accepted the veracity of this seventh-century Arabian man. *Iman* (faith) had entered my heart. "I was like, yeah, I believe in this man. Pass me the chips." It was subtle. I didn't realize what had happened. That night I went home like any other night. There was no party to celebrate my new faith. How could there be? No one was aware of my transformation, not even I. The next morning was the first day of many on the long road to Islam. It would be another year before I was to formally embrace Islam, that is, verbally express the testimony of faith--*shahadah* before witnesses. Once I accepted Islam, it meant that praying and fasting in Ramadan would become incumbent upon me to carry out—practices that I wasn't ready to take on yet. Besides, I still had questions. The place where many of those questions were answered took place at a small mosque in Fremont.

Before there was a Zaytuna or Ta'lif, two important Islamic institutions in the San Francisco East Bay, there was the P.Q. Crew. It was a group of young Muslim men and boys that met every Friday night at a small mosque in Fremont, California, called Masjid Bilal, to learn the basics of Islam, and just hang out and have fun. Started up by Bilal, the P.Q. Crew (Prophet and Quran Crew) was thus based on the two most important sources of Islam. I don't think there was anything else like it in the Bay Area.

On some nights there were forty of us, mostly Afghan youth. Besides Bilal, I was the only non-Afghan. I was also the only non-Muslim. It's ironic because I really didn't care for Afghans. I first encountered Afghans in middle school and they left a wrong impression on me. They were a rough people, like the angry Arab with the scimitar that I imagined. I thought they were Gypsies. I couldn't figure them out. The city of Fremont has one of the largest Afghan populations in the U.S. and it is referred to as little Kabul. I never had one Afghan friend in high school, and I never took an interest in their religion. It never crossed my mind to ask one question about their culture and religion. One Afghan kid from middle school introduced himself as Muhammad and with pride and confidence said he was from Afghanistan. I remember thinking to myself, "With a name like that (i.e., Afghanistan) you should be embarrassed to be from there."

But there I was, years later, in the midst of this rough yet sincere group of Afghans in Fremont. Our paths would never have crossed otherwise except that we were at the same point in our lives where we wanted to learn about Islam and the Prophet Muhammad. In the beginning, I was afraid to meet with Afghans, and I wasn't sure if I'd fit in. But the warmth and hospitality of the group, qualities that they are known for around the world, made me feel welcome and a genuine member of the community. In those gatherings, the Afghans were an element of safety and comfort that I never experienced anywhere else, and this space of safety and security helped me to relax and be myself. I fit in well with the Afghans and they used to joke that they made me an honorary Afghan due to eating so much Afghan food.

Bilal conveyed Islam's teaching through stories. At the mosque, we would sit on the floor in a big circle on a beautiful Persian rug. The talks were based on the prophetic traditions of Muhammad and the Quran, thus keeping true to the group's name. Every night was a different theme, but Bilal consistently drew our focus to the remembrance of God and the importance of developing ethical character. Wisely, we never discussed politics; instead he routinely touched upon the importance of caring for and respecting people: one's brother, sister, neighbor, stranger, Muslim, and non-Muslim. And Bilal would cite an example of how Prophet Muhammad cared for people. The story that comes to mind is an example of Muhammad's chivalry for his neighbor, an elderly Jewish woman, and how he treated her with kindness. Bilal knew how to make learning fun. One of his talks that I'll never forget was about the role of the mosque, which he said in the time of the Prophet Muhammad was a place of putting the forehead to the ground before God; then he said it was also a space of physical activity. "The Prophet's companions used to wrestle," Bilal said, and then all of the sudden he grabbed one of the Afghan youth and took him down to the floor, just like a wrestler. All of us were in shock. It was a bold move to demonstrate, while in a mosque, the breadth and practical teachings of the Prophet Muhammad.

It was those days at Masjid Bilal that my understanding of Islam was shaped and when I formed close bonds with Muslims. There were many people who facilitated my path to Islam but one family, in particular, comes to mind: the Nawabis, an Afghan family in Fremont. Feroz used to attend the gatherings at Masjid Bilal; one evening he invited me to his family's home for dinner. One of the main dishes was *qabali pallow*, one of my favorites to this day. At the time, though, I was literally afraid of it. Large heaping mounds of rice served in large bowls were brought in from the kitchen and placed before me. But then I looked carefully and noticed seasonings and fruits like raisins, nuts, and shredded carrots. I was totally turned off by the mix of rice, raisins, and meat. I would have given anything for a burrito or pizza. Feroz, sitting beside me, noticed my hesitation and rhetorically asked, "Do you think we eat different foods than you? It's all the same ingredients, just cooked differently." I said to myself, "He's absolutely right." His point was simple but it pierced deep into my psyche, causing a paradigm shift, and from that point after, I began to think differently about Afghan culture and Islam. Feroz's mother, Habiba, was so patient with me—even to this day. She and her family allowed me to approach Islam step by step in my own time. Although I didn't become a Muslim during this period, I credit people like her for facilitating my path to Islam.

Later that year Bilal relocated to southern California. This meant the end of the P.Q. Crew. We tried meeting amongst ourselves but without his leadership and energy, the gatherings fizzled. Many of us parted ways and for a while, I stopped hanging out with Muslims. One evening while I was working my shift at a drug store, a friend from the gatherings came in. I hadn't seen him in months and I was happy to see him. He told me about an event that he was organizing. He quickly ran to his car and returned with a flyer of the event, the title of which read: "What is Islam? Thursday, December 1st, 6:30 p.m. at Chabot College. Speakers: Abdul-Malik Ali and Hamza Yusuf." I wasn't scheduled to work that evening, so I could attend.

It was almost a year from that night at Bilal's house. I had learned and studied so much about Islam that I was familiar with the themes and the terms used in the talk: *jihad* (struggle), *sunnah* (Muhammad's way), *taqwa* (consciousness of God). Abdul-Malik Ali spoke about social justice, the topic that drew my interest to Islam. He energized the audience with his charisma and articulate speech. It was the best talk. He was one of the favorite Islamic speakers of the Bay Area. After he spoke there was an intermission.

I walked out of the theatre and into the crowded hall towards the table where books were being sold. As I was looking at the titles, I bumped into a friend, Muhammad from Qatar, whom I had met at the beginning of my experience in learning about Islam. I hadn't seen him in months. I visited his home several times to have tea and talk about Islam. He was happy to see me and with a heavy Arabic accent, he immediately asked if I had converted to Islam. This question was frequently put to me. Many people in the community had known that I was learning about Islam for some time that it was assumed that I was a Muslim. In embarrassment, I said, "No. Not yet." He was disappointed.

I believed in God and Muhammad. Yet, there was the cultural question that I was dealing with, but I was also procrastinating in accepting Islam. Muhammad said, "You're not a Muslim? What is this?" "Do you believe in Allah and His Oneness? Do you believe in Muhammad as the last prophet? Do you believe in the angels?" I said yes to each question. Then he said, "Okay, you're ready now to take your *shahadah*! Let's go. You can take your *shahadah* on stage with one of the speakers, in front of everyone!" I told myself that I'm not going up there. "No way!" My mind was racing for answers—for an exit or back door. He noticed my hesitation. He asked me what the problem was. He was quite pushy, which I didn't like. He didn't let up. In an instant, I went from being shy and hesitant to being upset. I told myself that I'm not going to let anyone push me into being a Muslim. Then I said to myself, "Look, it's time. I believe. Now *is* the time to do this. No more procrastinating." I said to Muhammad, "Okay, I'll say the *shahadah*, but not on stage." He said, "Okay, no problem." "We'll go over to the corner and take it there." "Okay," I said. It was a compromise. Before I said the *shahadah*, I thought for a moment to make sure that I was going through with this because I sincerely believed and because I wanted to, not because I was being pressured into it. It felt right.

A small gathering had formed to witness the occasion. I repeated three times in Arabic, "There is no god but God and Muhammad is the Messenger of God." He said, "Okay, now you're a Muslim. *Mabruk* (congratulations)! Now you need a Muslim name. What do you want to be called?" As if converting to Islam wasn't sufficient for Muhammad. I was lightheaded due to the intensity of the moment. "I don't know," I said. Counting on his five fingers, he said "Okay, no problem. You can have Muhammad, Abd-Allah, Abd al-Rahman, Abd al-Hakim, Abd al-Rahim." "Definitely not Muhammad and Abd-Allah," I said to myself. I can't go home and tell my mom and friends that my name is Muhammad. That would have been too much to digest. I wasn't prepared for this moment; I hadn't thought of a name for myself. It is true that the Prophet Muhammad renamed several people whose names had adverse meanings; for example, he renamed a boy with the name

Hasan (Good) upon learning the baby had been named Harb (War). So what was wrong with the name Justin? I was again put on the spot, and in order to quickly move past this awkward situation, I hastily said, "The third one." "Okay, settled. Your name is Abd al-Rahman!"

The intermission had ended and as people were returning to their seats, an announcement was made that Justin, now to be called Abd al-Rahman, had just taken his *shahadah*. There were loud shouts of joy and many heads were turned to get a look at this Abd al-Rahman. Some of my good friends were in attendance at the lecture but were not present to see my *shahadah*. They were upset with me for not being present. They too had waited for this moment for a long time. I felt terrible but I didn't know I was going to say the *shahadah*. I had always imagined that Bilal would be the one to give me the *shahadah*. It made sense. If not him, then at least it would be his father. Just like that one night at Bilal's house, my conversion to Islam was unexpected.

It has been said that converting to Islam is the easy part; it is being a Muslim that is difficult. This saying is definitely germane to my situation. Unlike Bilal, who told the world about his conversion to Islam, I didn't even tell my family and friends. I'm not the type to bring attention to myself anyways, but I didn't tell anyone because I was really unsure how to share the news. "*¿Qué tal?* Oh, by the way, I believe in Allah." My mom found out eventually, as mothers always find out everything. One day she walked into my room and found me on the floor—forehead on the ground and butt in the air—praying. In the middle of my prostration, I heard a deep sigh and then the door slammed. She learned of it the hard way.

Unfortunately, we didn't have that needed follow-up talk about things. My mother realized something unusual was going on with me before she began receiving phone calls from people with heavy Middle Eastern accents asking for me. To my regret, I didn't open up to my parents about Islam. They had an idea that I was involved in something very different. It became the big fat elephant in the room that no one talked about. My mom was troubled by the subservient status of women in the Middle East, which, from her point of view, Islam sanctioned. It would be some years later when I married my wife that my mom felt comfortable with Islam. My mom and wife immediately hit it off and my mom learned more about Islam from my wife in just a brief period than she did from me in five years. At the time, I didn't know how to tell my parents. It was a struggle to express what was going on with me.

But if I had found the truth, why was there uneasiness regarding my conversion? Something within me wasn't right but I couldn't articulate the problem. Perhaps it was because I couldn't identify it and put my finger on it. I wasn't just dealing with a religious problem; there was a more profound and subtler issue confronting me. Conversion to a religion is supposed to mean that one has chosen a path because it brings peace within oneself. This wasn't my situation. I think the reason lies in the fact that Islam is a total way of life. It's not a personal lifestyle to be practiced in private. Its outward manifestation, reflecting the inward, is beautiful, and it is most beautiful when the two complement one another. The outer Islam that was being presented to me was a synthesis of Arab, Afghan, and Pakistani culture—and none of them jived with me. There wasn't harmony between me and Islam. It didn't make cultural sense.

There was never a feeling of doubt in my decision. I firmly believed in God and Muhammad but I couldn't separate Islam the religion from the Islam of the Middle East. To my mind Islam was, and still is in many ways, a Middle Eastern religion. In an effort to broaden and demonstrate the cultural scope of Islam, one will often hear a Muslim say that there are more Indonesian Muslims than Arab Muslims. This is true. However, Islam is predominantly Arab in culture. And, regardless, westerners are inclined to associate Islam with Arabs, not Indonesians. I felt I had not only embraced Islam but also Arab culture along with it. It was a struggle not to feel as though I had *punked* out or that I lost a little bit of who I was by changing religions. Catholicism is interwoven with Latino and Portuguese culture such that Catholicism and Latin American culture are almost synonymous. It would be like replacing the Spanish language in Latin America with a different language. Thus, there was a sense of insecurity about my identity. My rallying call had been "*No se venden*" (No Selling Out). Had I sold out?

For the first five years after converting, I lived multiple lives. I had a life as a Chicano activist, and I had another life as a Muslim with my Muslim friends. I never mixed the two worlds. If one would ask my mother, she would say that I had another life at home, because she didn't know much about my life outside of the house. My identity shifted according to whichever group I was with and I would move across the identity lines from Justin to Abd al-Rahman and back. On the same day, I would attend a MEChA meeting, discuss the day's business, and then afterward hang out with my Muslims friends or meet up with them to do the afternoon prayer together. I lived in two parallel worlds.

I couldn't join them because to my mind there wasn't a historical relationship between Mexican-Americans and Islamic culture.

In college, I came across a book that changed the way I viewed Islam in a significant way. It was Carlos Fuentes' *The Buried Mirror* in which he stated, "Fully one-quarter of all Spanish words are of Arab origin." I was astonished to read this line. I didn't understand how the two languages intersected. Fuentes was calling attention to the inter-cultural connection between Latin American and Islamic histories, specifically to the history of medieval Iberia (Spain and Portugal), in which Iberian Muslims—or Andalusians as they were called—had ruled in the peninsula for more than eight hundred years. During this period, there were many influences and exchanges, including linguistic borrowings. Thus, Latin America's linguistic heritage, originating from Spain and Portugal, is also of Arabic origin.

Now I could point to a connection between my own culture and Islam. And this was very important for me because Islamic culture wasn't irrelevant to my own heritage, as I had otherwise assumed it to be. Both my Mexican and Portuguese roots were interwoven culturally with Islam. I didn't sell out. I was embracing a culture that was already a part of my heritage, a more diverse culture. Yet, this discovery was more meaningful because it was coming from Fuentes, an authority on the Spanish language, and importantly, someone from within the culture. But I experienced another insight from Fuentes' words. Until this moment, I had forgotten all about my grandfather's words he exclaimed on that sunny Californian day. I had buried his words deep within my psyche and they had remained forgotten all these years. He was right after all.

I wanted to study the history of *Andalucía* (Muslim Spain and Portugal), the source of the cultural synthesis. Like my grandfather, my love for history has focused on exploring the Islamic aspect of my roots. From that day—when I read Fuentes' words—until today, I have studied the history of Andalusia. During our undergraduate studies, my wife and I seized the opportunity to live in Granada, Spain for one year and explore the history of Andalusia—its literature, law, and art and architecture. It was a wonderful experience to be able to live and study the past in the land where it all happened. Today I am working toward my doctorate in Islamic studies at the University of Chicago, where I will study the legal scholars of Andalusia, particularly the Portuguese jurist, Abu al-Walid al-Baji (or Beja, a city in southern Portugal), and shed light on his contribution to Islamic law in Europe.

Despite the epiphany that day—of discovering my Andalusian heritage—complete harmony didn't occur between my identity and cultural Islam. Discovering my Andalusian roots has bridged the gap between who I am and Islam, but Andalusian culture ceased to exist 500 years ago. It's a part of me, but it's gone. I'm confronted with the reality of what exists today: how to be an American and a Latino and a Muslim and what those mean. The identity question is one that I continue to deal and struggle with today. I believe the path that I'm following will help me deal with the challenges along the way. The path of the Prophet Muhammad hasn't led me to something I'm not. Instead, it has led me to the source of who I am. In this way, I hope to reconnect with the Latino community and serve again.

Jesus Said: 'Follow Me,' So I Became Muslim

Kenneth Rodriguez

Religion was quite the paradox when I was a child. Growing up in a nominally Catholic home, my family's faith was limited to attending Sunday mass every few months, erecting a Christmas tree during the holidays, and blessing our home with a portrait of the Virgin Mary. That was the extent of our piety, and living in New York City during the 1980s, the same could be said of my neighborhood friends.

Yet despite the marginal role that religion had in our lives, being Catholic and being from the Dominican Republic were somehow seen as inseparable. If our faith was ever contested, even a non-practicing Catholic saw it as his duty to defend his religion. As a child, I remember hearing adults argue that Catholicism was apparently the one true faith, only to quietly admit that they themselves neither read the Bible nor regularly attended church. Our religion was the truth just because, well, it's the truth.

At the age of 13, I wanted to learn more about this peculiar religion that everyone believed in but disregarded only until Christmas rolled around. I always believed in the existence of God for the simplest of reasons: every building has a builder, every ship has a ship maker, and the universe is much more complicated than a building or a ship, so there was obviously a creator behind it. This was clear to me even as a child, but it was a religion that I couldn't quite understand.

So I went to the Bible for clarity, but instead of answers, I found discrepancies. Why wasn't Christmas mentioned anywhere in the Bible? Why is mass held on Sunday if the Old Testament says the Sabbath enters on Friday night? Why aren't there any passages that mention confession booths, Catholic saints, or even the Pope? When I pestered my friends and family with the granddaddy of all religious questions – "What happens after we die?" – the responses varied greatly.

"When a person dies, he becomes an angel and flies up to heaven," said one relative. "A dead person remains buried until he is resurrected on the Day of Judgment," said a priest. "His soul immediately goes to heaven or hell," said another priest. "There is no Hell, only righteous people are resurrected and admitted into Heaven," said a family friend. And the most common answer: "When we die, that's that – we just go to sleep forever."

I was still a child so I wasn't searching for any spiritual epiphanies about the afterlife. I just wanted to understand how followers of the same religion could have such conflicting explanations about what happens when we die.

Confused, I felt the Bible should have the final word on these kinds of matters, but the scripture proved to be a theological labyrinth. When is Jesus Christ called "the Son of God," is this to be taken literally or metaphorically? And when the Bible mentions "the sons of God" (Genesis 6:2, Job 1:6), what does that mean? I also found it strange that the Old Testament emphasized an unwavering belief in the One True God (Deuteronomy 6:4), only for it to be abrogated centuries later in the New Testament with the addendum that, on the contrary, God is one-third of a Trinity. Ultimately I was unsure whether Jesus was a man, the Son of God, or God Himself – or all three simultaneously – and because these ambiguous verses were open to interpretation, it all seemed somewhat subjective.

Even without a strict religious upbringing, one thing was clear to me: Jesus was born in Bethlehem, he spoke Hebrew and Aramaic, and he studied the Torah – therefore, Jesus must have adhered to the Mosaic Law. How could I claim to be a Christian while sidestepping the Jewish commandments that Christ undoubtedly followed? So I began focusing on the Jewish laws that were too straightforward to misconstrue, and I developed an affinity for Jesus "the Jew," as opposed to Jesus "the Christian."

So this eager 13-year-old did what he could: I stopped eating pork (Deuteronomy 14:8), set aside days for fasting (Matthew 6:16-18), washed up before praying (Exodus 30:17-21), and taught myself the Hebrew and Greek alphabet in hopes of one day reading the Bible in its original language. Living in a bilingual home, a good part of my childhood was spent as an English-to-Spanish translator for my parents, so I already knew the imprecise nature of any translation, nonetheless of God's Word.

Now with a hodgepodge of Biblical laws to follow which I handpicked during my daily readings, I faced the dilemma of actual practice. What exactly is "prayer," I wondered. I noted that Abraham and Elijah prostrated on their faces when they prayed (Genesis 17:3, I Kings 18:42), and Daniel prayed three times for each day he was in the lion's den (Daniel 6:10), so that sounded about right. But what constitutes "fasting"? How was I supposed to celebrate the Sabbath? And if I can't eat pork, does that mean I shouldn't eat food made out of pork gelatin either? The straightforward laws of the Bible weren't so straightforward after all, so I took a few liberties to accommodate my life as a teenager in New York, and I asked God to overlook any shortcomings.

A few years later in my early teens, now the mid-1990s, I was admitted to one of New York's specialized high schools, which meant I now had to commute from Manhattan to the Bronx for the next four years. During that time, I was fortunate enough to meet classmates from various nationalities, cultures, and religions that otherwise I would have never met in my predominately Hispanic neighborhood. During this time, I befriended several Muslims of Middle Eastern, Asian, and African descent who dispelled my misconceptions about Islam. Up to that point, I had only heard of Islam in passing and I assumed it was an Arab-only religion utterly foreign from the Judeo-Christian tradition. On the contrary, they explained, Islam was the religion of Abraham, Moses, Jesus, and Muhammad – peace be upon them – all of whom preached the single message of monotheism.

My curiosity led me to research this strange religion. I was astonished to find that by following those Biblical laws – adhering to clear dietary rules, fasting on certain days, washing and prostrating in prayer – somehow I was already practicing Islam. How is it that these practices are virtually neglected in contemporary Christianity, despite appearing in the Bible, yet they are still preserved in Islam? I learned that even Arabic, the language of the Quran which Muslims uphold as the final revelation, is a Semitic language similar to Hebrew – so when the Bible refers to God as Elohim in Hebrew or Elah in Aramaic, it is a linguistic cognate of Allah in Arabic.

It was indeed an enlightening moment when I revisited that framed portrait of the Virgin Mary sitting on our kitchen windowsill, only to realize that she was wearing a head-scarf indiscernible from those worn by Muslim women – a tradition mentioned even in the New Testament (I Corinthians 11:5).

Beneath the outward worship of Islam, the entire religion is based on a single statement that is cogent in its simplicity: "There is nothing worthy of worship except the One True God." Monotheism, in its truest sense, is to distinguish the Creator from His creation. I found it inconceivable that the prophets Abraham, Moses, and David would worship anyone other than God, and even Jesus professed that the greatest commandment is to "love the Lord thy God with all thy heart" (Matthews 22:34-37).

So at the young age of 15, I was convinced: in order to properly follow Christianity, I had to follow Judaism; and in order to properly follow Judaism, I had to follow Islam.

Zulu Nation, Popmaster Fabel, and My Journey To Islam

Khalil D. Salgado

I hardly speak about my days of jahiliyyah (ignorance). For those of you who are not Muslim, I am referring to my days before my acceptance of Al-Islam.

However, today I just want to shed some light on my experience with the hip-hop organization known as the Universal Zulu Nation (UZN). I remember when I was sixteen years old and going to that park on the Upper West Side. It was the Rock Steady Crew's (RSC) Anniversary. I would later learn that this very park was a historical place in hip-hop. This was where the RSC would practice, hang out, and battle other crews back in the late 70s and early 80s.

At this event, I picked up an application for the UZN. I was told about the universal (meeting) that was held at the Bronx River Houses in the South Bronx. This place too, as I would later find out, was also a historical place in hip-hop history. At this meeting and many others to follow, I would become part of a new generation of youth in New York City who would become part of the UZN. The UZN would spark my interest in different religions, because it would promote positivity for Black, Puerto Rican, Latino, and other inner-city youth, and encourage seeking knowledge.

It was through the UZN that I would come to an understanding of the "Oneness of God." Before that time, I was engrossed in 70s politics and had become an atheist. I liked the way that Zulus promoted a positive form of hip-hop. This was refreshing at a time when hip-hop was at the height of "gangsta" rap. I would learn from speakers such as hip-hop legend Crazy Legs that hip-hop was not just the deviant commercialized rap industry. Hip-hop is a culture that has different elements to it - MCing (rapping), djing, breaking (and other urban dance forms), and graffiti.

I was surprised by how many Latino (mostly Puerto Rican) youth were members of the UZN. Black and Latino unity was always stressed. The role that New York Puerto Ricans played in hip-hop was not hidden or overshadowed by the role of Black-Americans. Members who attended these universals were about 75% Latinos.

In these universals, there would be a prayer at the closing of these gatherings. Usually, the prayer would be Surah Al-Fatiha. I remember hearing the Quran for the first time at that very first universal. I can still remember hearing Mr. Wiggles (a fellow Boricua) of the RSC reciting Al-Fatiha. The UZN definitely inclined towards Islam.

I can remember many times going up to Bam's apartment. He is known to most of the world as Afrika Bambaataa. He is the founder of the UZN and one of the "godfathers" of hip-hop. It was at his jams at the Bronx River Projects, in the early 70s, where all the elements of hip-hop would come together. At Bam's parties, youth could forget about their gang colors and enjoy themselves. Bam, himself, was the head of one of NYC's notorious gang - the Black Spades. They were the predecessors to what would become the Zulu Nation. It was Bam's jams that these youth would give birth to a musical and cultural movement. We would discuss such topics as culture, religion, blackness, latinidad, politics, and many other vast topics. Afrika Bambaataa was the link between the Civil Rights/Black Power Movement and hip-hop.

One brother who would speak at many of the universals was Brother Jorge "Fabel" Pabon. He is known in the hip-hop world as Popmaster Fabel, the Vice-President of the RSC. At the universals, he would speak about Islam, Latinos, and the roots of Muslim Spain. I would learn a lot about the virtues of Al-Islam and the connection to Latino roots and culture, and the hidden Islamic connections. Alhamdulillah, I thank Allah for my experience with the UZN.

I thank Allah for my exposure to those who I have met. After thanking Allah, I thank Brother Fabel "Shukri" who is a true Muslim brother. I am still in touch with him. Unlike many in the UZN who were not really Muslim, he adheres to Islam. There were many like Bam, Mr. Wiggles, Afrika Islam, and others who lean towards Islam but are not really Muslim. Groups and individuals, however, may (with Allah's success) lead some like me to go and actually learn about what Islam is. I do not agree with the close ties that the UZN has with groups like the Nuwaubians and the NOI, but I understand the link that they have with my past and my present.

May Allah reward Brother Shukri "Fabel" and guide those who may know about Islam, but have not yet accepted it yet. Ameen.

My Military Brat Muslim Story

Lena Lopez

I myself have always wondered when asked the million dollar question – "Why Islam?" And after much retrospective inquiry, I realized the answer. I grew up so wrong that I had to go right! It was in the 1980's that I was born on a Jummah (Friday) to star-crossed lovers whose taboo teen pregnancy and unforgiving families prompted a speedy marriage. Ironically, I was given a good Muslim name, Lena, despite that my circumstances had been anything but.

I remember growing up as the only child of high school sweethearts whose personalities made Bert and Ernie look compatible being that my mom became the breadwinner and my dad...well...he tried. From being born in an Army hospital to living on an Air Force base, military life was my norm. My friends were Black and Asian, and my multicultural surroundings allowed me to quickly adapt to new environments. I think my being naturally observant came with these new environments and people. After having been stationed all over the country, you come to realize that things are just relative - what's acceptable in one circle isn't in another and vice versa. This got me questioning customs, manners, laws, and ethics at a very young age.

Death and heaven were constant themes in my little mind just because my parents never discussed these unknowns that instantly sparked my curiosity. I was the only one; I mean the only one in our untraditional family who wasn't even ritually baptized. So, it was no surprise that over the years an abnormally curious teen would frequent her friends' churches:

1. The Filipino Catholic Church.
2. The Americanized Catholic church where I snuck Communion many a Sundays.
3. The Baptist Church complete with complimentary hand fans and a choir that could rival the "Queen of Soul" herself.
4. The Lutheran Church that taught Jesus through PowerPoint.
5. The Methodist Church that hosted food and faith services.
6. The Korean Baptist Church whose youth congregation was the product of military Anglo-Saxon men and Americanized Asian women who served seaweed after the sermon.

7. Pastor John Hagee's infamous church where I learned that Moses could be animated on teen movie nights.

8. The downtown Catholic cathedral where SNL church ladies shunned me from baptism because being 12 was too old to accept Christ.

And, trust me that I have tried it all from being booked at 12 (but charming my way out of jail) to my many failed attempts at athleticism and clubs to even being a Debussy groupie who lugged around her violin. Yea, if I got anything useful from my dad, it was his natural curiosity and youthful impulses to try out new things.

All through high school I could never find my niche, my place in the sun, my anything that clicked until here came Islam in the form of an Arab-Mexican mixed kid who instantly had me at hello...or should I say salaam? So, here came Islam to me in a most unconventional way. This foreign thing whose philosophy was an instant cult classic to me and answered everything I ever wondered in my 16 naive years of being. Of course, this didn't settle well with my single-military mother and I didn't care, because while kids were rebelling to be bad I was rebelling to be good. And, in a school of 3,000 students, I sure as hell stood out as the loner who wore that "thing" on her head. My conversion was simple. There were no hidden fees or public displays of bathing but the extensive questioning and reading was a challenge, trying to decipher culture from religion, fact from fiction.

Then cancer came. Well if a 2 cm nodule ready to explode out your appendix isn't bad, having both your parents not seeing the necessity of rushing you to the nearest hospital was. Now imagine two teens speeding down the highway just to make it to a faraway military base hospital because you know, even though you're going out of consciousness, you wouldn't want to incur the wrath of your mother for inconveniencing her schedule and pocketbook.

I realized after that fiasco that youth or great health doesn't matter to Death himself. Knowing a part of my bowel was pickling in a jar somewhere is when I knew that I wanted more out of my limited time. My family and I had experienced enough Maury storylines that influenced me to make the most out of life. I wanted to be a college student and a wife.

Through mutual acquaintances, I met my better half who was soul searching and bettering himself by rediscovering his inherited deen. After graduation, we got hitched and ditched Texas for New Orleans.

During my first stint at college, I got pregnant and then evacuated back home to Texas after the Hurricane Katrina phenomenon. The aftermath was my family's acceptance, which was free of hesitation and doubt, towards my conversion and marriage. They finally knew neither were phases. The storm had passed.

Now what I have learned in my 8th year of this deen is that Islam is not the "As Seen on TV" depiction. I have been overseas to visit my in-laws and my experience overseas has put those rumors to rest. Everyone speaks grammatically correct English. Burger King delivers. And, Arab hospitality isn't a myth. While we display our discounted wardrobe, they upstage us with their designer labels and some yanks still have the audacity to claim, "They hate us because they want what we've got." Healthcare was cheap, and I discovered this foreign land was also home to my grandma's first love, a Kuwaiti engineer stationed on a base in the states in the 1960's. And, take comfort in knowing that chances are when you're on American soil and you see a lady adorn a veil, chances are she's really an American like me.

The Process Of Learning Islam

Lidia Ingah

I met my husband eight years ago and I automatically fell in love with his personality. He was exactly what I was looking for: a man that respects me for my values, that loves me for who I am and that cares for me in a very responsible and consistent manner. He was so different from other men I met before - men that fall in love with women for their looks only. My husband was all different. He was too good to be true, but he was real, and I soon realized that he was a blessing that God sent to guide me towards a peaceful, happy and fulfilling life! Alhamdulillah!

As I am writing this story, tears are falling down my eyes because I feel very special and loved by Allah every time I remember how I was introduced to Islam. One day right after meeting my husband I saw he had a big book of the Quran. Automatically I thought that he could not be a Muslim because he was way too much of a beautiful person and he could not be one of them. I panicked and I wished that book was only a souvenir!

I was raised in Spain, in a very much 100 percent Catholic society, which was very much phobic towards other religions and ways of life. In school, my history teachers taught me terrible things about the way Muslim men treat their women and, as a female, I was terrified by the thought of falling in love with a man that would end up treating me as a subordinate and that would want to control all my actions and decisions.

"Yes," my future husband responded when I asked him if he was a Muslim. Oh no, he was really one of those! I felt sad and betrayed because I thought that he was acting out to seem to be respectful and caring. And, I was afraid that the "monster" inside him would emerge as soon as I seriously committed to him. However, because he seemed to be a pretty much rational person I decided that I could "help" him to see the "truth" about justice and equality. I knew that to convince him I needed to read the Quran and demonstrate that its teachings are all wrong and inhumane. So, I started reading the Quran.

Every time I opened that "so feared" book a sense of peace was with me. The feeling was so addicting that I could not stop reading and learning from it. Every night I would look forward to having some quiet time to continue learning. Rather than trying to demonstrate what a blasphemy the book was, I was now reading it to find direction and peace in my daily life.

When I married my husband, I told him that I was not ready to become a Muslim yet and that I could not guarantee him I would ever become one. His response was very tranquil and assured: "Take your time." That choked me up and at the same time motivated me to know more about "that way of life" that my husband was so convincingly following.

Today, all praise due to Allah, I accept Islam as the only path of life that is right for me and my family. My journey of learning Islam continues every day, slowly but surely. As my life becomes more and more permeated with Islam, a great feeling of peace and happiness grows inside me. Today, I am following my heart. I was full of misconceptions about Islam and Muslims. Now, I feel blessed entirely for seeing the right path, for letting myself be myself, and for freeing myself from external distractions that used to blur my eyesight.

From Mormon To Muslim

Marcela Mesto

My story begins in El Salvador. I was born in San Salvador, El Salvador, and at the age of 12, I migrated to Australia with my mother, my brother, and sister. From the moment we arrived in Australia, I remember visiting different Christian churches of differing sects as we used to do back in El Salvador. Unfortunately, none were solid enough for us to remain in. I was initially baptized in the Roman Catholic Church and as a teenager, I found that being a Catholic was too comfortable. I began looking for more guidance in following God's commandments.

At the age of 15, my family and I started to attend "The Church of Jesus Christ of Latter-day Saints" commonly known as the "Mormons." My auntie has been a long time member, and we found it was making a lot more sense than many other Christian teachings we had heard. Along with the good things came many that didn't seem to have a logical explanation at all, like the fact that there are prophets inspired with revelations within the church. So I just thought that with faith, one day I would understand them and they would make sense. A few months later, I was baptized. A few years went by and I really liked the Church but once again I found that I was confused at the fact that they didn't seem to think there was anything wrong with young people enjoying the nightlife as long as they didn't drink, smoke and make any bad choices.

As a teenager, can you tell me how it can be possible to enjoy all of this but yet keep away from temptation? Staying away from a lot of temptation was kind of hard, so I was "inactive" as they say for a while. At the age of 19, I met a guy who now happens to be my husband. He is a Muslim. He was not a practicing Muslim at the time, but what I liked about him was that he had principles and loved God dearly. We talked about marriage and concluded that we wanted to be together. At the time, being an inactive Christian and he being a Muslim, we came to a mutual agreement to be married only through the marriage registry to avoid any preference of our respective religious beliefs.

As the years went by, I actually thought about going back to church – any church, as my love for Jesus was there and I felt the need to be close to God. But the thought would soon go away when I thought about one of the main reasons I had stopped attending church in the first place. There was too much bickering, backstabbing, and criticizing. This has always been going on in the many churches that I attended, which I found made people forget the real purpose of being there. Going to church felt more like a Sunday social event rather than worshipping God.

I can honestly say that at that time Islam was of no interest to me and believe me, becoming a Muslim would never ever had been an option on my "preference list" of ways to get close to God. There was no interest whatsoever, until recently. A few months ago I had a dream that really shook me up. I felt quite scared and woke up praying and seeking guidance from God.

Two weeks later I had another dream very similar to the first. I woke up saying in Spanish "¡En el nombre de Dios todo poderoso y todo piadoso!" (In the name of God all-powerful and all-merciful). Again, I prayed and asked God for guidance. I asked him to show me how or what I needed to do to be closer to Him and to help me do His will. I continually asked Him if he wanted me to go to church to worship Him and if so, to please guide me to the correct one. I asked Him to make it clear how He wanted me to get close to Him. I asked Him to make it so clear that my heart could not deny any of His will.

Within that week I had a third dream. I was in a car heading up towards a very high mountain. I could not tell if I was the driver or a passenger. But as the car almost reached the top of the mountain, I had a horrible feeling that something terrible was going to happen. I looked out from the car window and noticed that I had reached the highest point of the mountain and could see a blue lake at the very bottom. It was so tiny that you could barely see the blue water in it. In that split second, the car lost control. I tried very hard to gain control of the steering wheel but it was impossible. I remember thinking that there was no chance of me surviving and thinking I was going to die as soon as the car went over the cliff. I felt really frustrated and scared that there was no chance of salvation. I felt as if I was actually facing death.

I began to feel extremely stressed from fear as the car was falling down towards the lake in the distance. As the car was falling, I then heard a loud voice echoing through the mountains. It was so loud that it made the mountains shake and tremble. The sound was loud but beautiful. It was so beautiful it gave me inner peace and made me lose the fear of dying but more importantly, what gave me this peace were the words being said.

I then heard the voice for the second time. This time it was carrying on for a more extended period. A bright orange, yellow light later appeared between the mountains – it was the sunrise. As the car was about to hit the ground, a road appeared out of nowhere. It was the road to my salvation. But what had really saved me were the words spoken by a voice through the mountains. Those words were "Allahu Akbar." It was the beginning of the athan!

I woke up instantly and was so emotional that I could not stop crying. I think I cried for a good two hours, but it was the most beautiful feeling ever. I couldn't even talk although my husband kept asking what was wrong. I told him my dream. I then told him I wanted to read the Quran. I felt this was a message from God who wanted me to seek knowledge.

The next morning I started to look into Islam. It's so funny because for the last 13 years I had been surrounded by many Muslims and was never aware of the real beauty of Islam. I remember my brother-in-law, a practicing Muslim, explaining the divinity of God alone without partners and how no other being should be worshipped along with Him or instead of Him, but my heart was completely sealed. I was never interested in knowing anything about Islam. In fact, I would get offended and at times I felt like telling him how misguided he was. I was convinced that it was not the right religion – definitely not the one for me anyway.

While seeking knowledge, I learned a lot about the deen (religion). I even began emailing people with knowledge from the other side of the world. It's for those who genuinely love Jesus' (peace be upon him) teachings just the way I do. It is for those who love all the servants, messengers and prophets of God, and most importantly for those who acknowledge the importance of the benefits that follow when you genuinely worship God alone. Islam is for everyone regardless of his or her race, nationality or ethnic background.

My heartfelt the complete opposite of the rejection I had for Islam. Alhamdulillah (All praise is to God). I was very fascinated by the treasure I had just discovered - the beautiful truth, the evidence and benefits of the teachings of Islam. I read not only from the Islamic side but the real history of all of the beliefs that had blindfolded me for so many years.

Who would have thought that hearing the call to prayer not only saved me in my dream but also was the truth and salvation I had been asking for in reality? God had answered my prayers. I put my spiritual feelings aside and looked at the evidence that I had in front of me, and my conclusion was this:

"Ashhadu Alla Ilaha Illa Allah Wa Ashhadu Anna Muhammad un rasulullah."

"I bear witness that there is no true god but God, that none has the right to be worshipped but God alone, (and that God has neither partner nor son) and I bear witness that Muhammad, may the blessings and mercy of God be upon him, is a true Prophet (and messenger) sent by God."

So after 13 years of being married to my husband, I have reverted to Islam. My husband is still shocked that I have reverted to Islam, so is his family and of course mine too. But when you know that all that you are doing is for the sake of Allah, and no one but Him, it feels so right.

Some of my closest friends were very supportive, as they know that Islam has given me inner peace and humility. Others think I have become an extremist just because I pray five times a day and have changed my dress code completely. Alhamdulillah. When I started to pray, I remember feeling so strange at first but it seemed so right at the same time. Islam is not just a religion but also a way of life.

Wearing a hijab now makes me feel so free and so respected. People who don't know me automatically get the impression that I'm Middle Eastern and when they find out I'm a Latina, they get shocked. They ask me why the dramatic change, but it's a good thing because it gives me a chance to actually give them a small explanation of the beauty and wonders of Islam.

Wearing the hijab gives me a sense of pride because I feel I have contributed to the good values most of us have forgotten. The hijab is not a responsibility, it's a right given to me by my Creator who knows us best. I definitely feel as if I'm contributing to today's society in stopping women from being oppressed by having to dress or behave in a certain way to fit in. I cannot say how happy I am that Allah has guided me into His path and I know that we plan things but Allah is the best planner. Just like the ayah (verse) from the Quran says: "He it is Who gives life and causes death. And when He decides upon a thing He says to it only: "Be!" and it is." (Quran 40:68).

Reverting to Islam helps me to strive to be by His side in the hereafter. My life on Earth is not forever. Therefore, I have to strive to be a good servant of God to be in Paradise one day. The happiness I get here is not eternal, but if I return to my Creator's side I will have everlasting happiness.

Please ask God alone with full submission for guidance and seek knowledge because you will be rewarded by our Creator.

Searching For Guidance

Maria Echandi

I was born and raised in Houston, Texas. My parents tried hard to raise me in a "better" part of town instead of the ghetto area. Even though my family's income was not enough to buy us everything we wanted, my siblings were close, my relatives kept in touch, and I had school friends, etc. And, I thought I had everything in order to live happily. As I became a teenager, everything changed. I found out the hard way that I needed God/Allah (SWT) in my life. And, so I began to turn to the spiritual and religious part of my life. It has been two years now since I've said my shahadah. Thanks to Islam my life has made a turn for the better. The best of all is that I am getting to know our Creator. Alhamdulillah. I have changed for the best.

Members of my family are Roman Catholic but they are not very religious. We rarely went to church. My parents made me go to church school but it eventually stopped altogether. I sincerely told my parents that I disagreed with the church school because it taught Christian beliefs like the Trinity (the Father, the Son, and the Holy Spirit). All I could think of was "Ok… so who's God?" And, I was told that all three make up God but I would say that I don't believe or understand that. Then, my parents would say to me that I'd get my answers in church school. As I had no guidance in my life, I looked for other things that interested me and somehow I turned to be interested in gothic. I soon became a rebel and a burden to my parents. I would talk back and yell at my parents. I was aggressive and short-tempered.

One day something snapped inside me, and I became very vulnerable. I would cry every time I made my parents mad. I always wanted to be alone and left alone to think, but that's when the Devil started whispering and made me feel that I was useless and a pain to my parents. I would have flashbacks to the worst moments and a wave of guilt, shame, and depression filled me. And, I would start to think that it'd be better if I died because I was causing nothing but pain. I literally thought of stabbing myself but I wimped out because I knew that it would hurt. So then, I had the idea of having an overdose. The pills were in my hand but then suddenly all sorts of questions popped into my mind. The question that caught my attention was "What happens and where will we go when we die?" I also thought of my family and my little sister. I wanted to see her grow up. I got angry with myself for being incredibly selfish. I would have caused my family a massive debt and maybe left them all heartbroken.

After this experience, I did my best to keep myself busy. I even started watching the news a lot, which was almost all about the war in Iraq and Afghanistan. I saw how the media was showing Muslims as the bad guys by calling them terrorists, extremists, and other exaggerated names. I knew that no religion would encourage hate or violence except maybe Satanism but I really didn't know anything about Islam either. I even did my research during school. I learned that it was Muslim women who wear the beautiful headscarves that I liked so much. What interested me a lot about Islam was the similarity in beliefs, such as the prophets, and I was impressed how women are raised high in status. Instead of blaming Eve for losing the garden, Islam says that both Adam and Eve had disobeyed God because Satan had tempted them and not just Eve.

One day while doing research about Islam during class, I came across an online Quran. I thought of listening to Surah Al-Fatiha, which is the first chapter of the Quran because I had just read it in English and Arabic. When I pressed play, I was so deep in thought. And, while listening to the beautiful voice reciting, I began to cry until I became aware that I never cry in class! So, I copied the website and I looked it up on my computer. I began to love and understand more and more about Islam and Muslims until I thought one morning about what was holding me back. Islam felt like a place where I really belonged and had all my values. I said my shahadah on the web with the help of a Muslim.

After that, I went to the mosque nearest to me. While there, I asked a sister what time was prayer. Somehow she knew I was a convert because she started telling me all the basics of salat and asked if I said my shahadah. After explaining how I did mine, she asked if I wanted to repeat it and I found out that I had made simple mistakes. After that, she provided me with a prayer rug, prayer dress, and books about Islam. I am very thankful for how Allah provided for me, and it was much unexpected. I wish that one day my family will respect my beliefs more because they are not so different from theirs at all. Instead, all they hear are exaggerations and things irrelevant to any religion. If people knew the true Islam, how could they hate this beautiful religion?

An Unorthodox Path to Islam

Maria Rodriguez

In the year 1999, I worked as a bi-lingual customer service manager for the largest remanufacturer of automotive parts. A wholesale customer representative named Brian in his phone calls kept sharing his Islamic faith and asking me some spiritual questions. I know now it was dawah and to be perfectly honest, it was annoying. I was a devout Christian and I did not welcome his remarks, but I remained polite on the phone. Out of the blue, I received a copy of the Qur'an mailed directly to my company! My initial response, without reading it, was that I could not bring it home. I was afraid of it! So I gave it away to a colleague a few weeks later. However, the seed of faith was planted, as it was my first introduction to Islam and a Muslim. I believe that you should never minimize any effort in sharing Islam. You may just be a planter for Allah in that moment.

Moving forward the year is now 2002, one year after 9-11. I had a vision that I did not quite understand, but thought it was important enough to write down. I shared my dream with some close Christian friends, but they too did not understand it. So, I just saved it on my computer and forgot about it for another two years.

This is the dream: "I found myself walking into a very old church. The wooden pews were lit by the natural light beaming through candelabra style windows. There was no artificial light. I felt I was in Spain at a different time. As I approached closer to the front of the church, I noticed a group of women to the right of me. They glanced at me with curiosity and they were fully covered, but they never spoke to me. They were separated from the men. At the time, as a Christian, I thought they were the old-fashioned Christian women wearing 'mantillas' typical of Spanish women. On the left, a group of men was speaking to each other. The language they all spoke was foreign to me. Only one man made eye contact with me. He came forward with a smile but did not speak. He had a sharply defined nose and very kind eyes, olive skin and dark black hair. As I could not understand his language, I addressed him in French for some odd reason. Three years later, I would marry a Moroccan Muslim who spoke both Arabic and French.

My childhood was not ideal as it was full of responsibility at a young age and religious in nature. My parents were born into Roman Catholicism but later converted to the Jehovah's Witness faith. My father's conversion was more serious thus becoming the spiritual leader of our family. From the age of nine years old until eighteen, I was nurtured and guided in this faith. I left home after completing my formal education and enlisted in the US Air Force. Having had made this decision, I was ex-communicated from my religious affiliation. They do not support the military, as they are conscientious objectors. I felt lost and empty inside as my spiritual support system was taken away.

However, I moved forward with my life. I went to Basic Training in San Antonio, Texas where I experimented with mainstream denominations starting with Catholicism then Protestantism. I continued with the Protestant services during the remainder of my training. After completion of basic training and my specialized career training, I was given orders to Germany. While in Germany, I was again looking for spiritual fulfillment. I attended few services, but still, my heart could not surrender. Some time passed, I met someone I could share my life with in Germany to fill the void, we married and then we were assigned back to the United States.

It was there where I thought I found fulfillment and attended Christian services. However, one year in Michigan, we decided that the military lifestyle was not conducive to raising a family, so we both opted to end our commitments. We started a new life and settled down in New Jersey. At first, we struggled as any young couple would, but we managed to do well. I had everything. A new religious community and a secure home to share our values with our children. I thought I had heaven on earth. It was shattered when my husband and father of three wanted to end our relationship and did not want to pursue counseling after thirteen years of marriage.

It was the darkest period of my life. Negative thoughts passed through my mind, but my faith in God would not allow me to succumb to them. I chose to live and make a life for me and my children. Ten years passed, and I worked hard to provide for my children. I went to school at night and was close to finishing my second degree. At this stage in my life, my heart wanted to embrace marriage again. So, after a few unsuccessful dates, I signed up for a Christian dating service and told God that if this doesn't work, I will remain alone and accept my fate.

Weeks later, government refund money came in the mail, so I decided to take my children to Disney World as a treat. This is where things turned mystical. I love Epcot as it has an international flavor, so I visited the Morocco site with my children. The young man employed there intrigued me as he spoke multiple languages and I was impressed. We talked briefly, took some pictures to remember the moment and went our separate ways. The very next day, we found each other again in the safari park. What are the odds for this to happen! We waved and said hello and continued with our fun. The third day, my children and I went to a gift shop in yet another park to buy some souvenirs and we meet him again. This time he introduces us to his cousins from France.

Now, I am wondering why God has brought this young man into my life three days in a row. Was it a message? If it was, what did it mean? If we meet him tomorrow, what should I say? None of this was planned; however, I did not see him again and brushed it off. We returned from our trip and I remembered to check my dating membership status to see if there were any messages. I was not optimistic as I hadn't completed the profile and it had no picture. However, to my surprise, I received a message from Morocco!

Logically, I wouldn't entertain the thought in engaging in a conversation with a foreigner as a local contact would be way more easy, but because of my mystical experience in Disney and the connection to Morocco, I began a dialogue with him to see where it would lead. Here is where Islam starts to enter into my life. We corresponded by email and letters for five months without pictures, then we decided I should meet his family if our time together had any chance to become a serious relationship. It was essential to know if the chemistry would work between me and his family.

There was still one obstacle. As a single mother of three, how could I spare money to buy a ticket to fly to Morocco? As God would have it, I unexpectedly received a check from the government for some error they committed in the past and reimbursed me in the amount I needed to travel. I took this as a sign from God and booked my ticket! The timing was too perfect to deny. It was easier for me to visit first without a visa, so I leaped in faith and set off on my new journey. However, before my departure, we had exchanged pictures and I was glad that we did not share them before as mutual feelings blossomed from our conversations. To my surprise, he was not the man I pictured in my head, but he was handsome. He had sharply defined features precisely like my dream two years earlier. I became more apprehensive about what he thought of me. Alhamdulillah! He called, and let me know all was well.

He met me at the Casablanca airport along with his sister, Hikma. The train ride home from Casablanca was a welcomed experience as it helped ease some of my anxieties before meeting his entire family. Once

I got there, the family received me warmly and made me feel right at home. This was my first time in an Islamic country and realized that their culture was similar to my culture as a Spanish-American woman. They were sociable, warm, and family orientated; the only difference was the religion. Despite the differences in religion, they treated me kindly. I spent seven days with them and the engagement was announced a couple of days before my return to America and was quickly followed by a party. This was a fantastic experience! I was dressed like a queen! First time in a long time, I felt like I mattered!!

Sadly, as I left Morocco and my fiancée behind, my mind kept reliving the last couple of days with delight. It had left an impression that I could not shake. Once home, I had to figure out if it was God's will that I follow through with this commitment of bringing him to America, so I knelt in prayer to ask for his divine wisdom on the matter. The answer came from my fiancée himself. Unknowingly to him, he made a remark that gave me pause, and I knew God was leading this man to my life. I did not share this with him but thanked God for answering my prayer. It would take another eight more months and precisely one year from the time we first met when he arrived in America.

I still remember the day. It was a beautiful, hot August summer day, and I was excited to start this new page in my life. My brother Jose and his wife accompanied me to the airport to pick him up. Shortly after, we married in 2005 in a simple ceremony with the mayor of our town. I remained Christian for the next four years. During this time, my husband was introducing me to Islam gently, but never demanded conversion and would recite the Quran: "There is no compulsion in religion." Basically, only Allah leads people to the faith. If Allah wants you, it will happen. He led me to watch Ahmed Deedat on YouTube. He is an Islamic scholar from South Africa who debated Christian scholars. The first video I watched was titled, "Is Jesus God?" That video opened my appetite to listen to all of his debates and to continue my research on Islam.

Four years later in 2009, I received a small box with Islamic literature from California. It came from my sister-in-law Amina who became a Muslim four years before me. I read a pamphlet teaching me how to pray as a Muslim. I found myself practicing the movements alone in my home, and wondering at the same time, why am I doing this? Actually, laughing at myself. However, Allah had plans for me!

My husband and I went to Morocco as I had just finished my second degree and I wanted a big trip! I did not know I booked it during Ramadan! I was introduced to fasting and prayers. I was amazed how Muslims would attend their communal prayers at the masjid and though there was no room inside; the humanity overflowed into the streets! I wanted to know what drives these people! Allah was working on my heart, but as a devout Christian, I could not turn my back on Jesus! He was the core of my beliefs and abandoning him was not an option. Not knowing Islam embraces Jesus (Isa) (PBUH).

However, Allah is the best of planners. The night before I would give my Shahada, profession of faith. I had another mystical experience. I had a vision in my sleep. I found myself behind tall black iron bars, and I had my hands on them trying to see clearly what was ahead in the alley. I saw movement ahead and some light, but it was far away. Somehow I knew I was looking at a Christian procession. I could not draw closer. At that moment as I was distracted, I felt a light kiss on my right cheek. Surprised, I turned my head to the right and I saw Prophet Jesus (PBUH). He was a bearded man wearing a white thobe and sandals. He left and disappeared as quickly as he went behind me.

Prophet Jesus (PBUH) knew I needed his blessing to accept Islam. By giving me that vision, it readied my heart to receive Islam. Allah knows best! The very next day, my husband asked me to join him in prayers (not Muslim yet) but I willingly accepted the offer. It was a good thing I read about Muslim prayers from my package that I received from Amina, my sister-in-law. Now it made sense! As we began to pray and made Sujood (prostration), I prayed to God, "Lord, this will change my life and everything I know, please give me the courage to accept." As we stood up again, my husband turned around and said, "You need to do Shahadah." We stopped praying and he called his mother over to be a witness. I knew that Allah was leading this process. There I stood in front of him and his mother repeating the profession of faith. So I began to utter, There is no God but Allah…tears flowed gently down my cheeks. I fully embraced Islam during the holy month of Ramadan 2009 in Morocco.

That same night, Allah gave me another vision. I was in the most beautiful mosque. Words are inadequate to describe its beauty. The ceilings were very high and ornate in gold. The marble floors were like glass as I could see my reflection so clearly in them. I felt so small in scale compared to the structure around me, but it was full of light and I felt safe. I looked to my right and I saw a covered woman standing on the balcony, and then suddenly to her left descended a winged bat-looking creature. He landed on the banister of the balcony. I then heard a small still voice saying, "Keep praying!" My mother-in-law told me that woman was you, Maria! You are going to be tested, so keep praying! I took her message to heart.

A couple of days later, I accompanied my husband and his family to the local mosque in Kenitra. My husband and father-in-law went to the Imam to ask him if I could publicly announce my Shahadah to the community. That moment in time will forever be etched in my memory, as it was very special. I heard the gasp from the audience, and it was later explained to me that I was the first American to revert to Islam in their mosque. Although in the back of the mosque, the women let out a "yu-yu" (native chant) and their joy reached my ears. I was moved as well.

After my public shahadah, my reversion became the talk of the community of believers, so much so that it reached the ears of a government official. He came to visit my in-laws at their home to find out who was this American that reverted to Islam. Unfortunately, I did not meet him, as my husband and I just returned back to America the day before, but my in-laws were more than happy to share the news with him. The important thing was that I was now a Muslim and my new spiritual path had just begun.

My reversion story was a bit unusual and it was a process, so it is my prayer that whoever reads my testimony is inspired and comforted to not lose hope for those you love as there is no compulsion in religion and Allah guides whom HE wants! I am living proof of this. Yes, the answer or message may even sometimes come in an unorthodox manner, but it's for his or her understanding. Nothing is difficult for Allah as HIS mercies are great! Allah Akbar!

My Revert Story

Marta Galedary

I am a Mexican immigrant and a US citizen. I was born in the state of Guerrero in a small village located three and a half hours south of Mexico City. My father owned a ranch, and every year the people from the village would come to my father and trade corn for renting a piece of land so that they could grow their own corn.

I am the 11th daughter in my family. My father realized that women were not a great help in the ranch. He believed working in the corn fields was a man's job. Therefore, he purchased land and built a home in an urban area where schools were available. He wanted his daughters to learn a skill. He feared that his daughters might marry unproductive husbands. My father's wise decision was crucial for me and my sisters, because had he followed the local cultural tradition our lives would have been reduced to getting married as young as fourteen or fifteen.

My mother raised me with strong Catholic beliefs. I used to go to catechism every Saturday, attend mass every Sunday, and confess to the priest, and receive communion.

During Easter week, I was not allowed to go to the movies or listen to music nor was I permitted to eat meat on Fridays. Culturally, the practice of Catholicism was left to the mother. The concept of God at this time was punitive only.

After I finished secondary school, I moved to Mexico City, where I started preparatory school. I was away from my mother and moved with my two sisters into an apartment. I was making decisions by myself on how to behave and take care of myself. My mother was able to afford a private Catholic school for girls only, El Colegio Hispano Americano.

In my third year of college, I decided to focus in the area of humanities and French literature. The area of humanities required reading at least four books a month followed by a written report. My readings were about Western literature, psychology, and contemporary philosophers. Marxism and Existentialism were introduced to me. I eventually earned a baccalaureate in Arts and Humanities at El Colegio Hispano Americano.

The influence of Marxism, Existentialism, feminism, and friends took me away entirely from practicing Catholicism, to the point that I was doubtful about God's existence.

I felt that I could survive with no God and no rituals. As a consequence of my actions and beliefs, I found myself lost, confused, and living an extremely conflicted and painful life. I could not see the reason for my existence or mission in this world. The feeling of emptiness in my heart occupied my mind as well.

In the middle of this turmoil, I got married in Mexico City to a man more conflicted than me and we had one son. I ended my university years and enrolled in a technical skills school. I earned a diploma in the medical field as a Registered Nurse. I started working in one of the Medical Centers in Mexico City for seven years.

I carried nostalgia for not obtaining a Master's degree from a university but I continued pursuing my own personal intellectual growth. Therefore, I enrolled at the Anglo English Institute/Instituto Anglo Mexicano, which was founded by the British Embassy in Mexico City. After three years of intensive English courses and working full time in Mexico City, I decided to take a summer English course in England in 1982. I was in advanced level and conversation but needed more practice with my English. At that time, the process of my legal divorce started.

My trip to England was the most important event in my life. God had reserved for me the opportunity to meet three Muslim students from Brunei. Suddenly, the world opened up to me. I was able to look outside from the small window of my apartment, and I tasted the importance of traveling as a source of cultural awareness and learning.

My new friends from Brunei never talked to me about Islam. Their actions toward me got my attention. I was treated with respect, kindness, caring and a clean attitude while feeling safe with them. The only question they asked me was if I believed in God and after giving an affirmative answer, I was told that I was a Muslim. Muslim was a word that I had never heard in my life and I did not ask the meaning.

The summer English course ended so fast. I returned to Mexico City. I had to face the lifestyle of a divorced woman in a country where being a divorcee is not welcomed in the society. My mother supported my divorce. Because I did not get married by the Catholic Church, he was never considered my husband in the eyes of God, my mother stated.

I kept in touch with my Muslim friends by regular mail. I asked them to teach me how to talk to their God. I did not know what the words "Allah" and "Islam" meant yet.

In reply to my question, I received the book "Islam in Focus." Also, I was told that communicating with God was done by praying and the section on prayers was marked in the book, and I started reading the book. The transliteration of Arabic to English was very difficult for me. The fasting sounded too long and unhealthy. However, I was going through such difficult times and I needed something to make my difficulties easier.

I did memorize two sentences from the Arabic transliteration: There is no god, but God (La Illaha Illa lah) and I seek refuge in Allah (Audhubillah). Every time I pronounced those words my problems seemed to be solved smoothly. I could not explain the reason, and I considered these words to be powerful and supernatural because I always obtained an immediate positive response to my problems.

In 1983, I decided to travel to the USA on a summer vacation. I enrolled in a public adult school to continue practicing my English. I met Muslims from Turkey and Bulgaria. I became friends with a Muslimah teacher, a convert. I asked her to take me to a mosque, because I was reading "Islam in Focus" and had many questions. My teacher friend took me to a mosque on a Friday to Jummah prayer. As soon as I stepped into the mosque, I experienced mixed feelings of peace and fear. My heart started beating faster. I was very impressed to observe so many men praying and prostrating their faces on the floor. I said to myself that this must be a powerful religion to have so many men praying. Culturally in Mexico, most of the men do not regularly attend church.

After my first visit to the mosque, I attended Introduction to Islam classes for non-Muslims and new Muslims at a local mosque on Friday evenings.

In December 1983, close to Christmas time, I gave my testimony of faith by saying "I bear witness that there is only one God and Muhammad is His last messenger." My English teacher was my witness. I was in tears during my first prayers. Finally, I had found peace in my heart. I knew that Allah was with me. And, I found out my role in this world and the reason for my existence. I have returned to the One God and I will never be lost again. As it is stated in the Quran 51:56 - "I (Allah) created the jinn and humankind only that they might worship Me." And, worshipping Allah is not only the Five Pillars of Islam, such as performing the five daily prayers. Worshiping Allah is every minute of life and performing actions with the intention to please Allah.

My family did not accept my decision to become a Muslim immediately. My mother had no idea about Islam. It was an unknown religion in Mexico in 1984. I advised my mother to talk to the local

Catholic priest and ask him about Islam. She was amazed and content when the priest told her that Islam was an ancient religion and that I was on the right path.

He did not need to elaborate more! My mother had a relief and no more worries. My older sister who was a Catholic nun blamed herself for not teaching me enough Catholicism when I was a child, but even she eventually came around to my embrace of Islam. My visits to Mexico were different because my family would not cook pork for me. And, they respected me while I was praying. I talked to my family about Islam when they asked me questions.

Presently, I am married to a loving husband who was born in California and whose parents immigrated to the United States from Iran more than fifty years ago. We have one son who is the first generation of Mexican-Iranian parents and who effortlessly traverses the cultural boundaries of the Latino, Iranian, and multi-cultural Muslim communities of Southern California as a native-born American Muslim.

Islam has given me a new way of living. The more that I learn about Islam the more I strengthen my faith in the One God and Muhammad as the last messenger. I have embraced the duty of sharing my experience with the large population of non-Muslim Latino Spanish speakers by providing them with information on Islam. This has been embodied in the formation of LALMA.

Most of the Latinos living the United States and Latin America are unaware of the legacy of Islam in our culture, language, and architecture. The Spanish language has thousands of words derived from Arabic. And the design of the homes in much of Latin America was inspired by an art form known as "Mudejar," which was developed by Muslims in Spain and Portugal. In Arabic, we say "Insha'Allah" and in Spanish, we say "Ojala," which is virtually identical in meaning.

My plea to the existing Muslim community: When meeting a new Muslim, be patient, and do not be judgmental and overwhelm the new convert with multiple rules. Remember that Prophet Muhammad did not introduce laws as a priority. For 13 years, he taught the belief in one God (tawheed).

Finding My True Self In Islam

Melissa Morales

I have always been a God-fearing person. Growing up in Puerto Rico as a Pentecostal, I was sure about my faith and had no intention of changing my religion. I used to go to church eight times a week - once every day and twice on Sundays. I enjoyed youth retreat camps and I even participated in mission trips to Central America. I was sure I was in the right religion because I felt in my heart an overwhelming peace and happiness of my trust in the blood of Jesus. I had always been a religious person, not a perfect person because nobody is perfect except God, but I did try my best to follow what I perceived to be the right path.

I had a strong feeling inside me that I should be learning more about theology. I wanted to teach people about God and share with them the message of Christianity. I didn't see myself as a preacher but rather as a teacher of theology. On 1995, I started an Associate Degree in Theology in a Christian institute. I was very happy for that opportunity to learn and study different books about God and the history of the Church. It was then when I first came in contact with Islam. In the comparative religion class book, there was a small section about Islam. I thought it was a religion for Arabs only and it seemed strange and distant to me. The book referred to Muslims as Mohammedans and that is all I knew. While at the institute, I met an Arab friend who wasn't Muslim, yet I became intrigued with the religion of the "Arabs" and decided to read about it to inform my friend about her parents' religion because she didn't know anything.

After reading much literature about Islam, I asked my teachers in the institute to tell me something about Islam. I still remember one of my teachers who had many degrees in Christian theology and had traveled to many places preaching Christianity and had read the Bible many times. I asked him to teach me about Islam because I was reading and found it interesting, not much different from what I believed. My teacher's response shocked me—I don't know anything about Islam, all I see is that it is a religion of warriors; they spread their religion by the sword! (What a fallacy if I could tell him now!).

I never asked him again, but inside me, I began questioning the truth. How can he be so sure about Christianity being the only right path if he knows nothing about other faiths?! How can he preach to thousands of people to believe in Jesus as God if all he knows is what he had learned from his youth and the religion of his country and parents? Perhaps he could be misleading thousands and he is not aware of that! I thought all of these things and decided to then read about other religions with the purpose of strengthening my Christianity. I loved Jesus from the bottom of my heart and never had put in doubt the doctrine of the Trinity. All I wanted to do was to increase my knowledge so I could teach and empower people to go as missionaries and help bring souls to Christianity. However, the more I learned about Islam, the more I liked it, and the more it felt that it was like my own nature being exposed in front of my eyes.

After a while, I stopped researching and continued with my life's routine. I had never talked with a Muslim, never had I seen one. I decided to go to the United States to practice my English skills and it was then that I met Muslims for the first time. These Muslims taught me a lot about Islam and I made futile attempts to convince them about Christianity. It seemed they always won all the rounds! All of my background in Christian theology was ineffective against these people. They told me that they believed in Jesus as the Word of God and the Messiah but not as a God because there is only one God - the creator of everything, the Almighty, All-Powerful. They also taught me about Muhammad, peace be upon him, and that he was a righteous man who helped the pagan polytheist Arabs to believe in only one God whose name is Allah in Arabic, the same Almighty, All-Powerful God of Judaism and Christianity. The same God that used Moses, peace be upon him, to liberate the Jews from the captivity in Egypt; the One who sent Jesus, peace be upon him, to teach his people that they should obey only God.

When I went back to Puerto Rico, I had already experienced a change inside me. I didn't want to give up my religion, but I couldn't feel the certainty I felt before. I started doubting and noticing all the mistakes that I tried to conceal before. I started going to church only occasionally. I saw people speaking in tongues and dancing in the Holy Spirit and knew that peoples' own emotions were involved in the process. If the music was playing, all the people were involved in the dancing and the tongues, but as soon as the music was over, the Spirit or emotion was over also. This didn't make sense to me especially after seeing many youths involved in the "Spirit" and weeks later they were back into drugs and sins.

I stayed for one year in Puerto Rico knowing in my heart that I was a Muslim, yet I didn't want to accept it and leave the dogma I grew up with. After finishing my studies, I went back to the United States and became Muslim. Later I married one of the Muslims who introduced me to Islam. I have been very fortunate because my family has been very supportive of my choice. I think because they have always known that I am a religious person and that Islam is not much different from what I have always believed. I have always been Muslim, just now I know Islam!

My Journey To The Truth

Nylka Vargas

Conversions never happen overnight; mine sure did not. I had a few early childhood experiences that really had me thinking of life and death. I was in a major car accident when I was five years old. Being run over by a car at that age was traumatic for my entire family. I was just getting out of kindergarten. It was summer. I was playing outdoors and all I remember was a red large object coming at me. The next thing I remember, I was in a hospital bed clinging on to life and holding my mom's hand so very tightly. I found out later that it was a month into my coma that I woke up.

The second experience that got me thinking about life and death was my father's death when I was seven years old. My father's death was very shocking. I had already experienced hospital days and hours upon hours of rehab to then later learn that my father was in a car accident. The family was again in panic and hysteria, and I at seven years old said my goodbyes with tears running down my face while by his side. Latino families are very open. They allow their children to experience their emotions out in the open. They do not censor as much as society in general does, and the children often grow up much faster than their counterparts in the modern world do.

Growing up in a South American family (Peru-Ecuador), I was surrounded by a loving and caring mom named Patricia and siblings named Nury, Ayisa, and Dayana. Thus, I grew up in a house of women representing all varying types of personalities and interests. I was loved and I am thankful to Allah (SWT) for providing me with this comfort of security in my young formative years. I traveled a lot to Peru. My mom, as you may have figured, was a single mom and primary breadwinner of my family. She worked several jobs, went to school, and had the ability to take all her daughters to see our family overseas every summer. We went on trips, we went shopping, we ate out lots of times, etc. She instilled in us values, moral ethics, and the importance of family. It was because of that we grew up cultured and bilingual in Spanish and English. My mom today is sick, and I see this as actually another blessing in disguise. It's her long deserved break. It is as if she just lies in her bed and has no worries. I pray for her but I too realize that Allah (SWT) is the Best of Planners.

When I was 19 years old, I reverted to Islam by uttering the words: La Illaha Ila Allah, Muhammad ar Rasullulah. It was then that I abandoned associating partners with Allah (SWT) and accepted our Prophet (SAW). Up until that point in time, I was Christian, believing in Jesus as both God and son, with some doubts about the entire process but nevertheless, that is what I believed. There were incidents in between where I showed some signs of religious rebelliousness. At 12 years old, I did not join the line of worshippers as they paid homage to Jesus on the cross, and I never confessed to a priest. At visits to other Christian churches with my family, I found it distressful to see individuals dancing and fainting at the Holy Spirit's touch, sending good luck messages to a named Saint, etc. Nevertheless, I was committed to God. He had something in store for me. I thought so then, except I did not know of any other way to find him but through the church.

It was also during this period that my eldest sister died in an accident. She went away to visit family in Arizona and as her fate was written the car she was in went off a cliff. It was thus at 15 years old that I found myself a lost shepherd out in the wilderness, nowhere else to go but the church. Without pressure from family, I signed up and completed Sunday confirmation classes and then graduated. My confirmation name was Christina after my great-grandmother. I was confirmed, and now I was officially stamped sealed and approved. No more doubting. Or so I thought. However, as one may guess, we can lie to the outside world, our loved ones, but lying to our soul and self is impossible. No one is ever successful at that. A sure sign of an imbalance of the mind-body-soul is that the symptoms will manifest themselves in one definite way or another.

During the summer of 1995, I was your typical idealistic young woman going to school for a better tomorrow. It was then that I met many foreigners, students participating in the international student exchange program - from Colombia, India, Spain and Saudi Arabia. My nature drew me to this crowd and curiosity got the best of me. It was not apparent nor did I openly mention any of my doubts I had for years. And as Allah (SWT) would have it my friends were Muslims. Something was different about them: the prayer, gender-interaction, and no drinking.

In retrospect, I am thankful for these Muslim ambassadors from overseas who came to teach me something about Islam rather than just confined themselves to their circle of friends or MSA's. I may have missed my chance! Alhamdullilah, I figured this out before the semester ended. As soon as I found out about Islam, which was the likely alternative that I was searching for, I immediately asked about the concept of God, Jesus, his birth, his mission, and Mary. These significant points were of interest to me. I was handed a dawah starter pack, and after much thought and research, I converted a year later. Allahu Akbar!

My journey is one that continues to this date. My long journey makes me appreciative of being a Muslim. I have met many Muslims who were not practicing Islam, and so for many years, I was misinformed. No less than the working of the Shaytan who maximizes on our weaknesses. It is not always so clear-cut. Things are seldom handed to us ready-made. We have to work for them. With every positive step I took forward, more obstacles blocked my path. But all of this only strengthened me to move more fiercely and to turn to Allah (SWT) for guidance. Although I was not trained in the proper manner of calling Allah (SWT) nor was my Quran recitation intact, I called in my dua to the Creator of All Worlds the way I knew how: hands held up, tears flowing down my face and a helpless disposition.

Many years ago, while I lived in Pennsylvania, I came into contact with a woman by the name of Mariam. I was interested in improving my understanding of Islam and seeking to better my personal faith in Islam. This was before the many Islamic programs found throughout the country. Sister Mariam who came to help me a few times taught me how to wear a hijab, perform wudu, and offer salat at the small masjid in Pennsylvania. Yet, I did not look like your typical Muslimah. I was still growing, and had not yet understood "the concept of hijab."

I have heard many similar stories of Muslim converts and those searching for the purpose of life. They are stuck for one reason or another, perhaps battling their nafs (inner selves) or unable to make that commitment. I believe it was a longing and earnest prayer that unveiled my heart and brought me to embrace Islam wholeheartedly, eventually to see Islam in its entirety. How true it is that Allah (SWT) hears us when we call Him and He draws near us when we take a step toward Him. Allah (SWT) has commanded us to remember Him always. He says, "Remember me and I shall remember you." (Quran 2:152).

Today as a Muslimah, I still remember how long it was and how many obstacles I had to face to get to the point where I am today. Knowledge is a powerful weapon. Without knowledge of this way of life, our personal faith in Islam remains deficient. Without sincerity to please Allah (SWT) alone, to put Him first, we are sure to lose sight of our goal and will thus lose sight of our goal. We will not have the courage and patience to deal with the challenges that we face. It was this small but significant knowledge that allowed me to see the truth of the matter. When the time finally came to choose between pleasing my loved ones and society or pleasing Allah (SWT), I stood firm.

Today I am a daie (a caller to Islam). I learned I was one after the fact. What began as helping out on small errands, grew into a full-time commitment. One thing led to another and the responsibilities dawned on me. I accepted the challenge. I am truly blessed that I was placed in a position to help newcomers and those inquiring about Islam. Our duty as Muslims is to convey the message of Islam.

Naturally, spending a significant amount of time at the masjid and attending Islamic study circles warmed my heart to crave religious knowledge. Alhamdullilah. I am proud to say that I learned how to read and write Arabic, and I am currently a student of the Quran. My goal is to memorize as much Quran as I can. Insha'Allah, God-willing. I will join the ranks of protectors of the Quran. I also teach new Muslims the basics of prayer and assist them in their transition.

I work in mental health counseling and social services. I am married to a Syrian Muslim from Homs, Syria. He has taught me much in our five years of marriage. The beauty of intercultural marriages is that we have the best of both worlds. As a convert, I believe what happens is that we are rightfully cautious and conscientious of minute details of our faith, and thus, lose sight of the natural every day-to-day element of Islam. My husband, alhamdullilah, has brought to light a side of Islam that I could not have learned through reading alone or informal relationships. For that, I am genuinely grateful to the Most-Wise, the All-Knowing.

My Revert Story To Islam

Pablo Calderon

I am a Chilean revert to Islam. Growing up in Los Angeles's San Fernando Valley, I was exposed to a lot of gang activity, mostly in school. As a young boy, I had a tendency to put classmates into groups and give them names. I remember my elementary school principal announcing our so-called gang in an assembly and this feeling of 'wow' came over me. Since then I started to run with a crowd of people and joined the neighborhood gang when I was 12. Statistically, I should have never been involved in gangs because I come from a very loving and supportive family.

I went through a lot during my teen years because of my choice of lifestyle. I became outraged and had no remorse for any of my negative choices in life. Because of my violent lifestyle, I moved up the ranks in the neighborhood becoming a shot caller. A shot caller is a person in the gang that basically makes the decisions on what goes on in the gang.

When I was 22 years of age, I started to work at a car dealership where my brother was a sales manager. That is where I met Muslim coworkers. One day I was walking by one of my coworkers and decided to sit in on a conversation they were having with other coworkers. They were talking about Islam and stating that they believe in only one God and that Jesus was a very important prophet.

Something clicked inside of me and I remember telling myself that's what I believe. I asked my Muslim coworkers to tell me more. At the end of our conversation, I asked one of my coworkers how to become a Muslim. He told me I had to recite the shahadah. I said ok I'm ready. He directed me to go to the Tampa Masjid in Northridge, CA.

I went there right before evening prayer. I drove up and met two Muslims brothers that happened to be sitting outside the Masjid. I walked up to them and told them that I wanted to be Muslim and told them what I needed to do. Their response was not something I was looking for. They asked me how I heard about Islam. I told them that earlier that day I had heard Muslims talking about Islam and that I felt that was my path. The Muslim brothers said to me that I should read up more on Islam and then make my decision. I told them I already knew my choice and felt it in my heart that I wanted to be a Muslim.

They told me ok brother let's go show you how to make wudu and that after that they would take me to see the Imam. The brother kindly did so and later that evening I made my shahadah and reverted to Islam. My life completely changed after that. I stopped gang banging and started to read Quran and make salat (the Muslim prayer). All I could think about was Islam and how much more knowledge I was hungry for.

I thank the highest Allah for his gift of Islam every day. My life has been blessed ever since with most of my family taking shahadah later including my wife. I am also blessed with two lovely Muslim children. Thank you, Allah, for guiding me to your religion (deen). Allahu Akbar. I'm proud to be Muslim of Latino heritage.

A Change Of Heart

Paulo Silva

My journey to Islam started a long time ago when I was in junior high in a small town in the central valley of California (Merced, CA). I lived with my father and grandmother. They were the religious types. I come from a Latino Catholic family. We had Santos (statues of saints) all around the house. We also had a table set as an altar with statues of Jesus, the Virgen de Guadalupe, and other saints. We went to church every Sunday, and I enjoyed going to church to visit God.

They gave me my first Bible. I read it twice and began to question it. I asked my grandma, "It says here in the Bible not to worship idols or engraved images." She replied, "We are not worshiping idols - the saints are messengers who give God our prayers." I knew this was wrong. Later in the New Testament, I had a hard time believing God himself would reincarnate as human or send down a son. To me, this sounded like a child's fairy tale. Slowly, I began to stop believing in the Santos and Jesus, but I felt there was a God out there but didn't know who He was. So still in junior high, I stop believing in Christianity.

One day, my dad was watching a movie about the Prophet Muhammad and I asked, "What is this movie about?" He explained it was about a man who claimed to be a prophet of God. I said, "So, they have their own God." My dad said, "No, they believe in the same God as us but Jesus is not God but a prophet and Muhammad is the last of the prophets and the Jew also believe in the same God but not Jesus at all." I thought to myself, "Wow, I think I should be Jewish since they also don't believe in Jesus."

Eventually, I forgot about religion all together through the rest of junior high and high school. Later, I went to Merced Community College where I met some Sikhs and eventually became friends with some of them. I remember a group of us, Latinos and Sikhs, would almost every Friday go to the park and get drunk after our last class. They would claim it was against their religion to smoke and drink, but we were young and wanted to have fun. They would tell me about their faith and their gurus and a couple of times I went to their temples (one in Livingston, CA and the other in Fremont, CA).

They would tell me how brutal and intolerant Muslims were. They talked about how most of their gurus were tortured to death by Muslims and how their children were chopped into pieces and the mothers were made to wear their chopped children around their necks like a necklace. At first, I thought to myself that these Muslims are no good, but for some reason, I began to wonder about these badasses who went around and kicked so much ass and I wanted to learn more about these people. I guess it was because I was young, and as a youngster, you want to be with the people who kick ass.

I was 19 at the time. I went to the bookstore at our mall and bought a copy of the Quran and read it. I found it confusing to understand and wished there were Muslims around to explain it to me, but I had nowhere to turn to for help. I kept the Quran and read it a few more times and a year later I joined the army.

I brought the Quran with me and read it during basic training and at my first duty station, which was Korea. One day a katusa (Korean soldier assigned to the US Army) asked what I was reading. I told him I was reading the Quran. He told me about a mosque in Seoul and showed me how to get there. I was happy because maybe someone there could explain Islam to me. I now understood that they believed in only God and no partners, which I also believed. Also, I got over not believing in Jesus after someone told me there was a group of Christians who didn't believe Jesus was a God or son of God but an inspired human being. And, I didn't have a problem accepting this also.

When I arrived at the mosque, the people there were rude and asked why I wanted to know about Islam. "You have your religion and we have ours." Also, they kept being rude, not wanting me there. So, I left thinking to myself, "Fuck these people. What is this religion? A religion of hate?" I put my Quran in storage and didn't pick it up for over 13 years.

In my early 30's, I began to think about God a lot again. I read the Quran once again, and I learned about Buddhism and Hinduism. I found Hinduism my ideal religion because it dealt with getting rid of the ego. I stayed as a Hindu for five years, and in my fifth year, I re-analyzed something in myself. I liked Hinduism, but I felt deep down inside guilty about bowing down to a blue God. It didn't sit right in my heart.

I knew I had to come back to one of the Abrahamic faiths. I didn't want to go back to Christianity because Jesus is believed to be God and I didn't want to become Jewish because Jews don't believe in Jesus. Muslims had the same beliefs as me but I couldn't get my previous encounter with them out of my mind. While searching the Internet, I found LALMA (Los Angeles Latino Muslim Association). I figured it would be better to meet up with other Latinos who could offer me a comfortable setting to learn Islam. Finally, I felt in my heart that I was where I belonged, as a believer that there is one God and Muhammad is His messenger. After leaving to meet with LALMA, one of my Christian friends was in my house doing some work on the house. I had told him I was going to meet up with some Muslims.

Later when I arrive home, my altar with all my gods and offerings were missing. At first, I thought I was robbed but that didn't make sense because only my gods were gone. I asked my friend if he knew where they were. He replied that I was a Muslim now, and so he put all my gods in the closet. I told him that I went for a visit, but that I am not Muslim. He said, "You're better off as a Muslim. I didn't want to tell you but I didn't like seeing all those idols in your house." A year later, my friend became a Muslim. I became a Muslim two months later. I am still a Muslim eight years later.

The Quran And My Decision

Raheel Rojas

In the Name of Allah, the Most Gracious, the Most Merciful

What made me become a Muslim was reading the Quran from cover to cover. Up until that point, I read secondary information about Islam and could not bring myself to read the Quran. But this was my chance. I read the opening surah (chapter). It sounded true and almost "Our Father" like. Then on to the next surah 'The Cow', "This is a book in which there is no doubt a guidance for those who fear Allah." What? How can a book say that? What kind of a book is this? Allahu Akbar. Only God can say this, if not God then a really, really arrogant person.

I continued to read about Moses and the punishment of liars and those who reject faith. The concepts hit me one after the other. Bang! I had to stop and think. Bang! I had to stop and think again. By the middle of it, I thought to myself, "What kind of a book is this?" I looked at the cover as if I would find the answer. I continued to read and realized that it was a book befitting of God's authorship.

Yes, what made me convert was how God presented Himself in the Quran. The Quran described God in a way that my heart knew to be true. This was the God I was looking for. This was the God my heart always knew but was never confirmed by my Christianity. In a nutshell, I took it as, "I am your God, and there is no other god besides Me. I have no partners and everything else besides Me is created by Me, therefore, I am the only one worthy of worship. Accept this message, and you will be successful and I will make smooth the path to paradise. Reject this message and I will make smooth the path to hellfire. It's all up to you; it makes no difference to Me but an eternal difference to you."

The Quran made me choose Islam. Allah guides whom He wills. I figured by the middle of the Quran I was ready to become a Muslim but I kept on reading. My conviction was further cemented with every page I read. After reading Surah 'Mankind', the last Surah, I was done. The next day I felt like I was floating on air. The world looked different to me. This book changed me.

When I started giving dawah to my family, I was astonished to learn how many of them already read the Quran. After seven years all my 30+ close family members are still Christian. It saddens me and at the same time increases my faith. It saddens me because my family might be destined to the hellfire. It increases my 'iman' (faith) and gratitude to Allah because out of all my family members He allowed me to be Muslim.

I think about how unremarkable I was compared to my family. How mean, rude, cruel, lazy and racist I was before Islam. But Allah allowed me to be Muslim. I used to wonder why He picked me. The only thing I could think of was how much I used to ponder over my own religion as a young child through my teenage years. There was one prayer I made often growing up. "Oh God, if you make yourself clear to me I will follow you."

I did not have a person teach me about Islam except that Jesus was a messenger and not God or the literal son of God. Before I read the Quran, I told myself that if there was anything that went contrary to what I felt in my heart was true I would not accept Islam. The Quran came and I knew that my prayer was fulfilled. I could not bring myself to reject it. There is nothing in this world that could sway me from la ilaha illallah. Snow is cold, water is wet, red is red, fire is hot, and there is no god but God. Allahu Akbar. God is great.

The True Guidance

Ramon Mejia

"He who leaves his home in order to seek knowledge, he is in Allah's path until he returns [to his home]." The Prophet Muhammad stated this. In due course with the teachings of the Prophet and the Holy Quran, I came to the University of Texas at Austin to seek knowledge in order not only to improve my knowledge of Islam but others through my life experiences. Although I converted to Islam in 2008, I have traveled a long winding path that has led me to where I am today. One can separate my life experiences before Islam and after Islam.

My father comes from El Platanal, Michoacán. El Platanal is a small village located in a southwestern state of Mexico. My mother comes from the small town of Pawnee, Texas. Both of my parents were raised in impoverished conditions and had to work in agriculture from a young age. My mother spent her youth picking cotton, strawberries, and other vegetables. My father spent his picking corn. My father would later immigrate to the United States in search of a better life. They then married. I have an older sister and a younger brother.

Growing up in both the United States and Mexico has exposed me to completely polar economical environments. I would transition from living conditions here in the U.S. where I had the ability to turn on a faucet and fill a glass of water to having to fill up buckets of water every two days due to the constant water shortages. My parents would collect clothes they bought here in the U.S. and would give them to my less fortunate family members in Mexico. When I was not in school, my parents would send me to Mexico. From the age of seven years old to my teenage years, I would help my cousins with the corn harvest and tend to other work that had to be done. Reflecting back now I see the lesson that I should have learned from it. This taught me an appreciation for what one has, as well as the compassion and ability to understand any difficulties or shortcomings that one might experience throughout their life.

Living in the neighborhood of Oak Cliff in Dallas, Texas has at times led me astray. Early on, I became self-aware of what kind of environment and people that surrounded me. I was surrounded by many bad friends and headed down the wrong path. We never worried about the next day or the consequences that would come from the decisions we made. Some friends were gang members and drug dealers. Some of my friends were murdered for their involvement in illegal activity. I myself was sent to juvenile detention and later sent to an alternative disciplinary school in 8th grade. I was fortunate enough to have been accepted to Townview Law Magnet. I think they liked the idea of an undisciplined youth wanting to change his life around. School has never been my strong suit. No matter how hard I worked, school has always been challenging. I graduated in May 2001, and I ranked 67th in a graduating class of 67 students.

My life could have been very different if my girlfriend at the time, now my wife, would not have become pregnant with our daughter Aryel. Getting married and having my daughter in my senior year of high school were two instrumental reasons for me enlisting into the U.S. Marines Corps in July 2001. I knew I had to be the one to support my family. In the Marine Corps, I learned about self-discipline, honor, responsibility, but most of all it introduced me to Islam. I first learned about Islam during recruit training at the Marine Corps Recruit Depot (MCRD) San Diego after the attacks of September 11. My first impression of Islam was not a religion of love and respect, but one of hate. During my deployment of Operation Iraqi Freedom in 2003 as part of the invading force, war exposed me to what life and death truly mean and signify. Although I had made inaccurate assumptions of Islam and the followers of this religion, in the beginning, it was not until I first heard the call to prayer (athan) on an early morning near Baghdad that my opinion about Islam would change. It went from one of hate to one of curiosity. A feeling overtook me that I will never entirely be able to explain.

The athan spoke not to my physical self, nor to my intellect, but to my heart. It was saying specifically to me, Ramon Mejia in Baghdad, Iraq, "Find out what this is, and what these words signify." Shortly after returning from Iraq, I suffered from unknown seizures and received an honorable discharge in November 2004. Until this day, I am required to take prescribed medication for seizures. Between 2004 and 2008 is a blur and a part of my life I am not proud of. I suffered from depression and addiction, which nearly cost me my family and my life.

Through it all, my wife stood by me and pulled me out of a downward spiral. In order to extract me from the environment and to support our family, she enlisted in the U.S. Air Force. As a medical technician, she has served two tours in Afghanistan. I made my shahadah on August 29, 2008. Later the same year my son, Ibrahim, was born. I chose the name Ibrahim for him, precisely because it is the name of Prophet Ibrahim (AS) and the name means "father of many." I make dua (supplication) hoping that insha'Allah, Ibrahim will be the first-born Muslim in my family that will stay a Muslim throughout his life and give rise to future generations of Muslims.

I looked at other religions in search of a connection with my spirituality in different ways, but Islam is the only faith that has ever and will ever make the greatest impact on my life. Islam has given me the correct definition of enlightenment and the ability to attain peace within myself. It is this knowledge that I continue to seek in every aspect of my life. Too much manipulation by people unwilling to learn for themselves what Islam indeed teaches is what brought me to the University of Texas at Austin. The ambition of instructing others has always been my quest. My goal as an academic is to become an educator and to teach people about the diversity of Islam, as well as other world religions. My thesis on Latino Muslims hopes to show another side of Islam that people so rarely learn about in the media. I hope that this is only the beginning for me. On my father's side, I will be the second with exception of my younger brother to have graduated from a university. I will insha'Allah continue my studies and return one day to the University of Texas at Austin to teach Islamic Studies.

All I have to show for myself is my experiences and my ambition. I was once asked what I loved about Islam and what I disagreed with in Islam. I responded with, "I LOVE everything about Islam, and disagree with NOTHING. Islam is the truth. It is perfect as ALLAH (SWT) has made it that way. Islam is the truth." Islam is the truth. Attaining, living, and dying in a state of Islam are my goals. I am a Muslim; I am a Mexican. It is my goal and I will insha'Allah one day educate others on its history and beauty, not as a religion and culture, but as this way of life. Insha'Allah one day I hope to travel to Mexico when I am better educated and have the ability and opportunity to do dawah to my fellow countrymen and assist others as well in knowing about Islam. Insha'Allah, todos puedemos estar en Jannah juntos. (God-willing, we will all be in Paradise together).

I make dua every day that my family and friends will look towards their spirituality in order to better understand their lives. We should not worry about worldly possessions since we are here temporarily in this life. We cannot take any of it with us. We only carry with us our good deeds and our bad deeds. We should worry and strive only in earning mercy from Allah (SWT). Only the mercy of Allah (SWT) will allow us to enter into Paradise.

A Newyorican Odyssey

Ramon Ocasio

My story begins on a Sunday night in June 1953. There, at St. Francis Hospital in the South Bronx, I was born Ramón Francisco Ocasio to newly-arrived Puerto Rican parents. They had come for the grand American adventure, to the city of Nueva York, the land of milk and honey, where the streets were paved with gold. But they had to settle for the fifth floor of an old tenement on 110th Street and Madison Avenue in the isle of Manhattan's Spanish Harlem.

The fabled ghetto, known to the locals affectionately as El Barrio, was at the time the cultural and spiritual heart of the Puerto Rican community in New York as well as the country. Boricuas slowly but inexorably were making their way from Fifth Avenue to the East River displacing and often fighting its former residents, the Italians, for every block. West Side Story was in those days as much a documentary as it was a musical.

My parents were Roman Catholic, as were most of those of the Boricua diaspora. But Espiritismo, the remnant of ancient African religions intermingled with Catholicism, was strong in my household. Our back room was a kind of altar replete with all the trappings of the African cult: velas, religious candles for various saints, busts of the black Siete Potencias, El Indio, and el Buddha pipón, dried out apples, corn, and palm leaves. This contrasted with the traditional religious training I was receiving from the Irish Christian Brothers at Commander Shea, St. Cecilia's annex on 111th Street. There pagan African traditions were denounced by my Catholic school teachers and orthodox Roman Catholic, teaching was put forward as a bulwark against encroaching heathenism.

I was comfortable with this orthodoxy, however. Confessions were heard every Thursday by visiting priests in preparation for Friday and Sunday masses. Sunday mass was absolutely obligatory with attendance being taken and summary beatings administered the next day if satisfactory excuses were not given. I found the annual street processions, novenas, Stations of the Cross, and deeply sentimental religious holiday celebrations warmly comforting. By the time I was in the sixth grade, I was contemplating the priesthood, eventually becoming an altar boy who would wake up on cold winter mornings to serve St. Cecilia's six o'clock mass to a surprisingly substantial crowd of devotees.

When I was about 12, I had a noteworthy experience. I was due to receive the sacrament of Confirmation on a Sunday and for some reason, I was not in attendance the previous Thursday at the chapel to make confession. We couldn't receive the sacrament unless we were free of sin so I would have to make a Saturday trip to St. Cecilia's, the parish church, to have my confession heard.

But I arrived too late, the priests had all gone home, and now I was in a pickle. I reasoned, however, that since God is all-knowing and ever-present that I would appeal to him directly to forgive my sins. I prayed to Him directly as it never occurred to me due to my Catholic religious training to direct any requests to Jesus or the Holy Ghost. The next day I was confirmed as a Christian soldier and received the toughening ceremonial slap with no misgivings about my direct appeal to God. Years later, I would reflect on the significance of that day.

My high school years were filled with challenging religious debate as this was the 60's and even our Religion teachers at my Catholic high school were questioning long-held ideas. I was having spirited discussions, also, with that half of my family that was Pentecostal, whom I viewed at the time to be anti-intellectual and close-minded. This was all going to change radically as I transitioned from high school to college.

In 1969, I met a young 14-year old named Mark Ortiz wearing a purple beret and spouting a barrage of socio-politico-economic aphorisms which left me dizzy. He was, as far as I could tell, the youngest member of a new force in El Barrio that would forever change it: the Young Lords Party.

Formerly a gang out of Chicago, it had adopted Marx-Leninist-Maoist political ideology and a tactic of community service which resembled in many ways the Black Panther Party. And the bewildering aphorisms my new young friend had spouted were beginning to make sense. In 1970, by the time I was 17, the former altar boy and priesthood aspirant was selling Palantes, its bilingual newspaper. I was now advocating socialist revolution, an end to capitalist imperialism, freedom for Puerto Rico, and the abolishment of that great opiate of the masses: religion.

Everything pointed to the fact that something radical had to be done. My beloved El Barrio had turned into a hell-hole of drugs and violence. Typically to get to the front door of my fifth-floor apartment meant stepping over a number of stoned, sometimes vomit-covered junkies who used my floor as a shooting gallery. Blood was smeared all over the walls and the floor was littered with discarded "duji" or heroin bags. The floors hadn't been swept or mopped in years. My apartment building had long been abandoned by the landlord and taken over by the City. We would see entire winters with no heat and hot water and a series of ceiling collapses injured both my mother and brother. And so much violent death surrounded us that we became eerily detached to its horror.

So a radical revolution seemed to be the solution along with its atheistic socio-political rhetoric. This was further reinforced by my college social science courses, SS10 and 11, which I call ATHEISM 101, i.e., religion is just mankind's way of explaining the natural world progressing from primitive animism and nature worship to monotheism with the implication that these mere explanations for natural phenomenon have been superseded by science. Now I was right at home on my soapbox in my neighborhood preaching atheism, helping tenants carry out rent strikes, taking the night watch at university building take-overs, marching by torch-light behind a hapless effigy, or demonstrating at the UN.

However, I started to feel something was not quite right. It was not with the revolution but the revolutionaries. With all the ideological training and good intentions, not enough attention was being paid to the development of character. Guys and girls cheating on each other and frequent drug use made me wonder what to expect from this brave new world re-made.

Dissatisfied with the direction of the "movement", I continued my search. It wasn't clear to me yet but I was searching for something. I was searching for answers before I even knew what the questions were. Now, with a friend's encouragement, I was exploring the beliefs of the Nation of Islam. Malcolm X had been dead nearly seven years but the movement he had helped build was still a force in Harlem and had captured the imagination of a great many people. It was based on the belief that the black man was the original man, father of civilization, god of the universe. A broad definition of black encompassed virtually all non-whites though it conferred a special status on those with purer black bloodlines.

I never became a Black Muslim (NOI) but I wound up joining a group that took their beliefs to their logical conclusion. The Five Percenters is a breakaway group started by a dissident Black Muslim named Clarence 13X. They teach that if the original man, the Black

Man, is God then all black men collectively is God personified. They believe that submitting to one Supreme Being as Muslims do is an absurdity. Thus, I became one who thought that there was nothing in the universe greater than oneself and that he was responsible for all. Eventually, I came to believe this was the ultimate in arrogance, the apex of delusion, the consummate atheist deluxe.

The news came to us that Mark Ortiz, that then young 14-year old who first opened my eyes to political struggle as a Young Lord, had become a Muslim. My friend John and I were furious and went promptly to his house and spent what must have seemed like hours deriding him for becoming a Muslim and telling him how stupid he was for doing so. John was especially furious. He once stood in front of him while he was prostrating in prayer and said to him, "You're praying to me!"

We hurled abuse at him non-stop for being such a jerk, but he merely smiled and looked totally unfazed. Nothing we could say or do shook him in the slightest way from his faith in Allah. To us, he was the biggest "sangano" in El Barrio. But our fury was met with a calm serenity that only true faith could bring about. It was something we had never seen before and it foreshadowed things to come.

One day, at a gathering at Pueblo, the Latino club at Fordham College at Lincoln Center, I was engaged in a spirited discussion with one Federico Lora. Federico was one of the mainstays of a progressive group called El Comite. He was intelligent and well-regarded. In one of the seminal blunders of my entire life, I tried to explain to him a tenet of Black Muslim belief; how white people were created out of test tube by a black scientist by the name of Yaqub on the island of Patmos in the Aegean Sea. He laughed in my face.

I had no retort. I realized how ridiculous I was sounding. I felt awkward, rudderless. My belief in the most bizarre of cosmologies had brought me to the emptiest of feelings. And the rationalization that I was the pinnacle of creation, a god of the universe, brought no solace or comfort. What do you do for an encore once you have been deified?

I had hit rock bottom.

Not long after, I attended a Kwanzaa celebration. Amid the gaiety of traditional food, dance, and song, I was oddly detached. I turned and looked up at a paper plate stuck to the wall with the words written in a semi-circle around it "You are what you eat, physically, materially, and spiritually." Spiritually. I remained fixated on that word. I hadn't contemplated anything remotely spiritual in years. I had been an avowed dialectical materialist now converted to the most atheistic religion on the planet. Cynicism and skepticism about anything remotely spiritual or esoteric was embedded in my personality. But it didn't feel quite right to be a dispassionate, unfeeling automaton. Cold logic seemed just that: cold.

The turning point came one day when I attended an event which featured a recently released Puerto Rican political prisoner. After the event, a man walked up who seemed familiar. I then remembered him from two previous occasions. His name was Abdullahi, a Boricua Muslim from the East River projects. Almost two years earlier, he tried to explain to me his religious philosophy so bizarrely that I thought he was advocating tree worship. The other occasion was entirely different. He stepped up to the microphone at a Young Lords rally at the Hunts Point palace in the Bronx and gave a stirring speech about the importance of social conscience.

Now this enigmatic man began to speak to me about a fascinating new way of looking at the world, a novel belief, and a new way of life he called Islam. This was not the custom-made, distortion of Islam espoused by the Black Muslims but something unique and intriguing. His words touched me in a way that is difficult to explain. His words were filling that gaping spiritual void in my heart and I was drawn to his message.

But I was still cautious. I was intrigued by his invitation to explore Islam but I was emphatic that I was not interested in anything "spooky." By that, I meant any fanciful, illogical religious hocus-pocus. I was still in many ways the skeptical materialist, on guard against anything mystical or irrational. If I was going to accept any new belief, it would have to be based on logic and reason. I didn't want to be hoodwinked again.

Abdullahi suggested my search for Islam start at the main 42nd Street branch of the public library, one of the most extensive reference libraries in the world. My trips to the library were fascinating. These were the pre-computer days of card catalogs and the Dewey Decimal System. Books had to be looked up in the card catalog and requests were written down and handed to the attendant who would then procure your books. The brother had apprised me of the fact that the truth of Islam was being carefully hidden from the general population, so the attendants at the reference section of the Oriental department would not be too cooperative in obtaining our requests. Just as he predicted, we only received about half to two–thirds of our requests. This intrigued me and

I wanted to know more about what I perceived was being deliberately kept from me.

I began to attend the mosque on a regular basis, even started to take Arabic classes. I spent almost all my spare time with Abdullahi and his Cuban companion Khalil (Carlito). One Friday evening, I attended a lecture at Ya Sin mosque in Brooklyn with my lifelong friend Johnny who had been with me during my days running the streets, my Marxist politicization, and pseudo-deification. At the end of the lecture, we were invited to accept Islam. There was a not so subtle "threat" that there were no guarantees in life or that we would even make it to the subway station, so we should consider becoming Muslims to safeguard our hereafter. One of our companions who brought us urged us not to bow to any pressure to accept Islam and to only do it when we were good and ready.

Later on that evening, it hit me in of all places, a grocery store, that there was no reason left for me not to become a Muslim. The comprehensiveness of the message had sealed it for me. My spiritual and religious questions were answered in the Unity of the Divine Being, Allah, and a coherent history of prophetic continuity, ending with the Prophet Muhammad, which showed clearly where both Judaism and Christianity, in fact, all previous religions, went astray and why Islam was the culmination of revelation. Islam also allayed my fears that it would create a withdrawn, anesthetized society unresponsive to the challenges and inequities of life. It was a comprehensive system that had answers for every field of life be it social, political, economic, juridical, or familial. It aspired to create a rational society based on faith in the One and devoted to justice and the common good. The altar boy and the revolutionary were now reconciled. It was time to evolve.

John and I resolved that the next day we would take the shahadah and become Muslims. The rest of that night I was restless. That whole night I practiced making the prayer and studying the little Arabic I had learned. The next day, March 10, 1973, John and I took our shahadahs and became Muslims at the 125th Street mosque, which we affectionately called 303. It is the place where Malcolm X prayed his last Asr salat before meeting his fate at the Audubon Ballroom.

My parents were very accepting of my conversion. Considering how things were in El Barrio at the time, they seemed relieved that I was not going to wind up a junkie or "un bandido." But one day, I can't remember how it started, my father and I got into heated words in my living room. I grabbed the bust of El Indio, a fixture for decades in our back room Espiritista altar and threatened to smash it against the floor. I asked my father if he really believed that if I had done so then a thunderbolt would come through the window and strike me down. I turned it over and showed him the Hong Kong manufacturing label. I told him that bust itself was a manufactured thing with absolutely no power. He merely said to me that he didn't deride my religion and that I had no right to ridicule his. That ended that argument.

Some time later we were moving to a new apartment and I showed him the idols that were now confined to a bureau drawer. "Pop, what do you want me to do with these?" I asked. He simply replied, " Dejalos." And with that, no idols were ever seen in our house again.

In time both my parents were to accept Islam, my brother as well as my father who was dying of cancer. My ex-girlfriend from college accepted Islam and we were married less than two months before our Fordham graduation. Three months later her sister took shahadah on the day I left to Washington, DC to join the Islamic Party and continue a struggle I had started long ago. But now I was armed with a powerful ideology based on truth and the guidance of the Supreme Being.

Several years after my return from Washington, my old friend John (Juan), now known as Yahya, and I fulfilled a dream we had of starting a Latino Muslim organization. Alianza Islamica in its heyday was the premier Latino Muslim organization on the East Coast and quite possibly the country. Though it is today a memory, it is one that is still fondly remembered. Now there are a lot more Latino Muslims than there were in the early days and they are more diverse. In those early days, there were so few of us and being Latino from New York was virtually synonymous with being a Newyorican. My hope, insha'Allah, is that succeeding generations surpass us in every way and that Islam among Latinos grows and develops its own unique presence.

Today, I am also known as Umar Abdur Rahim Ocasio. I have been blessed with eleven observant Muslim children, seven sons and four daughters, and grandchildren, alhamdulillah. A fine legacy and a blessing. But I feel humbled when I reflect that it all began on a Sunday night in the South Bronx, nurtured on the fifth floor of a tenement at 1648 Madison Avenue on 110th Street, with an insignificant, undeserving, nearsighted, brown-skinned, buck-toothed Boricua.

All praise is due to Allah, Lord of all the Worlds.

In A Word

Ricardo L. Pena

I was born and raised in Chicago to immigrant parents from Puerto Rico and Mexico, my mother being from Puerto Rico and my father from Mexico. I was raised as a Catholic and grew up on the city's northwest side. Up until I was about ten years old, my parents weren't very "into" religion, though they believed firmly in God and Jesus in their hearts. After that, my parents became increasingly interested in weaving God into our lives but by the time I was thirteen years old, I had grown old enough to question many things and old enough to resist.

My mother always encouraged me to pray throughout my teenage years but I didn't understand the point in doing so. I always thought that if God observed my ways and He was just, He would know that I've always been a pretty good guy and should, therefore, judge me favorably in the hereafter. I had always believed there was a God, heaven, hell, etc. and I believed Jesus existed and was the Son of God. But the buck stopped there. I felt there was no need to go beyond my faith and in general, my actions. If I believed these things in my heart and I tried my best to be a good person, I believed that I was on solid ground.

Throughout my high school years, I didn't think about religion much at all. My mind was always on other things. Having fun, meeting girls, skateboarding, and wrestling to name a few. I had pretty much the same attitude toward education that I had toward religion. I was a commercial art and design major at Lane Tech High School and planned to be a commercial artist for my future career. Why in the world would I have to learn the intricacies of English grammar? I didn't need to know what a prepositional phrase was in order to wave a brush on the canvas. Such was my reasoning. I was indeed young and ignorant.

Getting to school was a daily battle until I'd gotten my driver's license and actually had a car to drive. Till then, I took three buses over the course of 45 minutes every morning to get to school. In Chicago, the winters made it extremely horrible to have to do this every day. That's not to mention the three buses to get back. Every morning I'd go to the neighborhood quick mart to buy a drink (usually Gatorade), a pack of gum, change for the bus and the Chicago Sun-Times newspaper. I always read the Sun-Times starting from the back, which is the sports section. After catching up on all the sports, I'd continue reading toward the front of the paper looking for catchy headlines. Things like, "Plans to Build Mile High Skyscraper" caught my eye and I'd read the article with interest. I read the article first for the purpose of killing time and second because it was interesting. If it weren't for the former reason, I'd never have the latter reason. And so I read many things over the many bus rides over the many years. This was my custom but unbeknownst to me, this practice would bring about an interesting trend.

Around the end of my senior year and soon after high school, I began to notice that I was able to engage in a wide variety of conversations having to do with a wide range of subjects. I was able to contribute interesting tidbits of information that raised eyebrows or captured peoples' attention. I was able to do this because I had read so many articles in the newspaper that I knew a thing or two about a thing or two. I began to notice that people started to treat me differently. I was treated with a little more respect. People asked for my opinion on matters important to them and they showed that they sincerely considered what I thought. I had also begun to notice that girls were more sociable with me and took a greater interest in me. I had absolutely no idea this would come about through the simple practice of reading the newspaper every morning.

This trend occurred over a number of months when one day, I had a revelation. I realized that I benefited directly from knowledge that I had no idea I would use in the future. This was knowledge I had acquired to satisfy a short-term need, which was to kill time. How many things are out there that I did not know that I could benefit from? How much valuable knowledge was I missing out on? I don't think I spent more than five minutes contemplating this revelation before I realized the magnitude of what had just come to me. I understood more than ever, now, that knowledge is truly powerful and the more of it I had, the more of it I could use to my advantage.

I was about nineteen years old when this revelation hit me and as quickly as I had been excited I had plunged into sadness. I had wasted away my high school years thinking I was never going to benefit from most of the things I was being taught and so I chose to just do enough to get by and in reality, not even that. It was then that I decided to set forth and learn as much as I could about anything and explore ways to exploit that knowledge for my benefit.

I had become the proverbial "nerd." My friends were astounded when I'd show up to parties with a book, then sit in a corner and read it instead of playing cards or pounding beers. I had entered a new era of my life. Even as I write this story I'm in awe of God's power and mercy when I recall these times because it was around the age of eighteen-years-old, approaching my nineteenth birthday that I had begun my quest for God and He answered by granting me the attitude I needed about knowledge so that I would seek my answers with a vengeance. I think that if I had never come to love knowledge the way I do now as a result of this change of attitude, I may not have held the interest long enough to do what I had to do in order to find my answers. But God knows best.

Around the age of eighteen, I had begun to really question whether or not religion was right for me. I didn't explicitly call Catholicism into question; I called all religions in general into question. Were they just fabled stories of old? Ancient lore remaining from centuries of the past? If not, which religion was right? Are any of them wrong? What about science? What if God wanted me to practice a particular religion? That was the question of all questions for me. I was overcome with fear for a long time. This concern, that I may end up in the hellfire for eternity, combined with the eagerness to learn, fueled my passion to press forward in my quest for God and being quite the rookie, I was forced to start from scratch.

In short order, I began to read information about all kinds of religions. I learned about Buddhism, Hinduism, Judaism, the reasons why there are different branches of Christian religions, etc. The interesting thing was that I never took the time to learn about Islam and Muslims. It just did not occur to me to do so at the time. Little by little I began to narrow things down. I began to dismiss the possibility of adopting religions as my own when I came across things that didn't make sense to me. For example, I personally didn't like the raising of cows to a sacred level as in Hinduism. I don't mean to trivialize this belief or even to simplify the meaning behind it. I cannot give an exhaustive analysis into this Hindu belief and I'm not qualified to do so anyway but suffice it to say that I was not comfortable with it and it was things like that that made me say, "Okay, Hinduism is good and all, but it's simply not for me."

I had also begun to actually read the Bible. It's kind of funny to say "actually" since I was a Catholic but the reality is that most Catholics simply do not read the Bible. It isn't stressed that someone should do so by the church and in many cases, it is discouraged because one could be "led astray" if they don't understand what they're reading. Nevertheless, I read the Bible starting with the New Testament. I was captivated by the beauty of Jesus' teachings (peace be upon him). It really touched me to the core of my inner being and I had experienced a spiritual uplifting. I went on to read the Old Testament but I hadn't gotten halfway through before I felt most comfortable with the Bible and Catholicism than any of the other religions I had ever learned of.

I also began to read books that analyzed the Bible to supplement my learning and I took an extremely deep interest in prophetic revelation. It was the fact that many prophecies came to pass that was the clincher for me. I believed that the Bible was the actual Word of God based on the reasoning that only God could have let the prophets know what was going to happen in the future. I had also recalled from one of the many articles I'd read in the past (in some magazine actually) that a study of psychic people showed that they all had something in common. They all had a premonition in varying degrees of vividness and certainty of an apocalyptic end of the world. At the time I reasoned that the Bible must undoubtedly be the truth. It taught many good values, it was validated in my mind through the miraculous prophecies it contained and in general, it made sense to me. I also felt that all religions are basically different paths to God and we are free to choose one of those paths. God would then judge us based on how we did in our respective paths. It was then that I decided that I didn't have to explore any other religion and I chose to remain a Catholic and to try to practice being a better Catholic.

Over the next two years, I had become devout. I went to church every week and had grown accustomed to praying no less than a full Hail Mary every night. I was very much at ease with my decision and very much into my religion. I loved Jesus and considered him to be the true Son of God. I felt that my search had been concluded and I moved on to other things. There were other issues going on in my life and I had other passions that I enjoyed reading about, but God had other things in store for me.

In high school, I had a friend that lived right across the alley from me and we used to go to school together. He's Columbian/Mexican and had been a Muslim for a number of years. I didn't really know he was Muslim until well after high school when I was about twenty years old. One day, we had gotten together and we were talking. I was intrigued by the fact that he was a Muslim and wondered how he couldn't be a Catholic or Protestant. How could he not love Jesus? I almost felt sorry for him. I thought he was missing out on what I had found and I assumed that he didn't look as deeply into it as I had. Then he explained the most basic thing to me that I'll never forget and this little explanation marked a turning point that changed the rest of my life.

He explained that there are these three religions - Judaism, Christianity, and Islam. He went on to explain that from the teachings of Moses (peace be upon him) came the Jewish faith, from the teachings of Jesus (peace be upon him) came Christianity and from the teachings of Muhammad (peace be upon him) came Islam. Then he went on to explain that Muhammad is the last and final Prophet after Jesus. He said that Muslims believe in all the Prophets from Adam to Noah to Abraham to Moses to Jesus to the last Prophet Muhammad and all the Prophets in between (peace be upon them all). He explained that Muslims believe in the angels including the Angel Gabriel and the Angel Michael, that Muslims believe in Heaven and Hell and of most paramount importance, that Muslims believe that there is only One God.

That conversation entailed a whole lot of questions and answers to be sure, but that little explanation above is what really blew me away. If he had only told me that little bit of information and absolutely nothing, I mean absolutely nothing else, it would have been enough to send me back on my journey to learn about one more religion - Islam.

I had no idea that Islam was related in any way to the Biblical religions, namely Judaism and Christianity. I had always assumed that Muhammad was some Arab dude in the desert that invented his own religion based on whatever influences the Arab culture had during his time. I thought Allah was the name of "their" god and that's about it. I had always thought that Islam sprung out of the desert very much like Buddhism did in Asia. Buddhism had a founder that based his teachings on things that had absolutely no direct connection with the Biblical religions. I had always thought that Muhammad (peace be upon him) was kind of like the "Buddha" of Arabia.

This was a profound discovery to me. I wondered why this wasn't more commonly known. There are so many people who have no idea that this connection exists. I felt compelled to learn about Islam because I had to judge whether or not there is any valuable information in Islam that could benefit me. How different is Islam to Christianity and why is it different? Are they so different that they cannot co-exist as two legitimate paths to God? Is one right and the other wrong? Does Islam contain any prophecy that came to pass? Does Islam contain prophecy that has not yet come to pass? Fear and uncertainty struck and I was back on my quest once again.

Going into this extended journey, I felt very threatened and insecure but I kept an open mind and an open heart. Still, I loved Jesus, I loved

Christianity, and I was determined to defend my belief to the end. I asked many questions and read anything about Islam, even encyclopedias. I read books on comparative religion. Then I finally bought and read a paperback copy of the Quran, an English translation by Yusuf Ali. I must have read that book in seven days flat but I don't remember exactly. I just remember learning that Muslims believed that Jesus was not the Son of God, that he was a revered Prophet of God and that he would testify as such on the Judgment Day. I wanted for the Bible to prevail more than anything and I begged God for guidance. I prayed sincerely every night for months as I studied more and more. I asked for signs and I asked to be given clear understanding. I asked God to show me the truth.

The more I asked for guidance, hoping, that my prayers would be granted in favor of the Bible, the more direction I received to the contrary and it came to me repeatedly. The Quran, a marvelous book, was so much easier to understand. Its authenticity is proven while the Bible's originating manuscripts do not exist and are forever cast in a shroud of doubt. The Bible is riddled with contradictions, errors and questionable content. As time wore on, the difficulties with my own religion were too much for me to bear. I couldn't help but feel the insecurity of a child lost in a crowd, or an island in the eye of a storm, or a tree at the edge of a brushfire, or a man in a world of temptation threatening to cast him into eternal oblivion. My soul felt heavy, a burden heaped upon me in ways intangible, taxing the night and day where the wages of sleep and peace of mind were the prices I paid. As broad as Islam is in its teachings, so were the reasons for my accepting it as truth. But there was a particular beacon of light and guidance that brought my heart and mind a reconciliation of thought and emotion. A light that made Islam shine like the dawn of a new day.

Tawheed. It is an Arabic term that means the "Oneness of God." That there is only One God. There are no other gods beside God. That there is nothing comparable to God. That He has no beginning. He has no end. He is a single entity. He is not made up of "parts." He is a whole. He is The Originator of all that is. He is indefinable and anything that the five senses can perceive, that He is not. If you can feel it, that He is not. If you can taste it, that He is not. If you can smell it, that He is not. If you can hear it, that He is not. If you can see it, that He is not. If you can conjure it up in the most sensational of the artifacts of the mind...that He is not...no.

But yes. He is many things that are vivid nonetheless. He is The Creator. He is The All-Knowing. He is The Forgiver. He is The Compeller. He is The Opener. He is The Provider. He is The Light. He is The Guide. He is The Creator of Death and The Giver of Life. He is The Restorer and The Sustainer. He is The Bestower and Originator. He is The Guardian of Faith and The Source of Peace. He is The Loving. He is The Aware. He is The Most High and He is The Most Merciful. He is The Truth and He is The Wise. He is seventy-seven more names the likes of which none other than He is even remotely worthy of, and He is the Lord of the Prophet Muhammad, may the peace and blessings of God be upon him, who was sent to us to deliver this message.

It is a message so simple, so comforting - la ilaha il-Allah (there is no god but God). It can satisfy the erudite and make a wise man out of a simpleton. It is a concept that nourishes the mind, calms the heart, and feeds the soul and it doesn't matter who you are. You shouldn't have to be a scholar to understand your religion. Your relationship between you and God has no checkpoint in between. Until then I had never really noticed that although I always believed that Jesus was the Son of God, I always directed my prayers to "The Father." I was always on the right track, I just needed a little help to get there...and I wasn't alone.

My brother Marco was my confidant throughout this journey and we traveled it together. We shared our lives to such an extent that I don't know where his begins and mine ends or mine begins and his ends. One day I said to my brother, after seven months of soul-searching, "Let's go to the mosque." And so we did, by ourselves, nervous as children on the first day of school, not knowing where to go, who to talk to or even what to say if we did. We entered the mosque conferring amongst ourselves wondering whom the "sheikh" or "imam" or whatever you call him is. All of a sudden I heard someone call my name..."Ricky! Oh my God what are you doing here?!" I had not seen Syed Ahmed in almost ten years. I'd forgotten that he even existed for most of those ten years and there he was. "You're not going to believe this but my brother and I are here to convert to Islam. Do you think you can help us out? We don't know where to start." I cannot explain in words how relieved my brother and I were to have him there for us. He talked to the sheikh for us, described the process, and made us feel thoroughly comfortable and served as one of our witnesses as my brother and I declared our belief reciting shahadah and embracing Islam together.

Praise be to Allah! It was a long hard journey as we struggled down a path less trodden, but in the end, Allah was there...waiting for us, giving us strength, giving us courage, opening the door, guiding us through, to a friend whom He sent there and who ushered us in, our hearts at ease, filled with joy, He made it plain, He made it easy, for our submission, to bring us peace, all that, in a word, is...Islam.

Salaams From The Rio Grande Valley

Roberto Solano

I live in Brownsville, Texas. I came as a tourist to the Rio Grande Valley area and never left. For the first three years here, I lived in the southern part of the Rio Grande River in a Mexican city called Matamoros, which is about half a mile from Brownsville. There I met my present wife Ethel, and we have been together ever since. She was born in Mexico in a small tropical town near the Gulf of Mexico. We got married in July 1997. She has been in the USA since 1999 when my daughter Khadijah was born. My wife needed a caesarian so we left Matamoros to have it done in Brownsville. Our second daughter was born the following year. We decided not to have more kids because Khadijah and Aisha are equivalent to ten kids.

When I take the little ones to McDonald's for food and exercise in the play area, some people assume that I'm the grandfather. Probably because they think I am old because I have a gray beard and people can tell I'm not in my fifties anymore. Some even assume Ethel is my daughter because she is skinny and looks much younger than her age. I was a lawyer for about 12 years with a good practice in the New York City/New Jersey area. But now I collect rents and retirement checks, and I fix a pipe or a window once in a while.

I have attended about 300 classrooms in my life. I obtained my high school academic diploma in New York City, my BA at Arizona State University, and my Juris Doctor (JD) at the University of Baltimore. I also took 60 credits of Spanish literature and various sociology/psychology courses at West Virginia University in Morgantown. Yet I can only remember the names of about 10% of the professors and about 1% of the subject matter.

I worked for the Defense Department in Contract Compliance for about five years, four for the Federal Equal Employment Opportunity Commission, two for the Social Security Administration, and one for the Housing and Urban Development (HUD). I've served in the Army during the Vietnam War for about two years. I'm a 'disabled' veteran but still get around and take care of my children.

I am Latino. Both of my parents were born in Puerto Rico. Both were USA citizens at birth as were their parents and grandparents. None genuinely liked or appreciated the gift of citizenship but they were not disloyal. Everyone took my mother to be an Italian or a good-looking

Jewish woman with greenish-blue eyes and jet-black hair. She hardly ever spoke English, and she lived most of her life in the New York/New Jersey metropolitan area. My father, who looked like a Sefardi Jew, was proficient in three languages. He was a direct descendant of the Moriscos of Spain.

Some of you might ask why I became a heretic of the Roman Catholic faith. Why did I pick Islam? Why has my faith gotten stronger after 9-11? All I can say is that it is Allah's will. My birth name is Robert, and my Muslim name is Sulaiman. I do not have a confirmation name from the time I was a Catholic.

I became a Muslim in 1994. I was working at Jones Farm in Trenton, New Jersey and awaiting an appeal for my conviction on contempt of court. The judge had sentenced me to a consecutive sentence of 18 months plus 18 months for two counts of contempt of court. I had been a practicing lawyer in that state for over twelve years. My conviction and length of sentence were under appeal so this is probably one of the reasons that the Department of Corrections sent me to "the farm" to work with milk producing cows instead of sending me "behind the wall" at the New Jersey State Prison. While at the farm, I read the Bible many times. I felt very guilty for my involvement in my criminal activities.

I felt that it was my fault that the judge had put me behind bars. After all, I had jumped bail and went to Mexico for a few years instead of facing him for sentencing. However, I did the same in 1995 before my appeal was decided because I believed that I was going to win. I had to pay for my decision after the 9/11/2001 incident by being rearrested one day in November 2001 when crossing the bridge from Mexico to Texas. Previously, I had been apprehended in 1994 in Brownsville, Texas as I was withdrawing money out of an ATM machine. But everyone is entitled to an appeal, and I had filed mine only to have it denied two years after I was released on parole. The length of my sentence was not reduced, and the conviction was upheld. During this period, I was in prison. I read three or four translations of the New Testament. The smell of the cows did not deter me from this practice. While others played softball or watched TV, I read and read.

From my readings, I became convinced that the Bible had been altered and interpolated. Someone had taken things out. It was clear. And, someone had added entire sentences. It was clear as night and day even in translations. It became evident that Jesus (PBUH) was not a god but a Prophet. There had to be an explanation for the interpolations. I did not have a clue and to this day do not know why or by whom or when these changes were made to the Bible. Some weeks later in Surah 112 of the Holy Quran, I found some indication as to who Jesus (PBUH) really was.

It all came about one evening when a young African-American allowed me to read his English explanation of the Quran. But only after I had washed my hands did he let me hold his book. He explained that this was a translation and not the Quran itself, which was written in Arabic. This young man who had been a drug seller and user for years had reverted to Islam and was studying everything he could find about Islam. He wanted to change, and it was evident that he had. I read the Quran. Then, I purchased a Quran in the mail. It was a Spanish translation by Julio Cortes. This Spanish translation of the Quran was published by Tahrike Tarsile Quran of Elmhurst, New York. It was easy to read, and the footnotes were extremely helpful. Long after I took my shahadah in the fall of 1994, and became a Sunni did I learn that it was a Shia translation (Julio Cortes) that brought me to the truth and Islam.

I was released on parole pending the outcome of the appeal for ten months in 1995 after being flown from Texas to New Jersey. They did me a favor by putting me in jail because those months were a blessing in disguise. All the heavy work, heavy reading, and heavy praying (Salat - five times a day) made a permanent impact on my life. My first Ramadan as a Muslim was spent in part at a NJ Hospital where I was working with other inmates when I got transferred out of the Jones Farm to Garden State Prison.

My parents had been religious people. So, religion was not new to me. One of my brothers, who is ten years older than me, had converted to the Seventh-day Adventist Church when I was around six years old in Puerto Rico. I remember my mother cooking one dish for the family and one for my brother Juan because he refused to eat food prepared with pork lard. Seventh-day Adventists, like Jews, follow the Old Testament law. They are Christians in that they believe in Jesus being the only begotten son of God but in everything else they generally follow the Jewish teachings.

They worship on Saturdays rather than on Sundays like most Christians do. By the time I started the first grade in school, my mother began to go to my brother's church although she did not become a member. And, in no time, she had stopped smoking and threw away all the saints (idols) she had in the house. Furthermore, we all stopped eating pork. She had been a Roman Catholic from birth. We already had learned that we were descendants of Moors from Spain as a result of genealogy studies my father had done with some Mormon missionaries.

Therefore, we knew that we were direct descendants on both sides of the family - not only of Puerto Rican Indians (Tahinos) but also of Muslims from the Iberian Peninsula. It took me little time after reverting to Islam to re-investigate my genealogy and find a historical link between those ancestors of mine. Yes, my ancestors had been among those who were forced to eat pork and kiss the cross in Andalusia after they were forced to stop the practice of Islam after generations of practicing Islam in the Iberian Peninsula. Now, I understood why my relatives look much like those inhabitants of Palestine and southern Spain. Now, I realized why over 20% of all Spanish words have an Arabic origin. I have always said in Spanish "Ojalá" (hopefully/if God wills). I had known these truths years before. Allah knows best.

Submission To God, My Way

Rodrigo Perez

I cannot begin telling about my reversion without first explaining my early childhood before I decided my path in Islam. My family and I are originally from San Salvador, El Salvador. My father decided that the Civil War in El Salvador was too dangerous for his family, so he moved us all to the United States in 1981. My father was an economist for the government of El Salvador and my mother, a housewife. I have four sisters and a brother. The struggles my parents have had occur in order to support their family can provide an inspiring script for Hollywood, but I am content to just relive it in my memories.

Religiously, we were all brought up to believe in the followings of Roman Catholic preaching. Church on Sundays involved dressing up in your best clothes for an hour in the day and trying to stay attentive to the priest's sermon. Religion in my family was more like a cultural practice rather than a religious practice. What I mean is that Latinos are bound by such a historical precedence of indigenous and Spanish influence that we incorporate the attributes of each in our daily lives. Perhaps, I have always wondered if converting to Islam was my indigenous heritage attempting to release me from the oppression of Spanish conquest.

During my sophomore year in college at the University of California Davis and as a young college student, I explored the many new things having my own freedom. When I make this statement I speak for myself, but I have heard from many the same reasoning. In terms of my religious beliefs, I was just content to be a good person and knowing that I believe in God.

In dreams, many of our deep subconscious thoughts are released in sequences of images that in some cases expel our most profound concerns. In the waking mornings or in some frightful instance, we awaken to interpret their meanings. It is difficult to explain the meaning of dreams, let alone explain where they come from with such notions as divine intervention. Although I have had many dreams and attempted to understand the meaning behind them, there is one dream that I could not dispel as a random occurrence.

In my dream sequence, all my belief was converted to a dramatic moment that will evitably occur on the Day of Judgment. The images are still etched in the ripples of my brain. As the image of the end of the world happened, I saw the masses aiming for the clouds in the sky. People were hurrying to see the image that dispels the endless wait of knowing their true savior. I attempt to warn people that they are following the wrong path. God is telling me in his own way to save these people and tell them the truth of whom "He" is… and that is where my dream ends. Although I recognize this experience as only a dream, it was an essential beginning in my personal realization.

In my early discussion of my conversion story, I did not mention that I was familiar with Islam already. I had befriended a Muslim family near my neighborhood. I had been friends with the family for almost seven years. I was introduced to Islam by the parents, but I never honestly felt that this religion was ever going to be part of my life. I did not mention this part of my life for the reason that I wanted to show more of a relevance of my conversion to the divine intervention. That God is always presenting us with apparent indications of His existence. However, meeting the Muhammeds was God's will, but it was not until I was waking in dreams that I understood the meaning of religion and God's path. To this day, I defend Islam and try to help others understand the religion itself regardless of what path they have chosen. But living life without guidance is a path of true oblivion. As a Catholic, I was happy to have learned other religions and learned the scriptures. As a Muslim, I am overwhelmed to be practicing a religion that stands for submitting one's will to God.

The dream had a big effect on the state of my consciousness. It allowed me to think about my state of mind and my affiliation with God. At school, I had previously worked with a Muslim student in a lab and I had asked him if we could talk about Islam in order for me to learn more about it. I decided to give this brother a call and to meet him at the local mosque near campus. I had intentions to only learn about Islam. However, that day I decided to convert and I took shahadah there. Although I did not truly understand my actions, I do not regret them. From that day on, I would call myself Muslim.

Everything I say that is correct is from Allah, and any mistakes are from me.

Welcoming The Change

Samantha Sanchez

Allah Guides Whom He Wills, (I'm so glad He guided me)

As far back as I can remember, I questioned religion. I was brought up Catholic but my parents were non-practicing Greek Orthodox and Lutheran, who attended Catholic Church. At seven years old, I vividly remember having a verbal disagreement with my Catholic school teacher about the Immaculate Conception. It was at the time of my First Communion when the teacher was explaining the concept. She said Jesus was born without a father. Even at seven years old, I was questioning when I didn't understand. Unfortunately, she became irate and said I just have to believe. She referred me to the priest who said if I didn't say I believed I could not make my First Communion. All I wanted was some explanation to make me understand how this could be so. I reluctantly agreed.

When I was thirteen, I began showing curiosity about other religions. But not just as a hobby, instead as a search. A search for the spirituality of my own. Through the following eight years, I would read books about and experiment with all kinds of religions, such as Buddhism, Hinduism, and Wicca. Then there was agnosticism. But agnosticism couldn't last long. Once I reflected on life and breathed in fresh air, I wondered how I ever could have doubted God. So again I set out on my search.

In college, I met again with this same resistance. I was kicked out of a religion class because I questioned how my professor, a religious scholar, felt he could rewrite the Gospel of John in his own interpretation. He told me to get out. I was expected to accept everything the priests and religious teachers said, without question. But I had so many questions.

I began reading a world religions book. I had learned the basics about Islam, but at the time I did not know a single Muslim. Then, one day an acquaintance and I ran into each other on campus. There she was with her head covered, in modest clothing, in the middle of our Jesuit college campus. How? When? Why? I asked myself. I asked and she began to tell me and said she would give me a book about it. We broke for summer and I read that book. We promised to stay in touch. Once I read that book I was hooked. Not hooked on Islam. Hooked on finding out why a Latina chose Islam. I had to know. So I delved into the Quran.

Throughout that summer I surfed the net reading everything possible, talking to Muslims, asking questions. It was then that I was hooked again. Hooked on Islam this time. Every word made sense. Although questions popped up regularly, reading the Quran was like reading the book that my mind was writing all my life. How I felt on social, political, and moral issues. All here in this very book along with the most beautiful poetry I ever read. How could it not appeal to me and how could it not be directly from God? I longed to know more.

Through a variety of sources, the Internet and new friends, I met several Muslims who answered my questions and explained things I didn't understand. Little by little I was changing the way I dressed, ate, etc. And not only did I not really notice or mind, it was all before I had even converted, or accepted Islam as my way of life. That summer I spent most of my time reading the Quran and nearly completed it. I found a new sense of spirituality. I was reborn.

When school began again, I immediately contacted my acquaintance and told her of all the information I had found and my hunger to know more. I was accepted into her study group at the mosque as if I had been there from the very first day. With no pressure, no questions, just love. In this open and comfortable space, I asked the questions I had been longing to understand. I asked, "How can Jesus have been born without a father?" I was directed to read the following in the Quran,

"She said: My Lord! How can I have a child when no mortal hath touched me? He said: So (it will be). Allah createth what He will. If He decreeth a thing, He saith unto it only: Be! and it is…Lo! the likeness of Jesus with Allah is as the likeness of Adam. He created him from dust, then He said unto him: Be! and he is." (Quran 3:47, 59).

Every page I turned led to more discoveries and further affirmations of what my heart already knew. It was then that I was sure; I had found it. I wanted to be Muslim. I *was* Muslim. After trying to console my parents, who at first, understandably had reservations, but later, by the Grace of God understood my choice and wanted me to be happy, I took shahadah. I declared my faith in the presence of my parents and old and new friends. I embraced Islam and it embraced me.

On Becoming Muslim

Shariffa A. Carlo

In the Name of Allah, most Compassionate, most Merciful

The story of how I reverted to al Islam is a story of plans. I made plans, the group I was with made plans, and Allah made plans. And Allah is the Best of Planners. When I was a teenager, I came to the attention of a group of people with a very disturbing agenda. They were and probably are still a loose association of individuals who work in government positions with a plan to destroy Islam. Although not a governmental group, they would just use their jobs in the US government to advance their cause.

One member of this group approached me because he saw that I was articulate, motivated and very much a woman's rights advocate. He told me that if I studied International Relations with an emphasis in the Middle East, he would guarantee me a job at the American Embassy in Egypt. He wanted me to eventually go there to use my position in the country to talk to Muslim women and encourage the fledgling women's rights movement. I thought this was a great idea. I had seen the Muslim women on TV; I knew they were a poor oppressed group, and I wanted to lead them to the light of 20th-century freedom.

With this intention, I went to college and began my education. I studied Quran, hadith and Islamic history. I also explored the ways I could use this information. I learned how to twist the words to say what I wanted them to say. It was a valuable tool. Once I started learning, however, I began to be intrigued by this message. It made sense. That was very scary. Therefore, in order to counteract this effect, I started to take classes in Christianity. I chose to take classes with this one professor on campus because he had a good reputation and had a Ph.D. in Theology from Harvard University. I felt I was in good hands. I was, but not for the reasons I thought. It turns out that this professor was a Unitarian Christian. He did not believe in the Trinity or the divinity of Jesus. In actuality, he believed that Jesus was a prophet.

He proceeded to prove this by taking the Bible from its sources in Greek, Hebrew, and Aramaic and show where they were changed. As he did this, he showed the historical events, which shaped and followed these changes. By the time I finished this class, my religious views had been destroyed, but I was still not ready to accept Islam. As time went on, I continued to study, for myself and for my future career. This took about three years. In this time, I would question Muslims about their beliefs. One of the individuals I asked was a Muslim brother with the Muslim Students Association (MSA). Alhamdulillah, he saw my interest in the deen and made it a personal effort to educate me about Islam. May Allah increase his reward. He would give me dawah at every opportunity that presented itself.

One day, this man contacts me, and he tells me about a group of Muslims who were visiting in town. He wanted me to meet them. I agreed. I went to meet with them after isha (night) prayer. I was led to a room with at least 20 men in it. They all made space for me to sit, and I was placed face to face with an elderly Pakistani gentleman. Mashallah, this brother was a very knowledgeable man in matters of Christianity. He and I discussed and argued the different parts of the Bible and the Quran until the fajr (dawn). At this point, after having listened to this wise man tell me what I already knew, based on the class I had taken in Christianity, he did what no other individual had ever done.

He invited me to become a Muslim. In the three years I had been searching and researching, no one had ever invited me. I had been taught, argued with and even insulted, but never invited. May Allah guide us all. So when he invited me, it clicked. I realized this was the time. I knew it was the truth, and I had to make a decision. Alhamdulillah, Allah opened my heart, and I said, "Yes. I want to be a Muslim." With that, the man led me in the shahadah - in English and in Arabic. I swear by Allah that when I took the shahadah, I felt the strangest sensation. I felt as if a huge, physical weight had just been lifted off my chest. I gasped for breath as if I were breathing for the first time in my life.

Alhamdulillah, Allah had given me a new life - a clean slate - a chance for Jannah (Paradise). I pray that I live the rest of my days and die as a Muslim. Ameen.

The Past- 'Mi Vida Loca.' The Present-'Hispanic Muslim.'

Theresa Vargas

My life was not comfortable. On the day I was born on July 24, 1959, in Detroit, Michigan, I was born into a world of cruelty and abuse. I was raised by an aunt and uncle who adopted me at the age of five years old and abused me physically, verbally, and mentally. At the age of 13, I was already smoking marijuana. One day while skipping school, my friends and I were at a park. I heard a sound coming from a large building that looked like a castle. I asked one of my friends and they explained to me that it was the Call to Prayer for the Muslim community.

To follow up, I asked, "So what do they do—just drop everything just to go and pray?" My friend said, "Yes!" I began to laugh and I said, "Boy I wish I could just drop and stop everything, and tell the teachers at school, 'Well, I'll be back... I've gotta go pray. See ya!'" I sat there for a while and watched everyone go inside this beautiful castle (not knowing what this place was called). After a while, we headed back to school.

Years passed by. At the age of 18 years old, I joined the Marine Corps. I was stationed in Iwakuni, Japan and traveled all over Japan. I went to Osaka, Kyoto, Nara, Hiroshima, Yokosuka, Yokota, and Okinawa. My life in the Marine Corps was crazy. New drugs were introduced into my life along with heavy whiskey drinking, not to mention more physical and mental abuse. I served my tour in the Marine Corps, and I was awarded an Honorable Discharge.

In 1982, I gave birth to a handsome baby boy in Lincoln Hospital in the Bronx, New York City. Three years later, I was divorced. In 1988, I gave birth to a gorgeous baby girl at Reno Nevada General Hospital. A year later, I married my daughter's father and had four more children. My marriage lasted 14 years. It was very abusive both mentally and verbally. We moved to Elko, Nevada from Reno. Then in 1999, we were divorced. My oldest son moved to Miami, Florida where his father lived and began his own life. Because my son moved to Miami, I felt that I also needed a new beginning in my life. I called my uncle in Tacoma, WA, and asked him if my children and I could come by. My uncle said, "Yes."

Meanwhile, I had to ask permission from the court to take my children to Washington. I filled out the proper paperwork and submitted my request. The court said that I was only allowed to take one child. Just the oldest child could go and the others would have to wait until they were 13 years old. The second oldest was not that far from being 13 years old. The twins had three more years to go until they were 13 years old. September 15, 2005, was a very emotional day for me because I was not able to take all of my children with me. Nevertheless, they knew that every summer they were able to visit and spend the summer with me and their sister in Tacoma. I left Elko, NV with my oldest daughter and drove to Tacoma, WA.

Finally, we arrived in Tacoma. My uncle was happy to see us but sad that I could not bring the other children. I found a job immediately and began to work. My daughter started school at Lincoln High School. After a while, I decided to look for a better paying job. A couple of months later I was hired at the Kaiser Plant. This was an excellent paying job. After two months, I was able to find a place of my own to rent. I found a house. My other children were able to come and spend the summer in Tacoma.

As time passed, I began meeting the people who lived around the neighborhood. I met a couple that I thought were nice. I used to go after work and have a couple of beers with them. After that, we began to smoke marijuana and soon enough crack cocaine was introduced to me. I started to smoke this drug and the more I smoked, the more I was hooked. My daughter began hanging out with the wrong crowd. She was skipping school and then she quit altogether. I began meeting more people who smoked this drug and started to hang out with them more. I left my good paying job and began to collect unemployment. The thing is that all my money went to this drug. My unemployment eventually ran out and I had to find a job. I found another job but it did not pay as well. I was barely paying the bills. I was having many parties at my house. Eventually, I ended up being evicted from my home. Everything fell apart—my life, my daughter left me, my son wanted to move back with his father in Elko and he did. Even my job ended.

I was homeless and I was too embarrassed to ask my uncle to move back. Ultimately, I did ask him and my uncle accepted me back. However, I was so ashamed and embarrassed that I later moved out. I moved in with a guy who I was dating. Not surprisingly, four months later we broke up. Now I was homeless again with no place to go and no place to live. I knew a couple that I had asked if I could stay with them. They agreed to let me stay. Later, I found another job and began working. I was later told by the couple that I could not stay with them any longer. They said that they knew of another couple that probably could help me. They introduced me to these new people. The couple accepted me, and I rented the couch I slept on in their living room for $25 a week.

One day, I was at the right place and at the right time. I met a man and we began to talk about several issues. We spoke about many things. On one particular day, we were discussing God. I had mentioned to him that I grew up Catholic. I also mentioned that my adoptive parents had converted to Jehovah's Witnesses but that I did not like the religion at all. I also told him that I had tried being a Christian and that I still was not happy or satisfied. He handed me a book called "Islam: A Brief Guide to Understanding Islam." I took the book home and read it over and over and over. I was amazed at what I was reading. It mentioned how a Muslim man is supposed to treat his wife—with so much respect and honor. I thought to myself, "If I ever found a man who would treat me like this that I would be on Seventh Heaven."

The next day I ran into the man that gave me the book. We sat down at a coffee shop and we began to talk about what I had read in the book. I asked him, "Is this how a Muslim man treats his wife?" He answered, "Yes." He began to explain to me that the name of God in Arabic is Allah. We talked about Jesus being a prophet and not the Son of God, the angels, and about the rest of the prophets. We talked for about two hours. I told him that I wanted to learn more about Islam. He said we could meet again tomorrow at the coffee shop. So for about a month, we would meet at the coffee shop to talk about Islam. He would give me simple books to read. One day he asked me if I would be interested in going with him to a community center where they held lectures and prayers. He explained to me how the men and women do not sit together. I thought this was strange but I accepted. I sat with the women and began looking around at how they were dressed and all. I thought to myself that I am not dressing like this. I asked myself, "What in the world am I getting myself into?" I am straight-up hood; I will not part with wearing my bandana and my colors. After the lecture, I asked my friend, "Do I have to dress like this?" He answered with a smile on his face. He said, "Right now you are just learning—one step at a time. Allah knows best." I answered, "Okay, I guess Allah knows best."

I went home and that night I thought about this man. He was very respectful. He was polite towards me and treated me with kindness. And to me, he was a brilliant man. Finally, I had met someone who I enjoyed talking to. One day, I saw him waiting for the bus. I crossed the street and told him to call me because I wanted to talk more about Islam. A couple of days later, he called me. I was so excited and nervous that he called that I dropped the phone when I answered. We talked for hours on the phone.

The second time he called, I asked him if there was a mosque in Tacoma. He said, "Yes." I told him that I was thinking about going to the mosque. My friend was happy to hear that I was interested in going but I told him there was one condition. I would go if something would be resolved. I made a prayer to God asking for an issue in my life to be fixed. If this issue was resolved, then I would go to the mosque and give zakat (Islamic almsgiving). Two weeks later, God answered my prayer and the problem was fixed.

Now I had to fulfill my end of the bargain. So, I went to the mosque. I was nervous because I did not know what to expect. I looked for the door that said 'Women Only' and I entered. I immediately took off my shoes and stood by the entrance. Now, here I was dressed like a gangster with my bandana and wearing my colors. I got the attention of one of the ladies so she could come to where I was standing. The Muslim lady came to where I was and then I proceeded to ask her, "Where is the zakat box?" She pointed towards it and I did what I had promised God. I told the Muslim lady that I would be back in two weeks because I had to go to the Veterans Hospital. The Muslim lady replied, "Okay."

Two weeks later, I returned to the same masjid. I entered, removed my shoes, and sat down. I listened to the sermon and then watched them pray. After the service was over, the same Muslim lady that I had spoken to before approached me and asked me if I would like to learn about Islam. I replied, "Yes," and told her that I was waiting for someone to approach me and that if no one did, I was going to leave and not come back. So, we sat down and began to talk. I explained to her that I did not like a religion that is forceful. Also, I told her that I did not like anybody telling me that I have to do this or that. And, since I was on that topic, I asked her if I had to wear the hijab. She explained to me that my heart will let me know when I was ready. For now, she just advised me to learn and with that answer I was happy.

Every Friday after Jummah, the Muslim lady would teach me about Islam. The man that I had met would call me and we would discuss much more about Islam. In addition, we talked about ourselves, our lives, our interests, our hobbies, etc. Eventually, we began to become more than just friends, even though we only communicated over the phone. During the times that I would meet him, there was always a third person with him. Sometimes I would bring my daughter with me so that I was not alone with this man, even though we would be in a public place. This went on for about six months.

One night, the phone rang late at night. This was strange because it was very late. It was my friend calling to ask me a question. I asked him, "What is your question?" He paused and then he asked, "Will you marry me?" I was silent for a little while. Then I responded. I told him that I would have to talk to my uncle who was my guardian and that I would get back to him with an answer. I went to speak to my uncle. My uncle had many questions and I answered them carefully and truthfully. My uncle's said that we should wait another six months to get to know each other a little more. My uncle wanted to meet this guy. I eventually did take my friend over to meet my uncle. My aunt asked my friend a million questions and my uncle just sat in his recliner observing each question that was being answered by my friend. In the end, my uncle gave his approval. The six months were up. Finally, we were able to get married.

Our wedding date was June 24, 2008. I also took my shahadah. Remembering the words I said, "If I ever found a man who would treat me like this that I would be on Seventh Heaven." On June 24, 2008, I was on Seventh Heaven!

I guess being in the right place at the right time does serve a purpose in life. Now, that I sit here thinking about my life, Allah (SWT) had my whole life planned out since the day I was born. *Mi Vida Loca* had its hardships with many life lessons. I give thanks to Allah (SWT) for choosing me to come into Islam. But, Allah had me fulfill another bargain that I had spoken of many years ago as a teenager. Those words were, "BOY! I WISH I COULD JUST DROP EVERYTHING JUST TO GO AND PRAY!"

Fast forward to the present. My name is Rahmah, and I am proud to be a Hispanic Muslim.

How Allah Saved My Life

Walter Gomez

My conversion to Islam has alarmed many friends and family members. It seems to them so strange and odd for a Latino like me to become a Muslim. Catholicism and Protestantism are the leading religions in Latin America so these are reasonable religions for any Latin American to convert to, but when my family follows either Catholic or Protestant denominations, why Islam? Well, my conversion to Islam was not introduced to me by any family member, like most of my family members whose parents' ideas of life were given to them and they adhere to that as truth, without searching. The journey to God is a beautiful road that was given to the Prophets from God to us humans. The Prophets are our ways, and that's the way I follow.

My story begins at my birthplace, El Salvador, a beautiful tropical country located in Central America, filled with exotic, delicious, and tasty fruits. The people are warm and welcoming to others and possess a very intimate culture. Our culture is a crossroads of the mingling of many rich cultures. If you mingle Spanish Arab intellect with the African tangy taste of rhymes, and the Native Indians love of the earth, you get the beautiful people of El Salvador. I was born in 1975, from the middle class of the poor, yes, we were poor but we had the blessing of food. My father was a farmer, whose family bought a lot of cheap land, so they were well off and my mother was from a very humble, poor family who lived by fishing and working for others to get by. Their families opposed of their marriage because one was poor and the other very poor. So my father did what most do, elope with my mother to my grandfather's house, even if my grandfather did not like it. Later, both families became okay with it and a house was given to my father by grandpa, and this is where I was born. The house was an old adobe house.

My father came to America in 1978 to make some quick money and he kept coming and going back for a period of four years until he bought a cargo truck with his brother and worked for a while. Then he felt the urge to come back again and because the war began he felt scared for me and himself. In 1983, he left El Salvador again but with an intention to bring the family and stay for good. After my father left, I spent a lot of time with my grandfather who was a Protestant, and I used to listen to the Biblical readings and I used to love looking at the pictures in the Bible. I used to ask, "Does anyone still dress like the people drawn in the Bible, with long robes, turbans, and beards." And, they would reply, "No, it was long time ago." I was fascinated with Noah, Moses, Abraham, and particularly with Jesus. I had this immense hunger to find people like Jesus, the way he spoke in the Bible and the way he dressed, his beautiful beard brought mystery and he looked very wise. I never saw this in my family who were very religious or in anybody else in the two Christian branches.

In 1984, my father sent a letter to my mother telling her to come to America and to bring me, too. When my mother told me about it, I felt sick and destroyed because I thought that I was in paradise and I didn't want to leave. I cried almost every day, pleading that my mother would leave me with grandpa, but my words were not heard. We left El Salvador in August and I did enjoy the trip to America, but it was very hard for my mom. My two sisters stayed with my aunt in San Salvador, the capital of El Salvador. We arrived in National Airport of Washington D.C. three weeks after we left El Salvador. After spending time here in America, I found out that religions are thrown away by society and are considered private, and not a way of life to many. I didn't feel the love of God as I did in El Salvador, but still tried to keep Him in my heart.

Most of my desires of God in my life were gone in America. I went to regular schools from second grade to high school, but my thirst for religion began in high school. My first year in high school was in 1990. What a joy! I was so happy the first day, and my cousin Ana warned me to be careful because seniors threw freshmen in lockers, but I didn't care, I was happy. Inevitably, soon I found out that seniors weren't the ones who beat and threw freshmen in lockers but it was the football team. The football team was not interested in freshmen only but in Latinos in general. We were terrorized so bad that we used to hide in bathrooms when we saw one of them coming. These guys were 6'5" tall when most Latinos are 5'6" so of course we were terrified.

In the middle of the year, we formed a gang to protect ourselves from the football team. We were becoming crazy to the point that the football team tried to offer an apology to us but we were having fun, and we did not accept to stop. We started going to clubs, drinking, using drugs, and of course, women were not excluded. This period of time was the most dangerous of my life. We used to fight for stupid things. I was almost shot on the metro (train) in Washington D.C. for a stupid argument between my friend and some young kids. The kids started shooting at me like I was the one arguing with them, and a bullet went by my head barely touching my hair. This was crazy and we went after the guys who shot at us, and they got beat up very badly. Twenty minutes later, I felt a drawling rush in my whole body; it felt like I was Superman. I just went through a dream and I thought that I was going to be known, recognized and respected by my homies that I called friends.

Next day, we told our friends and none of them believed our incident, but still, I felt strong. Another incident at a nightclub was our biggest fight ever. The fight was so severe that many of my friends left the gang that we belonged to. Three of my friends were stabbed badly inside the club, so a group of us went outside looking for them, and the cops separated us into subgroups. I was in a group of six guys. We were just walking around the club when a pickup truck came near us and they asked if we needed help, we said, "Yes." All of them got out the pickup truck. They looked fishy to me, but my friends were happy to see them. One of them asked, "What mara (gang) do you click (hang around) with?" We responded with our gang's name, and they said their gang's name, too. The bad thing was that these were the guys who stabbed our buddies and we were looking for them, also. We started to get ready and I told my buddies to run because several of them pointed guns at us, so we ran. I was too drunk to run so I got caught by six of them. They beat me severely. They kicked me with their boots and hit me with their fists all over my face and body.

The cops showed up right in time because I felt death on my throat. They could easily have stabbed me or killed me, and I looked up in the sky and said, "My Lord, save me, and I will serve you." One of my friends got thrown from a bridge and broke his hand while others got away. That same friend who was with me at the train shooting and the nightclub started to become more aware of life. After this incident, he began learning about different doctrines. His philosopher was Karl Marx, his sociology was communism, and his theology was Islam. To me, he was becoming unaware of life, and I myself started to search, but in the Protestant church. I found myself becoming religious again, once again praying to God for guidance. However, I did not want to become too religious of a person because I knew my family would ridicule me.

I had always been a person who seemed uninterested in life. My friend started preaching about his thoughts and beliefs. I told him that my love for the Protestant church was growing more so he could leave me alone. I told him Jesus is my teacher; not a black man named Elijah Muhammad or Farrakhan. My friend at that time was confused what the real Islam was; his Islam looked weird to me. He believed that the

Nation of Islam was the real Islam. He did not know the differences, such as that the real Islam was not racist like the Nation of Islam. I did accept his socialist belief in communism, and "Che" Guevara and Fidel Castro became our leaders for world modernization. At the same time, I was not too happy, because communism denounced God's existence.

He pushed on about Islam, telling me to read his Quran, so I did. I was amazed to see Jesus, Moses, Abraham, and many more Prophets of the Bible in the Quran. He told me, "We believe Jesus is a Prophet of God, not the son of God or God himself." And, I immediately responded that I believe in the same. He said, "Your church believes that Jesus is God and the Son of God and they make up the Trinity." I told him that is not my belief about Jesus and God. That made me think a lot more about Christianity and of their Triune god because I never knew that Jesus was considered this, even though I did go to church. I felt confused but happy that there was a religion that had what I believe in, but still, I wasn't too accepting of it.

A year after graduating from high school in 1995, I went to work at a cafeteria at a university. At work, I saw so many cultures and different religious people. I still had hatred towards non-Latinos, but my first week at work a group of students came to buy some stuff at the store where I worked, and they were fighting among each other because everyone wanted to pay. This incident was very touching to me because I was a very giving person yet my friends took advantage of that quality. I asked one of them later that week why Middle Eastern people were so generous with each other. He replied, "See, we owe it to Islam because Islam teaches us to be generous. Some of us don't practice that much but Islamic manners are embedded in our hearts."

This statement moved me. I replied to him that I used to study Islam for political reasons. He asked, "Why did you stop?" I told him that I didn't know where to get more information about Islam. He looked at me with joy and he said he had an American Muslim friend that converted six months ago. The next day they came to visit me, and I saw this white male dressed like the people in the Bible who looked like Jesus. My heartfelt this peaceful, calm feeling that I still feel. He started asking me about my health, my family, and my work. He didn't mention anything about religion. I was so happy that I told him to come teach me every time he could.

For two months, Muslims were coming to me with books, pamphlets, and just to talk. It went on for two and half months and then the store closed for the summer. Thus, for two months I just relaxed and partied all summer. However, I started to feel guilty while drinking. When I felt that way, I used to prostrate in asking for forgiveness. In September, I went to a party with my friend and I got really drunk that night and almost got into a fight, but my friend reminded me that I was studying Islam, so I stopped and asked him if we could go home. The next day, at 9:00 in the morning, I woke up with this sickening feeling and the phone rang. It was my friend from the university. I told him to please pick me up and take me to the mosque. He came to my house like a lightning flash.

I was nervous and happy at the same time. We arrived at this beautiful Mosque Darul-Al-Hijrah in northern Virginia, which was about ten minutes away from my house. At 10:00 a.m. the teacher came, very calm and not pushing, and asked me if I believed that God is One, I said, "Yes." He asked if I believed that Jesus is a Prophet and the son of Mary. I said, "Yes." Do you believe that Muhammad is the Last Prophet of God? With doubts, I replied "Yes." At that moment in doubts of Muhammad, I said to myself, "If I believe in the teachings of Islam, I must be a fool not to accept the one who brought it." I told the teacher that I was ready to become a Muslim (in submission to God). He told me to repeat: "Ashadu anla ilaha ilallah Wa ashadu ana Muhammadan Rasululah. I testify that there is nothing worthy of worship than Allah and I testify that Muhammad is the Messenger of Allah. Yo atestiguo que no hay nada digno de adoraci que Alah y Atestiguo que Mujammad es el Mensajero de Alah."

At this point, I could smell the mercy and the sweetness of heaven. I felt the presence of God in my torn and sick heart. I felt clean and brightness in my new way of life. My life was ready for the next journey on earth, the journey to Paradise. All Praises are due to Allah, Lord of the Worlds, that has invited me to Islam from among billions of people on Earth. My thanks are due to Allah, the Almighty, for inviting me to His House in Mecca in 1997 for Umrah.

My Battle For Peace Of Mind

Wesley Lebron

My name is Wesley Lebron. I am presently known amongst my Muslim brethren as AbdurRazzaq (the slave of the Provider) or Abu Sumayyah (the father of Sumayyah). I am of Puerto Rican descent, and I was born in Passaic, NJ in 1977. I will proceed to share my story of conversion with you and the process by which I became a Muslim after being Christian for 21 years. I will share how I lived a life that was in need of change and if that change would not have arrived, then only Allah (God) knows if I would have still been alive today.

I was raised in a Christian household. Pentecostal to be more specific. I was taught about the Christian faith through my grandmother (father's mother) who played a vital role in my life. My aunt (father's sister) always picked me up and my cousins on Sunday mornings in order to take us to Sunday school, because our parents were not very religious. Growing up I was taught to believe that Jesus was the Son of God and that he was God as well. We were taught to pray to Jesus, to turn to him in times of need, and to believe that he had died for all of humanity.

Once I reached the age of ten, I became a little more disconnected with the church. I rarely attended church at this point in life due to my commitment and love for baseball. I would dedicate my Sundays to playing and practicing for upcoming baseball games while spending much time with cousins and friends.

For the next eleven years, I removed myself from Sunday school and church in general and I did not want to attend or partake any longer. I began to wonder whom I should call upon for help in times of need. I started finding myself questioning the teachings that were taught to me by my grandmother and the church that we used to attend. I began to have doubt about worshiping and calling on Jesus whom at this stage in life I considered to be a man who walked the earth, a man who lived and died, and a man who ate and slept. I commenced thinking within myself that God had to be something greater than another human being like myself. I did believe Jesus as a Prophet of God and I did not raise him above this stance. I would re-direct my prayers and my pleas toward God alone. I would say, "O God, help me," instead of Jesus help me.

Since I was now removed from faith in general and I had no faith guidelines to live by, I began indulging in and trying many different things. By the eighth grade, I had tried drinking alcohol and that seemed to become more frequent the older I got, especially in my high school years. I was pretty good at concealing my newly founded hobby of drinking from my parents because most of the time my friends and I drank on the weekends in my room while my parents were downstairs asleep in their bedroom.

When I became a freshman in high school, I began to go beyond drinking and I tried smoking marijuana and taking tabs (little purple pills that made you hallucinate and laugh). I lost my virginity this same year and I found that this had become a new addiction that I was willing to continue exploring.

Marijuana for a while became the drug of choice because it was easier to conceal from my parents. I also began to sell marijuana inside and outside of school. By the time I reached my junior year in high school, I was frequently drinking alcohol, smoking weed, and selling it. I was making what I considered to be good money selling marijuana and the cash made from selling it allowed me to buy things I desired, e.g. clothing, sneakers, taking girlfriends out to do things, etc. My parents would ask me, "How did you buy that shirt?" And, I would say, "My friend bought it for me; I sold a Nintendo game, etc."

This same year, my junior year of high school, I decided to drop out of school and begin to work. I was uninterested in education and I was more interested in having girlfriends, partying, and making money. I was totally enveloped by the idea of making money both legally and illegally and I was caught up in this false sense of security. I used to think that I could make more than a college graduate if I continued to sell drugs and work full-time. I considered selling drugs would be safe because I knew my entire drug cliental, and I was not from those individuals who sold drugs on a street corner. If I did not know you, I would not sell anything to you and that was the motto I lived by. My cousin and I also tried selling marijuana wholesale to all of the drug dealers whom we knew, and we figured that this would keep us off the streets and it would be safer.

I lived this lifestyle until I was 20 years old - selling drugs, smoking weed, and consuming more alcohol after dropping out of school then I had in the years that preceded it. I found that I was drinking every day and that most weekends I would not even know how I arrived at my home and sometimes waking not knowing where I was for the first five to ten minutes. Drinking and driving was a regular practice.

I had my first kid when I was 20 and my second at 21 years of age. The two children were from different mothers and I was not with either of them. I began paying child support for both children. At this point, I had stopped selling drugs, but I did not stop consuming them. I started to drink more; the stress of having children and paying child support was something that I found to be heavy on my soul.

It was around this time that I had an unforgettable moment. I met a friend whom I had not seen in years and I went to visit him with two cases of coronas. I went to his home and along with two of his friends, we drank the coronas along with some other forms of hard liquor. We then proceeded to go to a club around 12 am and continued to drink and party. Upon leaving the club, I fell asleep at the wheel and crashed into a light pole at a main intersection in Hackensack, NJ. Thank God that we both survived, but after recuperating from the intoxication and being spared that night by a cop who was a friend of my friend. I then saw just how bad the car was and how we should have been dead. This was a moment that began a small change in my life. I still drank alcohol, but I tried not to drink as much when I was the responsible driver.

It was not too long after all of this that I was introduced to one of my mother's new foster children. He was around 17 years old and he had lived a rough life in New York City where he was raised. He and I became close friends and he introduced me to an organization that was called the Zulu Nation. He took me and another friend of my mine to their meetings, which were held in Harlem, NY. The leader of this organization was a man by the name of Afrika Bambaataa. He would teach about various things that contained faith, government conspiracies, etc. The two of us joined the organization while my friend who was the foster child was reacquainting himself with the organization.

We were introduced to the concept of Islam at these meetings. We were unaware of what Islam was and how it would soon change all of our lives for the better. We soon began researching it and studying its various forms within the multiple sects that connected themselves to it. We studied the Five Percent Nation, the Nation of Islam, Nuwaubian Nation, Islam according to the Sunni's, and we studied the books that were sold to us at Zulu Nation meetings.

At one meeting an old friend of the foster kid came and hugged him. He asked him, "Do you remember me?" And, my friend who was my mother's foster child said, "Yes, how can I forget." This man was someone who had just come out of prison and who accepted Sunni

Islam in jail and who was also Puerto Rican. He asked us to drive him home after the meeting, and he began telling us about Islam and its teachings.

We had been reading many different books and we had many questions. We asked him about God and what did he consider or who did he think God was. He told us that in Islam God was one whom no one has seen, He was not created, He was not part of his creation, He was not like His creation, He did not have children, He did not have family members, etc. At that point, I was still reluctant to believe in what I considered to be a new religion, Islam, but at the same time within myself, I stated, "Wow, this is what I have believed for the last 11 years of my life." My two friends and I soon began reading some books that he gave us and one, in particular, was all about Tawheed, the Oneness of God.

Upon reading this book on tawheed, we all believed that this was the true religion and that this was the religion that we wanted to ascribe ourselves to. We continued to go to both, the Zulu meetings and to the Muslim brother's home where we would ask more questions and learn more about Islam. The Muslim brother after two months of visiting him and learning from him, he told us that we could not have our cake and eat it too. He said that we must choose between Allah (God) and a gang and that we cannot mix the two. We decided to stick with the religion of Islam and we stopped attending the Zulu Nation meetings. At this point, he asked us not to come back to NY, instead seek out a mosque in NJ and to continue learning there and to call him with an update every now and again.

We proceeded to do as he said and we began looking for mosques that were close to our homes. One day we were parked in the projects waiting for a friend to come out of his apartment. While waiting, my friend who accepted Islam and I saw two African American men walking toward the projects dressed with what we perceived to be all white long-sleeved dresses. My friend said, "Those two men are Muslims," to which I replied, "I will never dress like that. They must be crazy." We continued after this to Paterson where we found a mosque, but we were too nervous to go in. We left and returned the next day and after building up some courage we entered the mosque.

My first impression upon entering the mosque was, "What did I get myself into?" All I saw were Arab men sitting around talking Arabic. Their leader stood in front of them and began delivering a speech in Arabic. I was even more convinced saying to myself, "What have I gotten myself into?" I could not understand what this man was saying, I again stated to myself, "How can I join this religion?" I looked at my friend and said that I was prepared to leave.

Upon exiting the main prayer hall, I saw two Muslim brothers who were dressed in baggy pants and had sweat hoods on. I looked at my friend and said to him, "Look! The two brothers over there look like they are from the hood, maybe we can speak with them." We introduced ourselves and they introduced themselves and we soon found out that they were from South America and that they had converted some years earlier. This brought a sense of comfort to both me and my friend because we were both from Puerto Rico and the brothers we just met were from Guatemala. It was also comforting to see someone who came from the same streets we came from.

They told us about another mosque whose congregants were mainly American. All their lectures and speeches were delivered in English. Soon after, we went to the American mosque only to find that same African American brother whom we had seen wearing a white dress at the projects giving the lecture. Glory be to Allah! It was as if Allah had shown us our future companion prior to meeting him. After introducing ourselves, we told him that we had seen him and his father at the projects, thereafter relating to him how shocked I was to see a man wearing a white dress (Islamic Garb for men). He began to laugh and this was the beginning of a fantastic relationship. Going to this mosque showed me the beautiful diversity that Islam had to offer. In it, you found African Americans, Hispanics, Whites, Arabs, etc., all worshipping and interacting with one another.

During this quest in search of a religion and a mosque, I was extremely oppressed by many family members. I would walk into my mother's home at times only to hear my grandmother (my mother's mother) screaming at me and calling me a devil worshipper. My friend, the foster kid, was sent to another home because of his conversion to Islam, but thank God that the new house was only a few blocks away. My family was upset that I left the religion of my forefathers for what they called, the religion of the Arabs. They told me that I no longer had an interest in being Puerto Rican, but that I now wanted to be Arab. They continuously tried to divert me from the path that I began to walk upon.

I continued to push forward worshipping Allah not allowing them to discourage me. I persisted in attending the mosque, learning and listening to the teachings of Islam. The teachings that called to the reformation of one's soul, the teachings that called to leaving off one's desires, to leave off illicit sexual intercourse, to leave off doing drugs, to leave off drinking alcohol, etc. It was a religion that was calling you to practice what you preach. It called to be religious in every instance and not just once a week, but that you were to be religious and God conscious every day.

To me, this was very different from the traditional Christian environment that I grew up in where people were religious on Sunday, but during the week they had girlfriends, illicit sex, did drugs, and drank alcohol. This is not to say that all Christians act this way, but the ones I interacted with did. I was shocked to see that Islam was a religion of practice and that speech meant nothing if it was not practiced and adhered to.

In the beginning, I would slip and drink alcohol and every now and then I would smoke weed. I also still had a girlfriend. The more I learned, the more I began to change. I started to teach my girlfriend about Islam telling her the importance of marriage while informing her of my intention to marry her. I soon stopped drinking and smoking weed. I stopped partying, and I began dedicating my life to Islam and the worship of Allah (God).

When my family saw this drastic change in my life while witnessing how I stopped drinking, hanging out, doing drugs, etc., it caused my parents to say, "Wow! This religion must not be as bad as we thought it was. It has changed our son for the better. He is a better citizen, he is a better father, he is a better son, he is more responsible, etc." Their attitude towards Islam and Muslims changed. They now loved the new faith, which their son had embraced even though they themselves had not. My father once met a Muslim man and told him that his son was Muslim. The man proceeded to ask my father regarding his sentiments toward his son being a Muslim. My father replied, "Now that my son is Muslim, I can sleep at night."

After all of the struggle and trials I have been through, life had started to taste sweeter and I began to feel the tranquility that I needed. My girlfriend had soon accepted Islam. By the grace of Allah, we were married and have been married now for over ten years. I continued to study Islam, and in June of 2001, I received a scholarship to study at the Islamic University of Madinah, which is located in Saudi Arabia. I was ecstatic at such an opportunity. My wife and I agreed that I should not turn down an opportunity of this magnitude. We decided that she would stay behind for the first year while I set up accommodations before her arrival. I left in August of 2001 to Saudi Arabia to study the religion of Islam.

Unfortunately, it was a fantastic opportunity that came to an end sooner than I expected. While I was studying in Saudi Arabia, the tragic event of 9/11 occurred. After seeing and hearing what happened in America, I knew that I would have to return home. My wife who had stayed behind was residing with her parents, but I did feel comfortable with her traveling by herself to and from work, to the grocery store, etc. We lived only a half hour away from the towers. Many people did awful things to Muslim men and women after 9/11, and I did not want my wife to be a victim of one of these ignorant attacks. Once the semester was over, I returned home with the intention of taking a semester off then returning with my family, but Allah had another plan for me and my visa for some reason was revoked and not given back to me.

I continued studying on my own. I also did not cease in calling my family to the teachings of Islam, which was now scattered all over the news. Islam was being falsely attributed to terrorism and the likes. I found myself more dedicated now than ever before. I felt as if I had to prove to my family that Islam does not promote terrorism, that their son would not be involved in a religion that was fanatical. I strove to be the best example I could be, illustrating Islam's beautiful teachings when it relates to family, especially when it came to the rights that parents have over their children.

With the help of Allah, two members of my family became Muslim. My family's outlook on Islam and its teachings were changed from negative to positive. They felt proud to know that we were Muslims and that we stood for justice, peace, and righteousness. They began more open-minded, asking questions about the religion.

I am now happily married with five children. Two of my children I had prior to Islam and three after my acceptance of Islam. I went from being reckless to being cautious, from being irresponsible to being accountable for all of my actions, and from being a boy to being a strong, responsible man.

I continued to study Islam by attending lectures and classes until I found Mishkah University in 2007. I enrolled in their Bachelor's Program for Islamic Studies, and I graduated in November of 2014 with my Bachelor's Degree. I strive to keep my intentions sincere when learning the religion of Islam. My first and foremost reason for learning Islam was and still is to get close to Allah (God). Then comes by intention to educate my family, community, and society at large, especially the Latino community which is an underserved minority within our faith. I am thankful to Allah (God) for giving me such a great opportunity, and I am grateful to my family for their continuous support and encouragement.

Through My Eyes

Yusuf Maisonet

I would first like to thank my mother for all of her hard work and also thank my oldest sister Miki and my older brother Jose for being my companions in this life. I ask Allah to bless them, my brothers and sisters, and the rest of my family and friends. I would also like to acknowledge my father Robel Torres Martinez and give special recognition to my son Robert, whom we grew apart due to circumstances.

And special thanks to my wife Hajja Amina Maisonet, my longtime companion whose wisdom and care made my life so beautiful and tranquil. Without her love and care, my life would have been complicated. With Allah's mercy, he gave me a beautiful partner to make my life full. All the experience I have received, I owe my wife with all of my love and gratitude.

I was born June 2, 1951, in Spanish Harlem, New York (El Barrio). I was the third of four siblings, all of them born in Puerto Rico. I was the only one who was born in New York, but at the tender age of three, we were separated from our parents due to a fall that they experienced. Heroin was king back in the fifty's and due to their being emigrants and needing the financial stability to survive in the concrete jungle.

They fell victims to the drug world, which did its job of breaking up families and incarcerating parents. On one of their drug dealings, they got busted and were sentenced to 7 to 15 years in the penitentiary and after they were sentenced, we were sentenced to an orphanage, St Joseph Home in Peekskill, NY where we remained until my mother's sentence was fulfilled. But by Allah's mercy that helped us become stronger human beings by being able to deal with life's ups and downs, which many people are not prepared to deal with.

At the age of sixteen, I was introduced to the Last Poets in Brooklyn, NY who are known for their hit "The Revolution Will Not Be Televised." They are considered as being one of the biggest influencers of hip-hop music. They were rehearsing in a shop that I used to go to on Myrtle Ave in Brooklyn. One of the members, Jalaluddin Mansur Nuriddin, started telling me about Islam then he read Surah Ikhlas 112 to me.

In the Name of Allah the Most Gracious, the Most Merciful

1. Say He is Allah, the One
2. Allah the Self-Sufficient
3. He begets not, nor is He begotten.
4. And there is none like unto Him.

And solely this Surah from the Quran had an everlasting effect on me until this present day. I went to a bookstore and bought a copy of the Noble Quran and took it home and started to read. The effect that the Quran had on me was very inspirational. Three days later I saw Jalal and told him that I wanted to become Muslim, so he prepared me and told me about taking a shower, and then to go and take my shahadah.

1. Testify that there is none worthy of worship but Allah and Muhammad is his Prophet.
2. Salat, prayer five times a day
3. Zakat, 2.5 percent of my annual salary
4. Ramadan, fast for 29 or 30 days the month that the Quran was revealed.
5. Hajj, pilgrimage to Mecca once in my lifetime, if I had the means.

It all sounded so easy until Ramadan started the following week and that is when the test began. It was hard changing my dietary habits from eating all of those Spanish dishes with pork in almost everything, but fasting from sunrise to sunset and making salat is when I realized that being Muslim was no game and that you had to be real and committed to this big change in your life. My Ramadan had its ups and down, but I didn't get discouraged. I knew that Allah judges by intentions and I knew that I tried.

In 1968 after my older brother was drafted, I felt alone so I volunteered in the Army. Soon after I realized that it was a mistake but it was too late for regrets, and to my surprise, I met a lot of Muslims in the Army. This surge of Muslims in the Armed Forces is not new. Even so, I had a lot of explaining to do about why I didn't eat pork, why I was always bowing down, and why I washed so much, especially my feet.

However, my Caribbean heritage had its good effect on me and by being exposed to the lifestyle of the concrete jungle, I knew how to deal with opposing forces. I never took any foolishness from anybody and I still do not. I speak what is on my mind and try to be as cordial as Allah allows me to be. I strive to be a good brother, but I do not bow down to anyone but the Creator of the Heavens and Earth. I recognize achievements and the realms of history, especially in America and the whole of the western world.

By Allah's mercy, he has allowed me to travel all over the world, from Rome to the Dome of the Rock (Jerusalem). I have spent Ramadan in different parts of the world, with Muslim families enjoying each other's culture. I realize that all this is Allah's doing, so I can share with the community back home.

My first trip abroad was to England after I got out of the Army. I was thinking a lot about experiencing Muslim hospitality. After arriving in London, I went to the big Masjid on Park Place. I was able to shower and eat at the masjid, where I met a white American Muslim. It was the first time that I met a Caucasian Muslim, and he directed me to a city called Norwich. It was a four-hour train ride from London. There was a brother waiting for me at the train station to greet me. That's when I was exposed to an entire community of white Muslims. Even though Islam is for all humanity, I was amazed to see an all-white community including the Imam. But the hospitality was 100% Islamic.

I was a little apprehensive in England, being brought up in a city like New York City, which pretty diverse with many Blacks and Latinos. They could sense my apprehension because they questioned me about why I was so uptight. And I explained to them why, and they made me feel at home with them. Because I had some money, I was able to share with some of the brothers who came from all over the world. They came from places like South Africa before the end of apartheid. There were brothers from Ireland with speckles on their faces and with red hair. There were people from Denmark, primarily from all of Europe, some Arab countries, the Philippines, and even Mexico. And here I was a Puerto Rican from New York on an international level, but little did I know that they were Sufis and every day they did their dhikrs and every day they were teaching me more about Islam. They also took me on trips around the country to see some of their history, castles about as long as Islam has been in Europe especially in England, a real education. I stayed in England for about four months.

Then I decided to travel to France because I heard so much about it and my last name was French. "Maisonette" means small house in French. I took a hovercraft across the English Channel and when I got to France I had to take a train ride to Paris but as I was riding I realized that my French wasn't up to par. However, by being fluent in Spanish, I was able to cope with the language barrier. I got to Paris and what a beautiful city it is. I asked a taxi driver from Morocco to take me to a masjid and he took me to the historical Masjid de Paris, an old Moroccan style mosque, and when I got there I made two rakat prayers.

I was amazed at the old style architecture. When I talked to the Imam, I told him I was from America. I also said to him that I needed a place to stay while in Paris and that I prefer to stay with Muslims and was willing to pay for any accommodations. He suggested that I stay with the brothers from Algeria or Morocco at Boulevard de Belleville and Courones. I took a taxi over there and talked to the Imam. He agreed to let me stay at the masjid. I stayed in Paris for three weeks. I went all over Paris and met brothers who were doing farm work for the picking season of strawberries.

We ate then made salat with them. Always to my surprise they would ask me, "Please brother Yusef recite Surah Al-Fatiha." Then they would start with the dawah. If a brother from America can recite Fatiha and go out on dawah, so can you. It was a pleasant experience. Crazy, but nice. It was all in the way of Allah. So I say to all of my Muslim brothers and sisters, especially those who just became Muslim, life is beautiful and people get what they strive for. You can do anything in life as long as it has some purpose to it and you are doing it for Allah.

One of my most memorial trips was going to North Korea. We went there to give food aid for them ending their nuclear program (Bush Plan). You all know what transpired then. When we arrived by Allah's mercy, I was the one to steer the ship to North Korea. They wanted the best helmsman to guide it into port and by Allah's mercy, I was the best. Being Muslim I try to perfect myself in everything that I do.

Alhamdulillah, that I was able to always keep myself as a Muslim. No matter where in the world I have been, I have always remembered that I was a Muslim and a proud Latino. I have traveled the globe like Ibn Battuta. By Allah mercy, I have been from the South Pole to the North Pole from East to West. By Allah's mercy, I was able to carry the banner of Islam wherever I went. Whatever you want to do, you can do it. There is no stopping me now until Allah in His infinite mercy makes that call. Travel through the earth and seek of Allah's bounty.

My Journey To Earthbound Paradise

Zeina Mena

How unpredictable life is! I never thought that I would be sitting here writing a conversion story about how I became a Muslim. Nevertheless, I never knew how much reflection doing so would cause in my life. I come from a broken family, which is almost standard in America. I was born and raised in New York City, and I am of Dominican descent. I grew up Catholic, went to Catholic school, and went to Catholic Church along with completing all of my rituals except for marriage. I always saw myself as a person who was close to God, especially after my parents' divorce, which devastated me emotionally in ways unimaginable. I needed emotional peace and often found myself seeking it through the church.

Two years after moving to Miami and graduating from high school, I met a Palestinian friend at a dental office at my work who taught me so much about the Middle East crisis and took the time out to explain things to me which were utterly oblivious to my knowledge. Then I began to realize how ethnocentric people in America are. Time passed and my learning of politics continued. At the same time, my empty heart kept screaming out for love and happiness. One Sunday while feeling depressed, I decided to go to church. I had not gone in a few months. I wanted to hear soothing words and know that someone cared. Forty-five minutes later, I walked out of the church, and I never went back again.

My interest in finding spiritual fulfillment grew stronger, so I decided to look into the various religions that were available. Although I was searching with an open mind, I did not want to go to anything that was not monotheistic. I chose to learn about Judaism. I read, went to a synagogue, and tried to learn and figure out if I could live my life as a Jew. I then decided that in order to grasp the essence of the Judaic teachings, I needed to read the Torah. After I finished reading the Torah, I went to bed and had my most confusing yet incredible dream.

In the dream, I wake up in a hotel room where I seem to be confused about why I am there. I decide to go to the lobby, and I find myself in a religious convention. I walked to my left, and there was a table about Judaism. I was trying to fit in with them, but they did not want me to be part of them. I then walked away and walked straight ahead from the room, and there was the Christianity section. Everyone in that section seemed to be in his or her own world and no one paid attention to me. I walked away again, and I wandered into the right side of the hallway and found people walking peacefully, all of them dressed in white.

This seemed weird to me. I did not know what it was, so again I walked away. This time I headed to my room. Suddenly, this man appears behind me and tells me "convert." Frightened, I told him "Leave me alone" and I started walking faster. Although he seemed to be walking slowly, he was able to keep up with me and again told me "convert" to which I again replied, "Leave me alone!" The man refused to give up and followed me all the way to the room. I hid behind the bed when he again told me in a stronger voice "convert!" Frightened and confused, I told him "Leave me alone. I am a Muslim!" For some time, I never knew the meaning of that dream. What puzzled me was that although I was learning about Judaism, I would actually say I am a Muslim in the dream. That night on I kept asking myself why I would say that.

A month passed and my Palestinian friend invited me to an Arabic restaurant knowing that I loved the culture. I excitedly agreed and went. That was three days before Ramadan. There I met her friends which all happened to be Muslims. My friend was a Palestinian Christian. I became friends with her friends immediately. One friend, in particular, took time to explain Islam and its teachings.

I learned about the Five Pillars and other basic information about Islam. Although I found Islam to be interesting, I still liked what I was reading about Judaism, and I did not want to change now that I had learned so much. That idea changed a few days later. During Christmas vacation, Ramadan started. My friend went back home to Syria to spend the last ten days of Ramadan there. Being the inquisitive type of person, I wanted to learn more about Ramadan and more than I already knew. I logged on to my computer and from the encyclopedia printed out information about the Prophet Muhammad (PBUH) and read it. It seemed really interesting and made me want to learn more about him and the religion itself.

I printed out the information about Islam and that too ignited my interest to speak with Muslims to see how they were and how they thought. I logged on to the web and went to a Muslim chat room where I just started a conversation. So many instant messages popped up on my screen asking me if I was Muslim or if I wanted to learn about it. They were all telling me about Islam, the Five Pillars, and everything but there was one particular person who took the time explaining everything. If I asked any question, it was answered. That person was a Muslim brother who was enthusiastic about teaching me. He taught me so much and even went on to explain the importance of covering.

He also sent me my first Quran and many books on basic Islamic information. As I read the Quran, my heart felt as though I was going to explode. I thought that I had found what my heart was searching for. So many emotions bombarded me that I broke down in tears. This holy book was speaking directly to me and with all its power it soothed my soul. I accepted Islam in heart on the 21st of Ramadan in the year 2000. It was then that the door to a new enriching world opened up for me. It was the day that marked the turning point in my life.

It was again time to go back to college for the spring semester, and although I was already Muslim and was praying on my own from a piece of paper, I needed someone to teach and guide me. God knows what you need before you need it because that first day of class while I was walking onto campus, a Muslim girl was walking out. I immediately ran up to her and asked her if she was Muslim, to which she replied yes. I told her I had converted and that I needed to learn how to pray correctly. She automatically offered herself to do the job. And, she also invited me to a get together at her house that day. I was so excited! After school, I rushed to the mall to find a headscarf to wear to her home. Wearing a headscarf was something that a month before I was debating because I felt that women shouldn't have to cover.

Everyone was amazed and happy to see that I had already worn the hijab. I felt so much happiness that day to have found her and the other sisters. They were very kind to me and eager to teach me. The next morning, I woke up for school, got dressed, and again put on my scarf. My mother watched me as I dressed and started laughing when I put it on thinking that I was joking. When I told her "bendicion mami" which is asking for the blessing of your mother in Spanish, she replied, "You are not planning to go like that to school, are you?" I told her, "Yes, I am." She couldn't believe it and thought I was going crazy.

I went to school that day and although people looked at me I felt good that I was identifying myself as a believing Muslim. My friendship and my learning passion grew stronger with my new friends. They taught me everything from the Surah Al-Fatiha to prayer, to ethics in Islam. I read so much and interestingly enough I learned more about my previous religion after converting to Islam than when I was a Catholic. I often found myself in situations in which people would ask me questions and that pushed me to learn more and to compare the Bible and the Quran.

Although that was the beginning of a new life for me, I never knew how much religion could affect my family just because I now believed something different. Every morning, I woke up happy to know that I was Muslim, but I also anticipated the challenge of my mother and stepfather, etc. My mother believed that I was going crazy. She would shout at me to take that veil off. She even told me that I needed to see a psychiatrist. My stepfather also made my life hard. One day he told me, "Either you take that off or you don't come into this house." That day I went to my friend's house, and I ended up staying there for two weeks. I never felt so much peace. I felt so loved and welcomed. I woke up to the Adhan every morning to pray with my Muslim sisters.

During this time I kept in touch with my mother although our conversations were bizarre. When she realized that it was not a "few days thing," she called me crying. She was asking me to return to the house and that she missed me. I must admit that I love my mother very much, and it was a hard decision. I did not want to hurt my mother, but I felt so happy where I was because I could be me. I went back home with the agreement that I was going to be allowed to wear my hijab. It was fine for a few days, but then other things started bothering them.

They were bothered that when a man came to the house I quickly went to my room and that I wouldn't share much time with them anymore. Yes, it is true. I did start drifting away, but not from them, just from the things that they did that are prohibited for me to be around. When my mother saw me praying, she would mock me. Not only that. I did not hear from my "friends" anymore and before I knew it, my life was heading in a different direction. My goal was not to be skinny and in fashion anymore; it was to please God.

Through it all, my faith was stronger. I knew in my heart that someday it would be ok. My first Ramadan was very emotional for me because I remembered all that I went through as a new Muslim. I realized how blessed I am to be a Muslim. I felt alone in my house because no one in my family celebrates Ramadan and no one cared. It was just me and God. This was the completion of my first year as a Muslim, but it was also the beginning of my second year as one.

After the first year, everything was easier! Although not convinced that Islam is right, my family acknowledged the fact that it was not a phase that I was going through and that whatever it was, I was staying with it. I learned to practice my religion, avoid the wrong, and still fit into my family. I realized that it was ok as long as they knew that I was only becoming a better person. Today, my mother knows many things that are "haram." My little sister can tell you about Judgment Day. My family cooks a second dish for me when I am visiting and best of all they accept the fact that I am a Muslim.

How amazing is the plan of God? So many things in my life seem to be clearer. Still, until this day, I ask myself, "Why did God choose me?" I don't know the answer, but I do know that I have touched the lives of many people around me even if it has been in small ways. They now know about a religion that they knew nothing about. And, it's no longer "those Muslims," because they have one in the family.

My struggle still continues. I am sure it will for the rest of my life. This experience has only taught me to be stronger, and it made me realize how much my belief means to me. I also know that I cannot ever imagine myself not being a Muslim. Islam has given me the peace that was taken from me. It has taught me to appreciate life. It has educated me in all aspects of life, but best of all, it has taught me that my journey on Earth is short. With all the hardships that I have encountered, my heart leaps of joy knowing that although I am not in paradise, I have found something like it on Earth. That is Islam.

Islamic Phrases

Al-Hamdu Lillahi Rabbil 'Alamin - Its meaning is: "Praise be to Allah, the Lord of the worlds." This is a verse from the Quran that Muslims recite and say many times per day during prayer. Another form is "Alhamdulillah," which means: "Praise be to Allah." Allah means God in the Arabic language. Alhamdulillah is a statement of thanks, appreciation, and gratitude from the creature to his Creator. If someone asks you how you are and you want to express that you're satisfied, you can say "Alhamdulillah."

Allahu Akbar - Its meaning is: "Allah is the Greatest." During the call for prayer, during prayer, when they are happy and wish to express their approval of what they hear, and when they want to praise a speaker, Muslims say this expression of Allahu Akbar. Muslims praise Allah in every aspect of life, and as such, they say, Allahu Akbar. Takbir is the term for this Arabic phrase. A speaker may call others to praise God by saying "Takbir!" and the audience will respond with "Allahu Akbar!"

Allahu A'lam - Its meaning is: "Allah knows best." Said when not sure about something, or simply don't know, could be the equivalent of "I don't know."

Ameen – Its meaning is: "O Allah, accept it." It is said at the end of a supplication (dua) or prayer as a way of asking God to grant that request.

Assalamu 'Alaikum - Its meaning is: "Peace be upon you." This is an expression Muslims say whenever they greet one another (instead of hi/hello). It is also used in farewells (instead of bye/goodbye).

There are two forms that are more polite and formal.

"Assalamu 'Alalikum Wa Rahmatullah," which means: "May the peace and the mercy of Allah be upon you."
"Assalamu Alalikum Wa Rahmatullahi Wa Barakatuh," which means: "May the peace, the mercy, and the blessings of Allah be upon you."

Astaghfirullah - Its meaning is: "I ask Allah's forgiveness." This is an expression used by a Muslim when he wants to ask Allah's forgiveness. When a Muslim abstains from doing wrong, or even when he wants to prove that he is innocent of an incident, he uses this expression. Commonly used when you think you have committed a sin, such as cursing, backbiting, etc.

A'uzu Billahi Minashaytanir Rajim - Its meaning is: "I seek refuge from Allah from the outcast Satan." This is an expression and a statement that Muslims recite before reading the Quran, before speaking, before making a supplication, before taking ablution, and before doing many other daily activities. This expression is also used when feeling unsafe or before entering unsafe places, or when scared by something, such as a bad dream. Satan is the source of evil and he always tries to misguide and mislead people.

Barak Allah - Its meaning is: "May the blessings of Allah (be upon you)." When a Muslim wants to say thank you to another person, he says "Barak Allah" to express his thanks, appreciation, and gratitude.

Bismillahir Rahmanir Rahim - Its meaning is: "In the name of Allah, the Most Beneficent, the Most Merciful." This is a phrase from the Quran that is recited before reading the Quran. This phrase is also recited before doing any daily activity. Another form is "Bismillah," which means: "In the name of Allah." You can say "Bismillah" when you are about to start something, such as driving, eating, walking, reading, etc.

Fi Amanillah - Its meaning is: "May Allah protect you." It is a way of saying goodbye.

Fi Sabilillah - Its meaning is: "In the cause of Allah." When you give charity or help people, you are doing something fi sabilillah.

Insha'Allah - Its meaning is: "If Allah wills." When a person wishes to plan for the future, when he promises, when he makes resolutions, and when he makes a pledge, he makes them with permission and the will of Allah. For this reason, a Muslim uses the Quranic instructions by saying "Insha'Allah." Muslims are to strive hard and to put their trust with Allah. They leave the results in the hands of Allah.

Inna Lillahi Wa Inna Ilahi Raji'un - Its meaning is: "We are from Allah and to Whom we shall return." A Muslim is patient and says this expression in times of turmoil and calamity.

Jazaka Allahu Khayran - Its meaning is: "May Allah reward you with goodness." This is a statement of thanks and appreciation to be said to the person who does a favor. You can use "Jazaka Allahu Khayran" instead of thank you.

La Hawla Wa La Quwwata Illa Billah - Its meaning is: "There is no might nor power except in Allah." This expression is said by a Muslim when he is struck by a calamity or is taken over by a situation beyond his control. It can be used to express dissatisfaction.

La Ilaha Illallah - Its meaning is: "There is no god but God." This expression is the most important one in Islam. It is the creed that every person has to say to be considered a Muslim. It is part of the first pillar of Islam. The second part of this first pillar is to say: "Muhammadun Rasulullah," which means: "Muhammad is the messenger of Allah."

Masha'Allah - Its meaning is: "Allah has willed it." This is an expression that Muslims say whenever they are excited, surprised, and amazed. When you wish to express your happiness, you can say "Masha'Allah," for example when you see a cute child or a beautiful sunset.

Muhammadun Rasulullah - Its meaning is: "Muhammad is the messenger of Allah." This statement is the second part of the first pillar of Islam.

PBUH - These letters are abbreviations for the words "Peace Be Upon Him" which is the meaning of the Arabic expression "Alayhis Salam." It is an expression that is said when the name of a prophet is mentioned, such as Prophet Noah (PBUH) or Noah (AS).

Radhiallahu 'Anhu (Abbreviated as: RA) - Its meaning is: "May Allah be pleased with him." This is an expression to be used by Muslims whenever a name of a companion of the Prophet Muhammad (SAW) is mentioned or used in writing. *Radi Allah 'Anha* is used whenever a name of a female companion of the Prophet is mentioned or used in writing. It means: "May Allah be pleased with her." *Radi Allah 'Anhum* is the plural form of saying companions of the Prophet. It means: "May Allah be pleased with them."

Sallallahu 'Alaihi Wa Sallam (Abbreviated as: SAW) - Its meaning is: "May the blessings and the peace of Allah be upon him (Muhammad)." When the name of Prophet Muhammad (SAW) is mentioned or written, a Muslim is to respect him and invoke this statement of peace upon him. Another expression that is alternatively used is: "Alaihissalatu Wassalam." This expression means: "On Him (Muhammad) are the blessings and the peace of Allah."

Subhanahu Wa Ta'ala (Abbreviated as: SWT) - Its meaning is: "The Most Glorified and the Most Exalted is He (Allah)." This is an expression that Muslims use whenever the name of Allah is pronounced or written. Sometimes Muslims use other expressions when the name of Allah is written or pronounced. Some of which are: "'Azza Wa Jall": He is the Mighty and the Majestic; "Jalla Jalaluh": He is the exalted Majestic.

Subhan'Allah – Its meaning is: "Glory be to Allah." This expression is often used when praising Allah or exclaiming amazement at His attributes, bounties, or creation. If you hear something amazing and you want to express your amazement, you can say "Subhan'Allah."

Wa 'Alaikumus Salam - Its meaning is: "And peace be upon you." This is an expression that a Muslim is to say as an answer for the greeting. When a person greets another with a salutation of peace, the answer for the greeting is an answer of peace. The other expressions are: "Wa Alaikums Salam Wa Rahmatullah." and "Wa 'Alaikums Salam Wa Rahmatullahi Wa Barakatuh."

The list just provided does not distinguish between masculine/feminine or singular/plural. More Islamic phrases can be found online.

https://islamicink.wordpress.com/basic-islamic-phrases-terms

http://arabic.speak7.com/islamic_expressions.htm

Selected Bibliography

Barzegar, Abbas. "Latino Muslims in the United States: An Introduction." The High Plains Society for Applied Anthropology 23.2 (2003): 126-129. Print.

Bowen, Patrick D. "Early U.S. Latina/o - African-American Muslim Connections: Paths to Conversion." The Muslim World 100.4 (2010): 390-413. Print.

Bowen, Patrick D. "The Latino American Da'wah Organization and the "Latina/o Muslim" Identity in the U.S." Journal of Race, Ethnicity, and Religion 1.11 (2010): n. pag. Web. 21 May 2014.

Bowen, Patrick D. "U.S. Latina/o Muslims Since 1920: From 'Moors' to 'Latino Muslims'." Journal of Religious History 37.2 (2013): 165–184. Print.

Chitwood, Ken. "Hispanic Muslims? An In-depth Look at a Little Known but Growing U.S. Minority." Sightings 31 Oct. 2013. Print.

Chitwood, Ken. "Islam en Español: Narratives of Reversion among Latina/o Muslims." Waikato Islamic Studies Review 1.2 (2015): 35-54. Print.

Diaz, Wendy and Juan Galvan. "The Growing Visibility of the Latino/ Hispanic Community." Islamic Horizons July/August 2016. Print.

Espinosa, Gaston, et al. "Latino Muslims in the United States: Reversion, Politics, and Islamidad." The Journal of Race, Ethnicity, and Religion. Volume 8, Issue 1 (June 2017).

Levy, Rachael. "Another Growing Component of the Muslim Fabric." Islamic Horizons January/February 2014. Print.

Maria del Mar Logroño Narbona, et al. Crescent over Another Horizon: Islam in Latin America, the Caribbean, and Latino USA. University of Texas Press, 2015. Print.

Martinez-Vazquez, Hjamil. Latina/o y Musulmán. Eugene, OR: Wipf & Stock, 2010. Print.

Morales, Harold Daniel. Latino and Muslim in America. Oxford University Press, 2018. Print.

Morales, Harold Daniel. Latino Muslim by Design: A Study of Race, Religion and the Internet in American. Diss. University of California at Riverside, 2012. Print.

Many articles are available online at LatinoDawah.org and HispanicMuslims.com.

About The Editor

Juan Jose Galvan is the editor of *Latino Muslims: Our Journeys to Islam*. He embraced Islam in the summer of 2001. Juan served as the executive director of the Latino American Dawah Organization (LADO) from 2005-2013. He was the editor of its online newsletter, The Latino Muslim Voice, from 2002-2012. Through his role as editor, he actively contributed articles to the newsletter including: Jesus and the Virgin Mary in Islam and FAQs about Latino Muslims. In his career, he has actively written about various Latino Muslim events, organizations and leaders. Juan manages the LatinoDawah.org and HispanicMuslims.com websites.

Juan Galvan advocates for the inclusion of the Latino Muslim voice in the mainstream Muslim narrative. He pushes for increased visibility of America's Latino Muslims in religious publications. Juan has assisted dozens of students, professors, and reporters with research and has provided access to the Latino Muslim community through interviews and his writings. He has been invited to speak at various Islamic conferences.

He has developed a growing national reputation as a content expert on the Latino Muslim community through newspaper interviews and publications. Juan has been quoted in many publications including the New York Times, the Houston Chronicle, and the Los Angeles Times. Hernán Rozemberg of the San Antonio Express-News wrote in 2005, "After becoming a Muslim, (Juan) Galvan made it his personal mission to inform the country about Latino Muslims."

In 2002, Juan Galvan spearheaded the first ever issue dedicated to Latino Muslims in *Islamic Horizons*, a highly recognized magazine dedicated to the North American Muslim community. He has also coordinated two issues of *The Message International* magazine focusing on Latino Muslims in 2004 and 2005.

Juan is a third-generation Mexican-American and the son of migrant workers. He is the third of eight children and spent his early years hoeing cotton in the rural Texas Panhandle. Juan was the first in his family to pursue a higher education and has a Bachelor of Business Administration in Management Information Systems (BBA-MIS) from The University of Texas at Austin. He lives in San Antonio with his wife and three sons. Juan encourages others to expand their views on the Latino and Muslim identity as he has learned through his own personal experiences.

Juan would love to hear your reactions to the stories in this book. Please let him know what your favorite stories are and how they affected you. You can also share your own story. He can be emailed at Juan.Muslim@yahoo.com.